Child Support

Child Support
The Next Frontier

Edited by J. Thomas Oldham
and Marygold S. Melli

Ann Arbor

THE UNIVERSITY OF MICHIGAN PRESS

Published in the United States of America by
The University of Michigan Press
Manufactured in the United States of America
⊗ Printed on acid-free paper

2003 2002 2001 2000 4 3 2 1

A CIP catalog record for this book is available from the British Library.

Library of Congress Cataloging-in-Publication Data

Child support : the next frontier / edited by J. Thomas Oldham and Marygold S. Melli.
p. cm.
Includes bibliographical references and index.
ISBN 0-472-11057-8 (cloth : acid-free paper)
1. Child support—Law and legislation—United States—Popular works. 2. Child support—Law and legislation—Popular works. 3. Child support—United States—Popular works. I. Oldham, J. Thomas, 1948– II. Melli, Marygold Shire.
KF549.Z9 C46 2000
346.7301'72—dc21 99-050667

To Chaille
—J. T. O.

To my husband and my colleagues for their continued support.
—M. S. M.

Contents

Preface

The latter part of the twentieth century has witnessed a revolution in the law of child support. A half century ago the public seemed to accept the idea that children in single-parent homes would be supported by their custodial parents or by the government; only minimal effort was made to obtain and enforce child support orders against absent parents. In the past two decades, however, as the number of divorces and nonmarital children increased, child support has evolved from a low-visibility issue to an important public policy problem. Major reform of the private child support system has been undertaken, driven by concerns about poor children and welfare costs. Formulas for calculating the amount of child support have been established, and public programs to collect child support have been instituted.

Today marks the threshold of a new era. Welfare, the public child support system, has been drastically revamped and limited. These changes have relied heavily on the recently reformed and strengthened private child support system. But although recent reforms have to some extent improved state private child support systems, a number of issues critical to U.S. child support policy remain unresolved. For example, a surprisingly large number of single parents do not have child support orders, and a significant percentage of orders are not paid; thus, new ways of establishing and enforcing orders are needed. What constitutes a "fair" amount of child support remains hotly contested. Finally, there is considerable evidence that the reforms have failed to accomplish one of the most important objectives of child support, that of reducing child poverty. Furthermore, some suggest that, because private child support will never be adequate to provide for children of poor parents, the United States (following the lead of other countries) should create more generous public benefits to alleviate the poverty of poor single parents and their children.

As the debate continues there is clearly a need for reassessment and more study. The essays in this book consider these problems. They examine, from a number of different perspectives, the role of child support in reducing child poverty, they consider the functioning of the present system and how it can be improved, and they offer insights into the implementation of changes in Europe, Australia, and the United States. Perhaps not surprisingly, given the controversial nature of these questions, the authors sometimes disagree about the best course for U.S. child support policy.

The first part of the book contains three essays that give readers an overview of child support regulation in the United States and set forth the multifaceted nature of this problem. In "Child Support Comes of Age: An Introduction to the Law of Child Support," June Carbone summarizes the history of child support rules in the United States, focusing on the changing mores of parental responsibility in a world of no-fault divorce and increasingly common nonmarital births as well as on the challenges of child support enforcement.

Marsha Garrison discusses the issue of what is an adequate amount of child support in "The Goals and Limits of Child Support Policy." She examines the reasons for child poverty in single-parent households and explores why recent public-policy reforms, such as child support guidelines and improved enforcement tools, have not significantly helped. She points out that, almost without exception, the child support guidelines currently in use were never intended to ensure that children did not suffer a diminished standard of living; rather, these guidelines were intended to ensure a continuity of expenditure by the noncustodial parent—that is, to require that a parent who does not live with a child continues to devote the same percentage of income to the child as when the parties lived together. Such a formula, Garrison points out, will result in a lower standard of living for the child if the expenditure base in the single-parent household is lower than that in the two-parent household, which it usually is, given the fact that most custodial parents are mothers whose incomes lag well behind those of fathers. Garrison also notes, however, that many children in single-parent families are poor because both parents are poor rather than because of any defect in the child support guidelines. But recognizing the inability of child support to take a large number of children of poor parents out of poverty, Garrison argues that properly structured child support guidelines could do much to provide more adequately for children and suggests a possible approach.

Paul K. Legler focuses on the effects of the recent federal welfare reform legislation (The Personal Responsibility and Work Opportunity Act of 1996) in "The Impact of Welfare Reform on the Child Support Enforcement System." Legler summarizes the revolutionary changes relating to paternity establishment and child support enforcement effected by the act. He describes the new system intended to make child support payments automatic and inescapable, like death or taxes. He describes the new national system for tracking obligor parents and predicts higher collections with resulting benefits for poor families.

In the second part of the book, "The Current Social Structure and Its Relevance to Reform," Professors Judith A. Seltzer and Daniel R. Meyer view the child support system from their perspective as social scientists. These two chapters give readers a sense of the complex family relationships in which the child support system must intervene. In "Child Support and Child Access: Experiences of Divorced and Nonmarital Families," Seltzer discusses the issue of whether noncustodial parents would pay more child support if they had more contact with their children. She also explores the converse of this argument—will increased paternity establishment and child support enforcement result in more contact between children and noncustodial parents? Seltzer attempts to determine empirically whether more aggressive child support enforcement would increase the level of contact between children and noncustodial parents and concludes that, to some degree, it would.

Meyer examines data on child support from the perspective of fathers, both as custodians and as payers of child support, in "Fathers and the Child Support System." Although women still receive sole custody in most cases, he refers to recent data showing that shared physical custody and father custody are becoming increasingly common. He summarizes studies relating to the amount of child support ordered and paid when mothers have sole custody and compares this information to what occurs when fathers receive custody. Meyer notes that, compared to noncustodial fathers, noncustodial mothers are ordered to pay child support less frequently and are ordered to pay a lower percentage of income when they are ordered to pay child support, an apparent difference in treatment that deserves further inquiry. Meyer concludes that, although payment of child support may diminish a father's economic well-being, it does not in general impoverish divorced fathers.

Part 3 of the book is entitled "Improving the Present System." It contains two chapters that address very important matters involving child support policy. In "Guideline Review: The Search for an Equitable Child Support Formula," Marygold S. Melli examines the federal initiative requiring states to review their adopted guidelines periodically to be sure that they remain fair and equitable and to be sure that courts do not deviate too frequently from the presumptive guideline amount. Melli concludes that the state guideline reviews have fallen short of achieving the objectives that Congress sought and recommends that the federal government provide leadership to the states in guideline review.

J. Thomas Oldham discusses the problem of updating the child support awards in "New Methods to Update Child Support." He notes the many barriers to creating an inexpensive and easy way to update child support awards. For a number of reasons, most states accept that child support orders should be expressed as a fixed amount. Thus, if the parties' circumstances change, some action is needed to modify awards to reflect new circumstances. Most states do not now have a very satisfactory way of dealing with this problem. Oldham discusses a few states' approaches to this problem and offers some potential solutions.

The fourth part of the book, "Child Support: The Experience Elsewhere," contains discussions of approaches to child support policy in other countries. In "Child Support as Distributive and Commutative Justice: The United Kingdom Experience," John Eekelaar thoughtfully explores the differences in approach to determining child support liability in systems that are primarily administrative and those that are primarily judicial. He outlines possible child support goals and their relation to two conceptions of justice described as distributive and commutative. Eekelaar describes the British experience of trying to change from a court-based system where judges had a great deal of discretion to an administrative system with no discretion and offers insights on the lessons to be learned from this experience.

Mavis Maclean and Andrea Warman compare national child support schemes from various countries in "A Comparative Approach to Child Support Systems: Legal Rules and Social Policies." They discuss current approaches in Australia and various European countries, comparing the policy focus in each support system and its location within the scheme of government. The authors note that these differences reflect variations in the assignment of responsibility for children and affect the distribution of resources.

The last part, entitled "Replacing the Current System," considers the proper role of government. Irwin Garfinkel argues that private child support cannot be expected to solve the problem of poor children when both parents are poor. He urges the establishment of a guaranteed minimum child benefit from the government in "The Limits of Private Child Support and the Role of an Assured Benefit." He argues that such a system would allow single-parent families more financial security and would not be too costly. In "Why Child Support Assurance Won't Work," Allen M. Parkman questions whether such a system of child support assurance would create socially undesirable incentives for prospective mothers. He also questions whether the benefits of such a system would justify its true costs. Garfinkel then offers a rejoinder to Parkman.

In "Child Support Is Not the Answer: The Nature of Dependencies and Welfare Reform," Martha Albertson Fineman criticizes current U.S. policy toward child poverty. She challenges the perpetuation of myths and symbols that underlie American family policy and calls for a reevaluation of gender roles and expectations. Like Garfinkel, she concludes that private child support will not provide adequate support for many poor single-parent families. Fineman advocates reconceptualization of public policy as it relates to support for children.

Part I

The Current Legal Structure

Child Support Comes of Age: An Introduction to the Law of Child Support

June Carbone

Child support has come of age. Once the stepchild of family law, child support has moved onto center stage in the modern effort to define and enforce family obligation. As congressionally mandated guidelines and strengthened state enforcement finally take hold, the issue is whether child support will mature into its new role or wither in the spotlight. The critics are growing in number and stature, and the success of the long-heralded reforms will ultimately depend not on the efficacy of collection efforts but on their ability to prompt a new ethic of family responsibility.

The prominence of child support is a critical element in a larger shift from the husband-wife relationship to parent-child ties as the defining element of family obligation. In an era in which nearly half of marriages end in divorce, one-third of American births are nonmarital, and 60 percent of American children spend part of their childhood in single-parent families, parenthood has replaced marriage as the more permanent part of family life, and the law has attempted to shift financial responsibility accordingly (Eekelaar 1991:90; Wong 1993; Beller and Graham 1993:2).[1] This legal shift is problematic at least in part because it proceeds from a public-policy consensus on the need for greater financial contributions to children without clearly addressing the relationship between fathers and mothers necessary to bring about such contributions. Reform supporters, an otherwise unlikely alliance of women's groups committed to greater equality and conservatives eager to protect the public fisc, agree only on a starting point—the principle that all parents should support their children. The almost universal support for the governing principle, however, begs the difficult questions of implementation: How does "natural" obligation translate into dollar amounts? Is it independent of the parents' relationship to each other? Of the circumstances of the child's conception and birth? Of obligation toward other children? Of ideas of equality and fairness between the parents?

Underlying these questions is the larger shift away from marriage as the defining element of family obligation. The older precedents in which child support has historically been rooted grew out of a conception of family centered on marriage. Older law drew clear distinctions between marital and nonmarital children, premised parental rights and responsibilities on the marital relationship, and subordinated parent-child issues to spousal obligations in the divorce context and public obligations in disputes involving unmarried parents (Fineman 1995). Modern child support practice, in contrast, erases the distinctions between marital and nonmarital births and treats parent-child ties as more lasting than spousal ones and independent of the relationship between mother and father. The most serious opposition to child support enforcement challenges the fairness of these results. Should a father with no more than a casual relationship with a mother and no say in her decision to bear and raise the child be charged with support on the same terms as a husband divorcing after a lengthy marriage? Should noncustodial parents who would have preferred to stay married and preferred sole or a greater degree of shared custody be charged with child support amounts that will significantly better their former spouses' standards of living? Should involved mothers who cannot support children on their own and consequently agree to fathers' custody claims be charged with child support in the same amount as noncustodial parents who spend less time with their children?

Existing child support enforcement proceeds from pragmatic considerations about children's need for financial support and the difficulties of individualized determinations. Yet the success of the new guidelines will also depend on their perceived fairness. This chapter examines the changing mores attending pregnancy, child rearing, and support in an effort to consider these issues and concludes that the guidelines are likely to be more successful in forging new norms for the middle class than in alleviating child poverty.

Child Support: The New Kid on the Block

Much of the tension between public policy and private norms arises because child-support enforcement takes place within the interstices of other forms of family obligation. Marriage has been the preferred source of provision for children, and support orders have historically represented the failure of other societal institutions to link effectively childbearing and marriage. As such, child support often constitutes more of a penalty for the violation of societal norms than a direct expression of parental responsibility for children.

In Anglo-American law, the first prominent child support enforcement involved the combination of rising "bastardy" rates and the availability of poor law relief in England centuries ago (Mason 1994:25; Stone 1979:382–404).[2] English ratepayers, much like their modern American counterparts, objected to paying for the support of children they viewed as the product of irresponsible behavior. Society brought considerable pressure to bear on young women to name the fathers of their children and on young men to marry the mothers of their children, pay support, or face imprisonment. Marriage was the preferred solution, and support orders were designed more to offset public expenditures than to provide adequately for children.

Nonetheless, as Lawrence Stone observes, the connections between law enforcement and customary morality were not always straightforward (Stone 1979). The conventional morality of the time would have condemned nonmarital births both before and after the eighteenth-century increase in child support enforcement. In the earlier period, however, public sanction punished fornication and bastardy more directly—use of the whipping post and the pillory were not uncommon (Mason 1994:25)[3]—and community disapproval encouraged men to marry the mothers of their children; if such was not the case, it encouraged women to hide, kill, or abandon their improvident offspring. As community controls on nonmarital sexuality relaxed, law enforcement shifted from physical to financial penalties. Direct punishment of fornication became less common, with the community interest "limited to ensuring that it was the father who paid for the support of the bastard child rather than the parish poor rate" (Stone 1979:398). Nevertheless, the purpose of the sanctions was to deter illegitimacy, increase the woman's leverage in securing a betrothal, and spare the public treasury, not to provide funds for the mother to raise the child on her own.

In similar fashion, postmarital child support became important only with rising rates of separation and divorce. As long as divorce was rare, the courts refused to intervene, believing support in such contexts unnecessary or, to the extent it would undermine patriarchal authority, undesirable (Scheule 1988–89).[4] Even with the initial nineteenth-century increases in divorce, child support took a backseat to other developments. Divorce, like illegitimacy, was a misfortune to be deterred, and the primary element in the financial allocation was assignment of responsibility for the breakup. Through the 1960s, divorce was available only if one—and only one—of the parties was at fault: that is, if it could be said that one party had so flouted the obligations of the marriage that the innocent party should be freed from the bonds of a union that had for all intents and purposes already ended. Within such a framework, the guilty party was responsible for those left behind. In practical terms, an innocent wife could demand (although not necessarily get) support in accordance with the standard of living enjoyed during the marriage, and an innocent husband could expect to emerge from the marriage with his resources intact (Carbone and Brinig 1991).

Child support was an incidental part of this framework. Although alimony, when ordered, might include an amount allocable to the expense of children, separate child support orders were rare, with Chancellor Kent observing in 1826 that the "obligation of parental duty is so well secured by the strength of natural affection that it seldom requires to be enforced by human laws" (Mason 1994:94). Into the 1980s, no more than half of divorcing couples had child support orders to enforce (Katz 1994). When Progressive-era legislation criminalized paternal failure to support children, the issue arose of whether fathers with no outstanding child support orders were off the hook. The majority concluded that parents had a duty of support even in the absence of a decree, but California courts agreed with the minority: "When a parent is deprived of the custody of his child, and therefore of its services and earnings, he is no longer liable for its support and education."[5] Even in jurisdictions in which the noncustodial parent's child support obligation was firmly established, Irwin Garfinkel and Marygold S. Melli (1990:163) report that "the courts operated on the premise that nonresident parents were entitled to spend their money as they saw fit, with the child receiving some of what was left."[6]

The net effect of this system was to reinforce marriage rather than to finance child rearing in cases of marital instability. The "honorable" obligation for sexually active people was to get married and stay married for the good of the children. The financial provisions the state enforced flowed from the duty to marry and the consequences of breach of the spouses' responsibilities to each other (Scheule 1988–89:832; Harris, Waldrop, and Waldrop 1990:689).[7]

No-Fault Divorce: Child Support's Rocky Adolescence, Part I

No-fault divorce, which swept through the fifty American states in the 1970s and 1980s, proceeded from two principles: first, the idea that where two spouses both wished to end their union, the law should not forbid it, whether or not either spouse had engaged in conduct that could be labeled fault; second, the conviction that the courts could not readily determine fault where the parties failed to agree. While the new legislation varied (Kay 1987),[8] the advent of no-fault divorces effectively rendered unenforceable the promise to remain married for a lifetime and remade the basis for financial allocations at divorce.

The Uniform Marriage and Divorce Act (UMDA), reflecting the no-fault reforms, embraced the principle of the clean break. The goal of divorce settlements in the new era was to end marriages as amicably as possible, with a minimum of recrimination for misconduct during the marriage and no continuing relationship between the spouses. Property division was accordingly preferred to alimony as the primary element in the financial distribution, and spousal support, if awarded at all, was designed to encourage the parties' financial independence. "Rehabilitative alimony," in the form of short-term transitional payments, replaced long-term support, and the custodial parent's child-care responsibilities were not to be a factor in the amount of spousal support. While the courts have since reversed some of the early decisions to insure greater support for long-term homemakers, spousal support continues to be awarded in less than a fifth of all divorces and rarely lasts long enough to be a significant factor in raising small children (Krauskopf 1988; Carbone 1994). The UMDA, at the same time it embraced a clean break between the adults, recognized child support as the remaining obligation from the marriage. Provision for child support, unlike spousal support, was to take into account the children's impact on the custodial parent's earning capacity, and child support was presumed appropriate in all cases involving children at the same time that spousal support was not. The combination of the small amounts of property available to most divorcing couples, the diminishing role of alimony, and the concept of the clean break left child support as the most prominent surviving obligation of the marriage (Katz 1994:52; Teachman and Paasch 1994).[9]

AFDC: Child Support's Rocky Adolescence, Part II

While public assistance in various forms is centuries old, aid that permits single parents to raise children on their own has been problematic. In the United States, by the beginning of the twentieth century, most states had some form of aid for dependent children, but, in all but a few states, nonmarital children were ineligible for aid, and mothers whose husbands abandoned them were suspect. The preferred solution to both problems was to bring the fathers to account for their offenses, and forty-six states passed separate laws criminalizing desertion and nonsupport (Mason 1994:95). The results for single mothers were nonetheless grim. In Boston in the early part of the century, only 13 percent of identifiable fathers were brought to court, and only 7 percent were ordered to pay anything (Mason 1994:99). Within one year of their birth, three-fifths of the nonmarital children born in Boston in 1914 would be wards of the state. In Minnesota, a Progressive-era model of strict child support enforcement, only 35 percent of unwed mothers in a 1921 study still had their children at two years of age (Mason 1994:100).

In 1935 Congress federalized provision for poor children with the adoption of Aid to Dependent Children (ADC, later Aid to Families with Dependent Children or AFDC) as part of the depression-era Social Security system. Congress envisioned the program as a temporary federal assumption of state efforts to provide for children whose fathers had died, and it permitted each state to impose "such other eligibility requirements—as to means, moral character, etc.—it sees fit" (L. Williams 1992:723n. 33; Gordon 1994). By the 1960s, however, the federal agency charged with administration of the program disapproved of barriers to aid based on illegitimacy alone, and the most common remaining restrictions focused on the presence of a "man in the house" (detected through unannounced midnight home visits) whose income would be deemed available to the recipient family (L. Williams 1992:723).[10] The U.S. Supreme Court invalidated these provisions in 1968, holding that

> Congress has determined that immorality and illegitimacy should be dealt with through rehabilitative measures rather than measures that punish dependent children, and that protection of such children is the paramount goal of AFDC. . . . [I]t is simply inconceivable, as HEW has recognized, that [any state] is free to discourage immorality and illegitimacy by the device of absolute disqualification of needy children.[11]

The Court further concluded that a state could deem a person's income available to the children in the household only when that person had a legal duty of support, not on the basis solely of a relationship with the mother.[12] Mary Ann Mason observes that with these changes, "for the first time in American history poverty alone was not an accepted condition for removing children from their parents, no matter what their marital status or with whom they chose to live" (1994:149).[13]

With relaxation of the barriers to assistance came renewed congressional efforts to secure financial contributions from absent fathers deemed responsible for their children's demands on the public purse. By 1975 Congress had established the Office of Child Support Enforcement (now located within the Department of Health and Human Services). AFDC applicants were required to assign their rights to uncollected child support to the state and to cooperate in establishing paternity, locating absent parents, obtaining support judgments, and securing payments. To keep their

AFDC funding, the states established enforcement agencies operating in accordance with federal standards (Krause 1989; Roberts 1994). While the early efforts were not always effective and local agencies sometimes spent more than they collected, the modern commitment to child support enforcement, much like its historical predecessors, started with the desire to cut public support.

Child Support Comes of Age: The Parental Obligation to Support Children in Accordance with Income

By the 1990s, the separate strands of child support enforcement—concern for the casualties of divorce and the demands children placed on the public fisc—had come together. Numerous studies documented the declining well-being of American children and attributed a substantial part of the result to the growing numbers of single-parent families and their straitened economic circumstances (Furstenberg, Sherwood, and Sullivan 1992; Hernandez 1993).[14] Other studies showed that child support awards were low compared both to the actual costs of raising children and to the ability of fathers to pay and that award amounts stayed low throughout a decade of legislative changes intended to strengthen child support enforcement (Beller and Graham 1993; Maccoby and Mnookin 1992; Garfinkel, Melli, and Robertson 1994).[15] At a time when American divorce rates had plateaued at world highs—with no viable movement to restrict divorce—and when nonmarital births continued to climb, increased child support was the one response that commanded nearly universal support.

Although advocates for the poor expressed reservations about child support enforcement in the AFDC context (Krause 1989),[16] child support as a partial solution to the problems of single-parent families was uncontroversial because it did not appear to break new ground. That parents should support their children was axiomatic, and that there was a legal obligation to do so, notwithstanding the historical marginality of the obligation, was well established.[17] The problems were the seemingly prosaic ones of amount and collection. To deal with these issues, the Family Support Act of 1988 required that each state (1) develop child support guidelines for determining the amount of the award; (2) implement automatic wage withholding without waiting for the noncustodial parent to default on payments; and (3) operate an approved computerized system for tracking and monitoring support payments (Garfinkel, Melli, and Robertson 1994:86).

The states proceeded pragmatically. In setting child support guidelines, states sought to increase the amount of the awards, their consistency and certainty, and the efficiency of the process (Pirog-Good 1993). Earlier cases had left child support to the discretion of the court, with the amount to be determined in accordance with the child's needs and the noncustodial parent's ability to pay. As a starting point for the new guidelines, however, the concept of need was problematic. First, any precise calculation of need, if defined in terms of basic expenditures on children, was likely to require a complicated assessment of individual budgets. Second, need would inevitably vary to some degree with income (Garfinkel and Melli 1990:164; L'Heureux-Dube 1994).[18] Guideline drafters therefore sought not only to attend to children's needs in some minimal sense but also to ensure that the child enjoyed support commensurate with the parents' income.

To accomplish these objectives, the states calculated income percentages that approximate the percentage of income that couples sharing a single household spend on their children. All but four states then determine each parent's respective share in accordance with one of two approaches: approximately seventeen states use a percentage-of-income standard that awards a fixed percentage of the noncustodial spouse's income irrespective of the income of the other spouse, while the majority employ an income-shares approach that bases each parent's portion of the total on his or her income, varying with the number of children (Oldham 1994:585, 592; Garfinkel, Melli, and Robertson 1984:87–88). The guidelines draw no distinctions between marital and nonmarital children or between welfare and nonwelfare recipients.[19] The new guidelines are intended in most cases to produce substantially higher awards than those in previous child support orders, although it is still too early for comprehensive data on the success of these efforts.[20]

This new child support system does not depart from previous practice in principle: parental obligation had been established in broad enough terms to incorporate the new guidelines. Nonetheless, the guidelines constitute a departure from centuries of practice in at least two respects: (1) the child support obligation is being treated as a serious one that if fully enforced could have a much greater impact on a noncustodial parent's standard of living than any sustained previous effort at enforcement; and (2) this imposition is independent of other family obligations. The historical emphasis in providing for children has been on marriage and the norms associated with it; the new guidelines allow parental obligation to trump other considerations. The results are most dramatic at the extremes. A father could find himself owing support for a child conceived during a one-night stand whose birth he would have opposed, and the support owed might be identical to that charged a father divorcing after a long marriage. A noncustodial mother could pay support that sustains the household of a former spouse whose affair and subsequent decision to leave precipitated their breakup. In earlier eras, practically, if not always legally, the claims tied to marriage would have been paramount; under the new system, the parental tie alone can determine obligation.

Child support enforcement is part of a wholesale shift in the legal regulation of the family and the balance of relationships between mothers and fathers. Child support starts from the need to insure that a larger percentage of the nation's resources are linked to children, but as Marsha Garrison, Irwin Garfinkel, and Martha Albertson Fineman point out in this volume, child support in itself is unlikely to solve the problem of child poverty. Rather, its greatest impact is likely to be on the middle class and on the conduct of relationships that never became the subject of court orders. Like many exercises in setting norms, the most visible aspects of the process may well be the sanctions against those who fail to comply. The success of the endeavor, however, is more likely to lie with the creation of a new ethic of parenthood that governs relationships offstage (Regan 1993).

NOTES

1. In John Eekelaar's words, "Indissoluble marriage has been replaced by the indissoluble responsibility of parenthood" (1991:90). In 1991, 34 percent of American births were to never-married mothers (Wong 1993).

2. Mary Ann Mason (1994) identifies the English Poor Law Act of 1576 as the first legal imposition of a parental obligation to pay for the upbringing of a nonmarital child. She also observes that the American colonies adopted similar laws. Lawrence Stone (1979) describes the English process in terms of cycles of increasing urbanization, adoption of greater poor relief by cities and towns, and corresponding public efforts to discourage nonmarital births. Stone begins with an initial cycle in the sixteenth century, declining illegitimacy rates by the early seventeenth century, and a second cycle of increasing rates of nonmarital childbearing toward the end of the seventeenth century. His description focuses on the poor law of 1733, but Parliament also passed similar legislation in the late seventeenth century. These statutes authorized the state to seek child support as compensation for state aid. They did not necessarily recognize a private right of child support enforcement.

3. Mason (1994) notes, for example, that the first Massachusetts laws punished fornication and bastardy and that the colony did not adopt an act requiring parents to support their children until the 1600s.

4. Indeed, the early cases did not raise the issue of support directly but rather involved the doctrine of "necessaries" in which creditors sued fathers to collect debts arising from the sale of provisions to children (Scheule 1988–89:809).

5. *Pacific Gold Dredging Co. v. Industrial Accident Commission,* 184 Cal. 462, 194 P. 1 (1920), cited in Mason 1994, 212n. 5. See also *State v. Langford,* 90 Or.

251, 176 P. 197 (1918) for a discussion of the different state positions. *Langford* involved a case in which the court had granted the divorce and awarded the mother custody without referring to child support in the decree. Ten years later, the father had paid no support, and the issue before the court was whether to construe a divorce decree that awarded the mother custody without mentioning support as absolving the father of any further obligation. The Oregon court observed that a majority of jurisdictions interpreted such decrees as leaving the father's "natural" obligation unimpaired, while a minority concluded that no support was owed. These practices have changed only in the last few years.

6. Garfinkel and Melli explain, "The rationale for this gentle treatment of nonresident parents was fear that the parent would refuse to pay anything at all by absconding or quitting work and the child would end up in an even worse situation" (1990:163–64).

7. As recently as 1965, the Oregon Supreme Court refused to order a father to pay child support in a case in which the mother left the father without cause, absent a court order giving her custody or evidence that the children would be harmed by the result. The decision reasoned

> The maintenance of family unity is regarded as an essential element in the preservation of our form of society. That unity would be impaired by an interpretation of the statute urged by plaintiff because, in permitting the wife to obtain support of the children taken from the home without cause, she would feel less constrained to remain at home and make an effort to keep the family united. (*Haight v. Haight,* 241 Or. 532, 405 P.2d 622 [1965])

See discussion in Scheule 1988–89:832; Harris, Waldrop, and Waldrop 1990:689.

8. England and some U.S. states continued to require the courts to review the desirability of the divorce or the irreconcilability of the parties' differences and added no-fault grounds for divorce without abolishing the existing fault grounds. Nonetheless, given judicial distaste for such determinations and the collusion of the parties, divorce is effectively available in most jurisdictions at will, and findings of misconduct play a relatively minor role in modern financial allocations. See Kay 1987.

9. By 1989, for example, the percentage of divorcing custodial parents with child support orders had increased from less than 50 percent to 72 percent. During the same period, the percentage of spousal support awards was much lower. Compare Katz 1994:52 with Teachman and Paasch 1994:75.

10. In addition, Louisiana deemed "unsuitable" homes in which the mother bore subsequent illegitimate children after acceptance of the assistance (L. Williams 1992:723n. 34).

11. *King v. Smith,* 392 U.S. 309, 324–25 (1968). The Supreme Court decision was one of statutory construction, and the Court based its interpretation on the AFDC amendments and agency rulings that took place during the 1960s, not on the original legislative history. The Court emphasized that the states could not both declare a home unsuitable for children (and therefore ineligible for support) and fail to take action to remove children from the home.

12. Id. at 326–32. See also *Lewis v. Martin,* 397 U.S. 552 (1970).

13. The "man in the house" rules, though designed to deter "immorality," were also thoroughly criticized for encouraging poor couples to split up. Under the AFDC system of the 1960s, mother and child might be financially better off on their own than with an impecunious father.

14. Fifty-one percent of all children in female-headed households were poor, as were more than two-thirds of children under the age of six living in such households (Furstenberg, Sherwood, and Sullivan 1992:1).

15. Garfinkel, Melli, and Robertson summarize the developments:

> Despite a decade and a half of child support reform, some indicators suggest there has been little progress. In both 1978 and 1989, only six of ten eligible mothers had child support awards. The proportion of awards paid increased only from 64 percent to 69 percent. Worst of all, the real value of child support awards declined by 22 percent between 1978 and 1985, and from $3,680 to $2,877. By 1989, average awards increased to $3,293, still 10 percent lower than awards in 1978. (1994:85–87)

Nonetheless, the reasons for these results are complex. For example, the percentages of both divorced and never-married mothers receiving child support orders increased during this time period, but the percentage of the total group that consisted of unmarried parents (a group with a much lower overall rate of child support orders) increased. Garfinkel, Melli, and Robertson conclude that "Like Alice in Wonderland, the U.S. child support system has had to go faster just to stay in place" (1984:87).

16. Reservations included concern about the risks poor women often faced in naming the fathers of their children, the utility of collection from fathers who themselves had very little income, the fairness of the government-imposed obligations in circumstances in which the fathers, in accordance with community norms, had no reasonable expectation of responsibility for the resulting child, and ideological objections to using payments from poor fathers to offset state assistance rather than to improve the lot of the children.

17. Cases from the fault era not only recognized a parental support obligation that was in most states dependent on custody rather than fault but also defined the obligation in generous terms. See, e.g., *Commonwealth ex rel. Kaplan v. Kaplan,* 344 A.2d 578, 579 (Pa. Super. Ct. 1975) ("The responsibility of the parents, to support the child to the best of their ability, consistent with their own station in life, is 'well nigh absolute.'") The problem was that the awards did not live up to the rhetoric.

18. To the extent, for example, that housing was likely to be the largest expense in most budgets, the amount "needed" for housing would vary with the family's socioeconomic status (Garfinkel and Melli 1990:164). Moreover, guideline drafters were often skeptical of need because of the extent to which parents and courts have historically understated expenditures on children (L'Heureaux-Dube 1994).

19. In addition, state guidelines tended to follow predominant case law and not give credit for additional dependents; however, according to a report prepared for

the state of South Carolina, guidelines in nineteen states now have formula adjustments that give credit for additional dependents, while thirteen states specify additional dependents as a deviation criterion (R. Williams 1994:1, 13).

20. The most recent federal report indicates that child support collection increased by 40 percent from 1992 to 1995 and that paternity actions increased by a comparable amount (U.S. Department of Health and Human Services 1995).

REFERENCES

Beller, A., and John W. Graham. 1993. *Small Change: The Economics of Child Support.* New Haven and London: Yale University Press.

Carbone, June. 1994. A Feminist Perspective on Divorce. *Future of Children* 4:183–209.

Carbone, June, and Margaret F. Brinig. 1991. Rethinking Marriage: Feminist Ideology, Economic Changes, and Divorce Reform. *Tulane Law Review* 65:953–1010.

Eekelaar, John. 1991. *Regulating Divorce.* Oxford: Clarendon Press.

Fineman, Martha. 1995. *The Neutered Mother, the Sexual Family, and Other Twentieth Century Tragedies.* New York and London: Routledge.

Furstenberg, Frank F., Kay E. Sherwood, and Mercer L. Sullivan. 1992. *Caring and Paying: What Fathers and Mothers Say about Child Support.* New York: Manpower Demonstration Research Corporation.

Garfinkel, Irwin, and Marygold S. Melli. 1990. The Use of Normative Standards in Family Law Decisions: Developing Mathematical Standards for Child Support. *Family Law Quarterly* 24:157–78.

Garfinkel, Irwin, Marygold S. Melli, and John G. Robertson. 1994. Child Support Orders: A Perspective on Reform. *Future of Children* 9:84–100.

Gordon, Linda. 1994. *Pitied but Not Entitled: Single Mothers and the History of Welfare.* Cambridge, MA: Harvard University Press.

Harris, Leslie J., D. Dennis Waldrop, and Lori Rathun Waldrop. 1990. Making and Breaking Connections between Parents' Duty to Support and Right to Control Their Children. *Oregon Law Review* 69:689–739.

Hernandez, Donald J. 1993. *America's Children: Resources from Family, Government, and the Economy.* New York: Russell Sage Foundation.

Katz, Sanford N. 1994. Historical Perspectives and Current Trends in the Legal Process of Divorce. *Future of Children* 4:44–62.

Kay, Herma Hill. 1987. Equality and Difference: A Perspective on No-Fault Divorce and Its Aftermath. *Cincinnati Law Review* 56:1–90.

Krause, Harry. 1989. Child Support Reassessed: Limits of Private Responsibility and the Public Interest. *University of Illinois Law Review* 1989:367–98.

Krauskopf, Joan. 1988. Limited Duration Alimony: Uses and Abuses of Limited Duration Alimony. *Family Law Quarterly* 21:573–89.

L'Heureux-Dube, Claire. 1994. Economic Consequences of Divorce: The View from Canada. *Houston Law Review* 31:451–98.

Maccoby, Eleanor E., and Robert H. Mnookin. 1992. *Dividing the Child: Social and Legal Dilemmas of Custody*. Cambridge MA: Harvard University Press.

Mason, Mary Ann. 1994. *From Father's Property to Children's Rights: The History of Child Custody in the United States*. New York: Columbia University Press.

Oldham, J. Thomas. 1994. The Appropriate Child Support Award When the Noncustodial Parent Earns Less than the Custodial Parent. *Houston Law Review* 31:585–616.

Pirog-Good, Maureen A. 1993. Child Support Guidelines and the Economic Well-Being of Children in the United States. *Family Relations* 42:453–62.

Regan, Milton C. 1993. *Family Law and the Pursuit of Intimacy*. New York and London: New York University Press.

Roberts, Paula G. 1994. Child Support Orders: Problems with Enforcement. *Future of Children* 4:101–20.

Scheule, Donna. 1988–89. Origins and Development of the Law of Parental Child Support. *Journal of Family Law* 27:807–32.

Stone, Lawrence. 1979. *The Family, Sex and Marriage: In England 1500–1800*. Abridged ed. New York: Harper Torchbooks.

Teachman, Jay D., and Kathleen M. Paasch. 1994. Financial Impact of Divorce on Children and Their Families. *Future of Children* 4:63–83.

U.S. Department of Health and Human Services. 1995. *Nineteenth Annual Report to Congress on Child Support Enforcement*. December. Washington, DC: U.S. Department of Health and Human Services.

Williams, Lucy A. 1992. The Ideology of Division: Behavior Modification Welfare Reform Proposals. *Yale Law Journal* 102:719–46.

Williams, Robert G. 1994. An Overview of Child Support Guidelines in the United States. In *Child Support Guidelines: The Next Generation*, ed. Margaret Campbell Hayes. Washington, DC: U.S. Department of Health and Human Services, Administration for Children and Families, Office of Child Support Enforcement.

Wong, Pat. 1993. *Child Support and Welfare Reform*. New York and London: Garland Publishing.

The Goals and Limits of Child Support Policy

Marsha Garrison

There can be little doubt that child support policy is an urgent concern. At least half of all American children will be eligible for child support at some point during their minority,[1] but most receive inadequate payments, and many receive nothing at all.

Inadequate support can contribute to welfare dependence and poverty (Bane 1986:231; G. Duncan and Rodgers 1988:1017 table 5). Almost half of welfare entrants become eligible for benefits as a result of marital separation or divorce. More than half of children in mother-only households are poverty stricken; in black and Hispanic mother-only households, more than two-thirds are poor (U.S. Bureau of the Census 1993:470–71, tables 737, 740).

In addition to these immediate adverse consequences, inadequate child support can produce expensive long-range effects. Children in single-parent households are more likely to experience poor health, behavioral problems, delinquency, and low educational attainment than are their peers in intact families; as adults these children have higher rates of poverty, early childbearing, and divorce (Hernandez 1993:58–64; W. Duncan 1994; McLanahan 1992:285–98; McLanahan et al. 1991:51–78). While these outcomes do not result solely from reduced economic status, this factor appears to be the most important of the identifiable causes (McLanahan and Sandefur 1994:3, 79–94).

Child support awards and payments also have a profound effect on the comparative well-being of family members. Under traditional support law, divorce typically produces an improvement in the living standard of the noncustodial parent, while that of his child and the custodial parent plummets (Garrison 1991:633n. 43, 721 table 56).

Although the problems associated with inadequate child support are not new, rising rates of divorce and nonmarital parenting have enhanced their visibility and urgency. The result, as June Carbone relates in her introduction to this volume, has been a succession of new laws designed to raise both the level and the payment rate of support awards. These laws have established new mechanisms for establishing paternity and enforcing support obligations. The new legislation has also altered the method by which the support obligation is calculated. Traditional support law was highly discretionary. Today, based on directives from Congress, each state utilizes numerical guidelines: while these guidelines need establish only a rebuttable presumption as to the child support amount, deviation must be justified in a written decision (Dodson and Entmacher 1994; Grimm and Munsterman 1991).

These various initiatives have thus far failed to achieve their goals. After almost two decades of government effort, fewer than six out of ten eligible women—and less than one-third of those never married—are awarded child support. The mean child support payment, in inflation-adjusted dollars, still falls short of its 1978 value.[2] Neither the poverty rate of children in single-parent households nor the disparity in postdivorce living standards of children and their noncustodial parents has declined.[3]

This dismal record raises fundamental questions about the goals and limits of government child support policy: Why have efforts to improve awards and payments had so little effect? How much poverty and living standard loss does child support policy have the capacity to avert? What level of awards and payments is achievable? Before undertaking new initiatives, we need to know why the recent reforms have failed and what child support policy can realistically be expected to accomplish. This chapter describes what we know about the failures and limits of government support policy and assesses current policy goals in light of that knowledge.

Why Have Efforts to Improve Child Support Outcomes Had So Little Effect?

What Has Been Achieved

In 1978, when the Bureau of the Census first collected national data on child support awards and payments, 59 percent of support-eligible mothers had obtained support orders. About half of those awarded support received full payment. The average value of child support paid ($3,865) represented less than half of what economists estimate as typical child-rearing costs and only 13 percent of average male earnings for that year.[4] State research also documented considerable variation in award values, even among families of similar size and socioeconomic characteristics.[5]

In 1991, after more than a decade of effort to improve these dismal results, 56 percent of eligible mothers had obtained support orders. About half of those awarded support received full payment. The average value of support paid ($3,011) represented less than half of what economists estimate as typical child-rearing costs and only 8 percent of average male earnings for that year. Research at the state level continued to document considerable variation in award values among families of similar size and socioeconomic characteristics.[6]

The introduction of numerical guidelines in the late 1980s appears to have modestly increased the value of new support awards,[7] but increases reported to date fall far short of those predicted (Haskins et al. 1985; Garfinkel, Oellerich, and Robins 1991). In some states award levels did not increase at all or increased only within certain income groups.[8] Children's living standards still typically plummet after family dissolution.[9]

This tale of failure masks some successes. First, the paternity establishment reforms enacted as part of the child support initiatives have improved outcomes for never-married mothers, whose award rate more than doubled between 1978 and 1991 (U.S. Bureau of the Census 1980, 1991:6). Never-married black mothers have done particularly well, obtaining a real-dollar improvement in the value of their awards, in contrast to the decline in award values experienced by other support-eligible mothers. Second, the child support enforcement program may have succeeded in enabling some women to escape welfare (Beller and Graham 1993:45). Third, given the rising number of never-married mothers over the reform period, the overall decline in expected payments "would almost certainly have been larger . . . without government efforts that helped raise award and receipt rates" (Beller and Graham 1993:53).

While government policy thus appears to have had some impact, its overall effect has been small. For most support-eligible children, the government initiatives appear to have achieved marginal improvements at best. Even for the group of never-married mothers helped most by the new laws, results fall far short of what is needed. These mothers continue to have the worst child support prospects of any group: more than three-quarters still do not have child support awards, and even those who receive support have payments that average only 51 percent of the average for the entire group of custodial mothers (U.S. Bureau of the Census 1991:18 table 2).

The Reasons for the Results

These discouraging results are sobering but not altogether surprising. One reason why the child support initiatives have not had more impact is simply that the guidelines states adopted in response to the federal mandate do not produce awards high enough to protect many children from poverty or a dramatic decline in living standard. One recent review, which evaluated all state guidelines in effect in 1989–90, concludes that none required lower-income noncustodial parents to provide enough child support to ensure a poverty-level or "minimum decent living" standard for two children; a significant number of states also failed to ensure that children in middle-income families enjoyed a minimum decent living standard (Dodson and Entmacher 1994:95–98). Moreover, awards under the guidelines reviewed produced a dramatic decline in children's living standards compared to that of the noncustodial parent: on average, children's living standards declined by 26 percent, while noncustodial parents' improved by 34 percent (Dodson and Entmacher 1994:98).[10]

Current guidelines do not do a better job of averting poverty or living standard loss primarily because they were not designed with these goals in mind. Only a few states utilize guidelines that take poverty prevention as an objective; none aim at maintaining the child's living standard or even at equalizing living standard loss.

What current guidelines do invariably seek is "continuity-of-expenditure." This approach, which aims to replicate typical child-related outlay in a two-parent family, is expressed in two different formulas, the "percentage-of-obligor-income" standard, developed in Wisconsin, and the more popular "income-shares" formula, developed by an advisory panel appointed by the U.S. Department of Health and Human Services, Office of Child Support Enforcement. Both of these formulas use standard "child-expense" percentages (derived from consumer expenditure surveys) that are applied to parental income and that vary depending on the number of children.[11] In the few states that aim for poverty prevention as well as continuity-of-expenditure,[12] a "primary support" value, designed to meet the minimum needs of one adult, is first subtracted from each parent's income; the remainder is then applied, in proportion to the parents' relative incomes, to the "basic child support obligation," designed to meet the minimum needs of one or more children. If the support obligor still has available income, a fixed percentage of that income, based on the percentage-of-obligor-income model, is then added to the basic support obligation (Williams 1994:6).

Among these guideline formulas, only the percentage-of-obligor income formula gives the child's interest in poverty avoidance the same weight as the parent's interest. The poverty-prevention model requires the court first to protect the support obligor from poverty; the child's needs become relevant only subsequently. The income-shares models similarly use a "self-support reserve" for the noncustodial parent that establishes an income level (typically the federal poverty level for a one-person household) below which a lower award than the guidelines would otherwise require is permitted or presumptively required.[13] Only a few states that provide the support obligor with a self-support reserve provide a comparable support reserve to the custodial household (Dodson and Entmacher 1994:49–55).

While the obligor's self-support reserve is a common feature of continuity-of-expenditure-type guidelines, it is actually inconsistent with the continuity-of-expenditure goal. Some studies have found that parents spend approximately the same percentage of household income on their children at all income levels; others have found that poor parents spend more on their children than their wealthier counterparts (Espenshade 1984). No studies have reported that poor parents spend less. As a result, percentage-of-obligor-income guidelines offer no break to low-income parents (Garfinkel 1992:134). Nor does the self-support reserve have any counterpart in traditional support law; empirical research has shown that child support awards under traditional standards were regressive, with low-income parents typically paying greater proportions of their incomes in child support than high-income parents (Weitzman 1985:462–69; Garrison 1991:718 table 53; McLindon 1987:371–72).

Abolition of the self-support reserve would ameliorate but would not remedy the inadequacies of current guidelines. Even without a self-support reserve, existing guidelines are inherently ill-suited to the task of preserving children's standard of living. The estimates of child-related expenditure on which the guidelines rely are based on predictions of how much more income a two-parent household, with a given level of expenditure, would need to add a new family member and maintain its standard of living. But single parents appear to spend a considerably larger fraction of their incomes on children than do two-parent households.[14] Moreover, more than 90 percent of typical household expenditures represents goods such as housing, transportation, and utility payments that cannot easily be allocated to specific family members (Betson 1990:3). The estimates thus describe only the marginal, or extra, costs associated with a new family member, not the per-person allocation of family resources.

These marginal cost estimates all rely on one or another household equivalence scale, devised by economists to permit living standard comparisons when households are not the same size.[15] Although their assumptions vary, such scales offer a basis for predicting how much more income a family will need to add a new member (a baby, for example) and maintain its current living standard (Blackorby and Donaldson 1991:164; Deaton and Muellbauer 1986; Nelson 1993). But the scales say nothing about the baby's living standard if her parents separate, dividing the family and its income (Tsakloglou 1991:354). Unless the same expenditure base is available in the baby's new household—an unlikely result given the prevailing gender-based wage gap—her living standard must, of necessity, change. The guidelines thus severely penalize children for being in the custody of a parent who has less income and reward them for living with the parent who has more (Betson 1990:19).

In sum, an important reason why current guidelines do not avert children's poverty or living standard loss is that the guidelines were not designed to do so. The guidelines' structure and goals are altogether incompatible with these other aims.

Deficiencies in the guidelines themselves are not the only problem, however. The individualized process by which awards are determined and enforced also plays a significant role. None of the support initiatives have altered the fact that each parent-claimant, through litigation or negotiation, must both establish the support obligation and make sure it is paid. Many parents fail to accomplish these tasks; indeed, one researcher has recently estimated that as much as $34 billion in additional child support could be collected if all children had support orders that were fully paid (Sorensen 1997).

Variation in award levels results largely from the negotiation process that determines the vast majority of child support orders.[16] Many parents who negotiate support awards are poorly informed about the relevant legal standards (Erlanger, Chambliss, and Melli 1987; Melli, Erlanger, and Chambliss 1988; Jacob 1992; Sarat and Felstiner 1989). In a large and apparently growing proportion of cases, lawyer representation is available to only one—or neither—parent (Pearson 1993:281–82; Murphy 1994). Under these circumstances, each parent's resources and attitudes toward the divorce may play important roles in determining child support outcomes and produce results that bear little relationship to those lawmakers intended.[17]

The failure of many support-eligible parents to seek awards also contributes to the problem. More than 40 percent of mothers—and almost 75 percent of those never married—have not obtained child support awards. While some women could not locate their children's fathers or believed that they were unable to pay, others report that they simply did not want or pursue an award.[18] We know little about the sources of maternal reluctance to pursue child support, and government initiatives have thus far done little to combat it. But given the increasing numbers of never-married mothers among those eligible for support, this problem demands sustained attention and research.

The failure of current child support initiatives to meet congressional goals thus derives from a combination of factors: the guidelines do not usually require awards high enough to avert a significant drop in living standard; for low-income families, they often fail to require enough support to avert poverty. This basic problem is exacerbated by inconsistencies associated with processing of individual cases: parents may forgo an award and, unless they apply for public assistance, that decision will be final; parents negotiate their own awards and may accept less support than the guidelines would require; and parents must individually collect unpaid awards, with varied resources and ability to succeed.

How Much Poverty and Living Standard Loss Could Child Support Policy Avert?

Poverty—How Much Is Preventable?

Current guidelines could be revised to increase their potential for poverty prevention: the obligor's self-support reserve feature of current guidelines could be scrapped; low-income obligors could be required to pay proportionally more support than those in higher income brackets (as they did under discretionary support standards) to avert their children's poverty; and support enforcement by government rather than individual parents could be extended to all poor families rather than focusing on public assistance recipients. How much poverty could such measures avert?

The quick answer to this question is simply that we do not know. These measures would undoubtedly improve the life circumstances of some poor children in single-parent households, but how many would actually be lifted above the poverty line is much less clear. Child support policy can avert poverty only if that poverty derives from an income loss associated with family dissolution or nonformation. If parents lack the resources to avoid poverty when together, child support alone cannot remedy the problem. Support policy may cause the child to experience deeper poverty by inequitably distributing the noncustodial parent's meager resources, but it cannot offer a cure (see Garfinkel, "The Limits of Private Child Support and the Role of an Assured Benefit"; Fineman, "Child Support Is Not the Answer: The Nature of Dependencies and Welfare Reform," both in this volume).

While there is a strong correlation between children's poverty and family breakup—the poverty rate of children in single-mother households is approximately five times that of children in married-couple households (U.S. Bureau of the Census 1993:470 table 737)—the evidence suggests that family dissolution is not in fact the most important cause of the current high rate of children's poverty. Indeed, even if the percentage of children living in mother-only households could be brought back to its 1959 low, experts estimate no more than a 10 to 20 percent reduction in the current children's poverty rate (Hernandez 1993:290; Bane 1986:231; G. Duncan and Rodgers 1988:1017 table 5).

Family structure has so little impact on children's poverty because the fathers of children in mother-only households are disproportionately concentrated at the low end of the income spectrum (Hernandez 1993:310–11). Although the earnings of low-income fathers may rise substantially over time (Phillips and Garfinkel 1993:236–37 table 3), divorce and nonmarital childbearing are both significantly linked with low socioeconomic status. Divorce is approximately twice as likely for couples below the poverty line as it is for the general pool of married couples,[19] and nonmarital parenting is even more highly correlated with low income.[20] Many children in poor single-parent homes would thus remain poor even if their parents were (re)united.

The primary source of children's poverty is simply low income (Ellwood and Summers 1986:81–83 figure 4.2; Hernandez 1993:325, 374 table A-9.1). For the period 1939–59, 43 of the 46 percentage points by which children's poverty declined are predictable based on the increased real value of paternal incomes over this time period; conversely, for the period 1969–88, the increase in children's poverty is strongly associated with the decreased real value of paternal incomes (Hernandez 1993:312, 325). Even for black children, who have consistently experienced the highest likelihood of residence in mother-only homes, income trends are a more important factor in producing children's poverty than is family composition (Bane 1986:231; G. Duncan and Rodgers 1987). Indeed, the available evidence suggests that movement into a single-parent household is a far more important cause of poverty for white children for than black children; white children whose parents are divorced have the lowest poverty rate among children in single-parent households but have the highest rate of poverty induced by family disruption (Nichols-Casebolt 1992:196–97 table 8.2; G. Duncan and Rodgers 1988:1012).

Family structure is not, of course, an insignificant factor in producing children's poverty. Given the declining real value of male incomes over the past twenty-five years, families increasingly need two parents in the labor force to stay above the poverty line.[21] Moreover, while family structure may be outweighed by parental income as a determinant of the overall rate of children's poverty, it has been an extremely important factor in producing the 40 percent increase in the children's poverty rate registered over the past twenty-five years. Because single-mother households have a higher poverty rate than do two-parent families, a larger proportion of children in such households ensures a rise in children's poverty (Hernandez 1993; U.S. Bureau of the Census 1993). Were the rate of mother-only households to be brought back to its 1959 level, the available data suggest that the post-1969 increase in the children's poverty rate could be reduced by anywhere from 40 to 80 percent and that welfare dependence could be reduced as well.[22]

Unfortunately, child support policy cannot achieve the same reduction in children's poverty as would a lower rate of mother-only households. The reason is simply that two households cannot live as cheaply as one; thus, the federal poverty level for a family of three is approximately 50 percent less than that of a family of one and a family of two. For the family that had barely averted poverty when together, dissolution ensures that some if not all family members will thereafter be poor. While recent estimates are unavailable, one expert has estimated that 16 percent of whites and 28 percent of blacks who became poor during the early 1980s as a result of movement into female-headed households did so simply because of the loss of economies of scale (Bane 1986:230).

No child support policy can raise the income of a child support obligor or re-create the economies of scale available to an intact household. One recent prediction thus suggests that even if all noncustodial parents paid child support based on current guidelines, the public assistance rolls would be reduced by only 9 percent and the poverty rate by 5 percent (Sorensen 1995:56–57). Given the disproportionate number of low-income families among those that experience divorce or nonmarriage, it is unlikely that even the best child support laws will achieve a dramatic reduction in the children's poverty rate or level of welfare dependence.

Focusing on child support as an antipoverty strategy may also increase the racial and marital status gap in children's poverty rates. One pair of researchers recently calculated that with "medium improvements in child support awards and collections" and award values set pursuant to the Wisconsin percentage-of-income child support formula, white custodial parents would obtain annual gains more than two and a half times those of black custodial parents. When the net benefits and tax savings of this program were aggregated by ethnic group, white families obtained a $481 million annual gain while both black and Hispanic families suffered more than a $200 million loss (Garfinkel, Meyer, and Sandefur 1992:518 table 3).

Child support policy thus has some potential for reducing children's poverty. That potential could be realized by eliminating the self-support reserve feature of current guidelines, improving poor custodial parents' access to enforcement mechanisms, and (within limits) employing regressive support schedules that tax poor parents at a higher rate than their wealthier counterparts. But the poverty reduction potential of these measures is severely limited by the disproportionate number of low-income parents among the support-eligible population and the impact of lost economies of scale. Because most poor children do not have "deadbeat dads" who can contribute significantly more to their support (Penkrot 1989; Michalopoulos and Garfinkel 1989), child support policy will offer the most help to the least needy: it cannot be expected to achieve a major reduction in children's poverty.

Living Standard Loss: Can Child Support Policy Prevent It?

Child support policy has more potential as a means of curbing the loss of living standard that children typically experience after family dissolution. While family dissolution necessitates a living standard decline because of lost economies of scale, that decline need not be borne solely by the custodial household. Unlike poverty, which cannot be prevented unless parents have income above the poverty line, living standard loss can be equalized—or allocated to the noncustodial parent—at any income level.

Child support policy aside, children have typically suffered the brunt of this inevitable loss as a result of two complementary factors: most children reside with their mothers, and mothers typically earn less than fathers. The result is that the larger segment of the divided family is left with the least income.

Child support policy could require that support payments be calculated to equalize living standard loss. Indeed, support policy could require transfers that would reverse the loss, imposing it entirely on the noncustodial parent. But while child support is theoretically capable of apportioning living standard loss in any chosen way, the ability to transfer loss from the custodial to noncustodial household is not, in fact, unlimited. Consider the case of Mr. and Mrs. A, who have six minor children and an annual income of $30,000, all earned by Mr. A. If Mrs. A assumes sole custody of the children postdivorce and continues to earn no income, it would be necessary to transfer $22,500, or 75 percent of Mr. A's income, from Mr. A to Mrs. A. and the children to equalize the family's living standard loss; to ensure that the children suffer no loss would require a transfer of $26,763, or 89 percent of Mr. A's income, leaving him with only $3,237 to meet his own needs.[23]

A law requiring transfers of this magnitude would produce several practical problems. One is enforcement. Researchers report, not surprisingly, that higher support obligations tend to produce a lower percentage of support paid.[24] Certainly most Mr. As would resist—mightily—a child support obligation amounting to 90 percent or even 75 percent of their income. Even if Mr. A could somehow be forced to pay, his incentive to keep earning $30,000 per year would be small: why should he work hard to retain only 10 percent or even 25 percent of his income? High levels of support obligation thus produce significant payment and work disincentives that will likely prevent, in a case like that of the As, realization of a living standard loss equalization goal.[25]

Another problem arises from the fact that to avert the children's living standard loss, Mr. A is pushed well below the poverty line. At this income level, Mr. A's ability to continue earning may well be impaired: he may be unable to maintain his residence or to keep the car he needs to get to and from work. He may even become eligible for one or another public benefit. In sum, in cases like that of the As, loss avoidance and even equalization may ultimately cost both the children and the public more than is gained.

The case of the As is, of course, extreme. Very few support obligors have six children: the vast majority have one or two.[26] Nor does the typical single mother have no earned income whatsoever.[27] In the majority of cases, with fewer children and some earned income going to the custodial household, loss equalization is a more realistic possibility. Consider the case of the Bs, who have one child and a $30,000 annual income. Mr. B earns $20,000; Mrs. B $10,000. In this case, equalization of living standard loss would require a transfer of $6,800, or 34 percent of Mr. B's income.[28] While payment and work disincentives are not negligible, they are also not extreme; indeed, the maximum percentage (utilized for obligors with many children) contained in current guidelines is typically set at this level or even higher (see Williams 1994). Not every Mr. B might earn and pay at this level of transfer, but more Mr. Bs would pay than Mr. As.

In sum, if guidelines were revised to aim at living standard equalization, that result could often be achieved. Unlike poverty prevention, equalization does not depend on a given level of obligor income. The ability to achieve equalization is limited by payment and work disincentives that are magnified at high support rates. But, while we cannot realistically achieve equalization in all cases, we certainly could do much better than we do now.

What Goals Should Support Policy Aim to Achieve?

Support awards and payment levels can be increased. The significant gap between children's standard of living and that of their noncustodial parents can be reduced. To achieve these realistic goals will require altered guidelines that do not prefer the interests of noncustodial parents to those of their children. Doing so will also require an improved and streamlined case processing system to reduce award variability and nonpayment.

Equalizing Living Standard Loss: Models and Problems

While current guidelines do not attempt to equalize living standard loss, there are several existing models—none more complex than current continuity-of-expenditure guidelines—that do. The best known is the "equal outcomes" model that some experts advocated in the early days of the guidelines movement (Cassetty and Sprinkle 1987:329; Eden, Cassetty, and Terrell 1987:353; Sawhill 1983:79). The central goal of this model is equalization of living standards. But because the model gives equal weight to the needs of all family members—eliminating the self-support reserve—it does a much better job of poverty prevention than do current guidelines.

Although policymakers frequently endorsed this model's basic goals, no state adopted it. This disinterest stemmed in part from the direction set by the federal government, which commissioned an economic analysis of child-rearing costs that produced the income-shares approach.[29] State policymakers also appear to have been confused about the limitations inherent in the income-shares model and how it differed from the equal outcomes approach.[30] And policymakers expressed reservations about equal outcomes based on the payment and work disincentives that arise when the model is used in certain cases; the Massachusetts state child support commission, for example, declared its preference for equal outcomes "as the method that best addressed the [problem of] disparity of living standards" before rejecting it because of the concern that the model "would provide a disincentive for both parents to work" (Smith and Laramore 1987:267, 273; Czapanskiy 1987:5, 6).

The original proponents of the equal outcomes model did not address these disincentives, but it is certainly possible to do so. Table 1 compares the results of an income-shares guideline incorporating a self-support reserve feature with those obtained under both a "pure" equal outcomes model and one modified to reduce work and payment disincentives. The modified equal outcomes model relies on the assumption that the initial support rate should not exceed 40 percent and that the modification rate should not exceed 33 percent.

These maxima are consistent with those contained in current guidelines and with current income tax rates, but I offer them simply as plausible "guesstimates."[31] Experts agree that high tax rates create significant negative payment and work incentives (Graetz 1983:273), but there is no consensus on the magnitude of the effect and almost no research on the magnitude of the disincentives induced by differing rates of child support. Using "plausible" labor supply elasticities, economist David Betson calculated the labor supply effect of switching from a continuity-of-expenditure child support formula to an equal outcomes model and concluded that for a family with one child and $30,000 in combined parental income, the net effect was a reduction in total income of about 11 percent. But Betson did not attempt to calculate the effect of nonpayment incentives or offer an optimal formula. The modified equal outcomes model offered here thus might require adjustment to achieve the best possible results.

TABLE 1. Results of Income-Shares and Equal Outcomes Child Support Models Applied to a One-Child Family ($ per month child support and % of obligor income), by parental income

Total Net Monthly Income Father's (F) and Mother's (M) Net Household Income Status Changes	Model A[a] (Income Shares with Self-Support Reserve) $ mo. / inc. %	Model B[b] (Pure Equal Outcomes) $ mo. / inc. %	Model C[c] (Modified Equal Outcomes) $ mo. / inc. %
Case 1: $800			
F $800; M $0	50 / 6	448 / 56	320 / 40
F's income up 20% ($960)	230 / 24	538 / 56	373 / 39
M's income rises to $500	50 / 6	228 / 29	228 / 29
F remarries (no new income)	50 / 6	400 / 50	320 / 40
M remarries ($800 new income)	50 / 6	160 / 20	160 / 20
Case 2: $2,5004			
F $1,667; M $833	400 / 24	567 / 34	567 / 34
F's income up 20% ($2,000)	480 / 24	753 / 38	677 / 34
M's income up 20% ($1,000)	400 / 24	494 / 30	512 / 31
F remarries ($833 new income)	400 / 16	834 / 33	834 / 33
M remarries ($1,667 new income)	400 / 24	375 / 23	375 / 23
Case 3: $5,000			
F $2,500; M $2,500	600 / 24	550 / 22	550 / 22
F's income up 20% ($3,000)	720 / 24	855 / 29	715 / 24
M's income up 20% ($3,000)	600 / 24	355 / 14	385 / 15
F remarries ($2,500 new income)	600 / 12	1,175 / 24	1,175 / 24
M remarries ($2,500 new income)	600 / 24	175 / 7	175 / 7

[a]Model A: For a one-child family, income-shares guidelines require a child support award ranging from 18 percent to 24 percent of net income: actual child-care costs are typically added to the basic award. To avoid individualized consideration of child-care costs, child support was calculated here at 24 percent of net income instead of the midpoint of the percentage range. The self-support reserve was calculated using the 1993 poverty threshold for a one-person family, the most common calculation basis. The minimum support obligation was set at fifty dollars, also the most common value.

[b]Model B: Child support was calculated to produce equal income-to-needs ratios for the custodial and noncustodial households using the 1993 poverty thresholds for nonfarm families with householders under age 65 if combined income did not exceed 200 percent of the combined poverty thresholds for both segments of the divided family; for families with higher incomes, child support was calculated to achieve equal income-to-needs ratios using the Bureau of Labor Standards moderate income budgets in 1993 dollars ($1,334 for one person, $2,072 for two, $2,915 for three).

[c]Model C: Child support was calculated to produce equal income-to-needs ratios for the custodial and noncustodial households using the 1993 poverty thresholds for families with incomes up to 200 percent of the combined poverty thresholds for both segments of the divided family; for families with higher incomes, child support was calculated to achieve equal income-to-needs ratios using the Bureau of Labor Standards moderate income budgets. Initial support awards were capped at 40 percent of net obligor income; modifications of the initial award were capped so as not to exceed 33 percent of new income, triggering a modification claim.

The results displayed in table 1 show that equal-outcomes models do a much better job at preventing poverty and raising award levels than does the income-shares model. Even if the self-support feature were eliminated, the equal-outcomes models, both pure and modified, typically produce higher initial award values at all income levels. But the results also demonstrate that, in contrast to what one might suppose, the equal outcomes models do not uniformly benefit the custodial household. For families in which parental income is fairly equal, both the pure and modified equal outcomes models produce slightly lower initial awards than does the income-shares approach. Moreover, because of its built-in sensitivity to shifts in family composition and income, the equal outcomes model benefits the noncustodial parent in common circumstances such as the custodial parent's remarriage to an income-producing spouse.

This built-in capacity for support modification consistent with the underlying goals and premises of the model is another, frequently overlooked, advantage of the equal-outcomes approach. The continuity-of-expenditure approach is focused on the past and thus provides little guidance to issues that arise when both segments of the divided family go their own ways, adding (or losing) members and income (Takas 1994). Such losses and gains are frequent. At least three-quarters of those who divorce remarry (Cherlin 1981:85; Wilson and Clarke 1992:131), and many have additional children; on average, divorced women who remarry regain their predivorce standard of living (G. Duncan and Hoffman 1985). Current state guidelines evidence no consistency on postdivorce shifts in family composition and income, with the result that both noncustodial and custodial parents often feel that support law is unfair and can point to cases in which the charge seems well founded. By having the capacity to consistently take account of changes in family composition in a way that treats the needs of both parents equally, the equal-outcomes model could enhance the perceived fairness of support law as well as improving its capacity to increase award levels and children's postdissolution living standards. Given its range of advantages, the equal outcomes model, modified to take account of work and payment disincentives, appears to be the best approach to child support determination currently available.

Case Processing: Improving Award Establishment and Decreasing Award Variability

The adoption of an equal outcomes model will not achieve optimal child support outcomes without complementary alterations in the process by which support orders are determined, updated, and enforced. Indeed, by raising support orders, the equal outcomes model might well increase the number of noncustodial parents who would attempt full or partial evasion of support obligations, making the need for improvements in case processing even more urgent (Beller and Graham 1993:52–53).

Case processing improvements are not simple to achieve, however. Some enforcement techniques, promising on paper, have failed to demonstrate any positive effects on collection rates or amounts. Others appear to have had a negative impact (Beller and Graham 1993:175–78). And some are simply not cost-effective. Over the past several years, for example, the federal Child Support Enforcement Program has had administrative expenses in excess of its collections (see U.S. Bureau of the Census 1993:386 table 613). Case processing innovations must be implemented and monitored carefully to achieve desired results. The precise limits of what is achievable are not yet known.

On most significant issues, far too little is known to design a complete reform package. An important source of the current low rate of award establishment, for example, is maternal reluctance to pursue awards. Such reluctance is far more common among never-married mothers than among those who divorce, and never-married mothers in the United States are unlikely to have cohabited with the fathers of their children (Bumpass and Sweet 1990; Cherlin 1988:303). There is also evidence that the lack of significant economic benefits from award establishment may play a role in producing award-pursuit reluctance among public assistance recipients (Adams, Landsbergen, and Cobler 1992). These data suggest that child support policy alone will be incapable of producing optimal results and that nothing close to universal award establishment is achievable.

The available data do not, however, tell us what we can realistically expect child support policy to accomplish. Researchers have found that organizational and legal change can significantly improve paternity establishment rates;[32] indeed, one research group has reported that change as simple as offering paternity defendants more than one opportunity to consent along with a bifurcated/administrative process might raise establishment rates by anywhere from 44 percent to 88 percent (Roberts 1994). Such successes warrant the new paternity establishment rules described by Paul K. Legler in "The Impact of Welfare Reform on the Child Support Enforcement System" (in this volume). But much more research will be necessary before realistic award-establishment goals and reforms can be fully developed.

Improving the consistency and payment rate of child support awards will also demand sustained research to identify realistic goals and an optimal package of reforms. And it is not even known how much of today's inconsistency is appropriate—the result, for example, of support-for-property trade-offs—and how much inappropriate. The individual settlement negotiations that generate most support awards enhance the difficulty of obtaining both accurate information and consistent outcomes. Centralized administrative case processing, like that envisaged in the new welfare-reform legislation Legler describes, might resolve many of the problems if applied in all cases. Other countries with guidelines typically utilize this form of case processing. But such a shift here would constitute a radical and probably unpopular change in divorce procedure.

Award enforcement poses many of the same problems. Some types of reform have consistently been found useful: wage withholding has been found effective in improving payment rates (Beller and Graham 1993: 177–78; Garfinkel and Robins 1994:160–62);[33] requiring payments to be made through a public agency appears to increase significantly not only the collection rate but also the level of awards. But the impact of a new enforcement technique often varies substantially from one population subgroup to another, and some support obligors—those who are self- or irregularly employed, for example—will be difficult to reach even with a broad array of collection devices (Pirog-Good and Amerson 1997).

In sum, far more research is necessary before an optimal case processing reform package can be designed. Award and payment rates can certainly be improved, but it is not known by exactly how much or at what price.

Reducing Children's Poverty

Even with a carefully designed package of case processing improvements, an equal outcomes guideline will be incapable of achieving a major reduction in the current high rate of children's poverty. An equal outcomes guideline cannot make up for the loss of economies of scale that accompanies family dissolution or raise the incomes of low-income noncustodial parents. Policymakers simply must accept the fact that child support policy cannot substitute for an antipoverty program.

A major reduction in children's poverty will require income supports for poor families with children. It is no accident that the United States stands virtually alone among developed nations in both the low level of benefits provided to its children and its high children's poverty rate.[34] The power of an income-support strategy is illustrated by the contrasting fortunes of U.S. children and the elderly. Over the same period in which the children's poverty rate has skyrocketed, that of the elderly has declined markedly. These divergent poverty trends reflect contrasting government policies. While policymakers pursued child support as a weapon against children's poverty, in the meantime allowing children's welfare benefits to decline in value (Katz 1989; Danziger and Danziger 1993:68), the elderly were the beneficiaries of inflation-adjusted Social Security payments and universal health care coverage through the Medicare program (Levy 1987). The result is that U.S. government cash transfers today reduce poverty among the elderly by more than 70 percent and among children by less than 20 percent (Danziger and Danziger 1993:66; American Bar Association 1993:9). Reductions in government benefits have, indeed, contributed to the rising rate of children's poverty.

To significantly reduce children's poverty will require income supports like those that assist the U.S. elderly and that assist children in the rest of the industrialized world. Such programs are expensive. But the cost of doing nothing—in reduced potential for many of tomorrow's adults and resulting expense to the society in which they live—may be even greater.

Conclusion

Policymakers have sought the impossible but also failed to pursue what is realistically achievable. We cannot substantially reduce children's poverty through child support policy alone. We can, however, increase the level of support awarded and paid. We can also do much to erode the significant gap between children's standard of living and that of their noncustodial parents. To achieve these realistic goals will require altered guidelines, like the equal outcomes model, that do not prefer the interests of noncustodial parents to those of their children. This achievement will also require improved case processing procedures that are less reliant on individual resources and initiative. Such reforms could do much to improve the level, consistency, and payment of support obligations. These changes could also improve the perceived fairness of child support policy. If we are serious about these goals, it seems clear that child support policy should take this direction.

What is not clear is whether policymakers are serious about improving child support outcomes. It is striking that, despite all the parental responsibility rhetoric that accompanied the recent child support initiatives, the guidelines adopted typically prefer the interests of noncustodial parents to those of children. In the end, policymakers must decide whether they prefer rhetoric or results.

NOTES

1. Researchers currently estimate that half to three-quarters of children born in the late 1970s or 1980s will spend some portion of their childhood years in single-

parent households. For a critical review of the estimates, see Hernandez 1993:69–71. As many as 90 percent of African American children will spend time in single-parent families. See, e.g., Haveman and Wolfe 1994:19n. 2.

2. In constant 1991 dollars, the mean yearly child support payment to custodial mothers was $3,865 in 1978 ($1,799 in 1978 dollars) and $3,011 in 1991. Compare U.S. Bureau of the Census 1995a:7 table B, with U.S. Bureau of the Census 1980:3 table B.

3. In 1979 the poverty rate of children in single-mother households was 48.6 percent; in 1991 it was 55.5 percent (U.S. Bureau of the Census 1993:471 table 740).

4. Child support obligors report paying even smaller proportions of their incomes in child support (Beller and Graham 1993:34 table 2.7, 38). Male Panel Study of Income Dynamics (PSID) respondents who had paid child support paid, on average, 9.5 percent of their current income (Fletcher 1989:414).

5. In a sample of fathers with one child who earned between $145 and $155 per week, support ordered ranged from ten to sixty dollars per week (Lieberman 1986:12). Sample child support awards ranged from zero to more than 100 percent of noncustodial parents' income (Nichols-Casebolt, Garfinkel, and Wong 1988:176–77 table 9.2). Alimony and child support awards to families in similar circumstances varied widely based on differing judicial philosophies (White and Stone 1976). Judicially ordered child support varied widely (Yee 1979). In a sample of stipulated child support awards, obligor's income, percentage of family income earned by custodial parent, number of minor children, custodial parent's net property award, and case duration accounted for 44 percent of case variation; among judicial awards, obligor's income, decision year, number of minor children, and the custody decision accounted for 54 percent of case variation (Garrison 1996:491–92). In the sample of stipulated and judicial child support awards, number of children, income of supporting parent, and couple's estimated net worth accounted for almost 50 percent of variation in child support values (Melli, Erlanger, and Chambliss 1988:1164).

6. Findings vary: 22 percent of sample child support orders followed guidelines (Ray 1994:54); 51 percent of sample child support orders followed guidelines; no determination was possible in 25 percent of cases (Melli and Bartfeld 1991:61 table 1); 12.6 percent of sample court-ordered child support awards followed Minnesota guidelines (Rettig, Christensen, and Dahl 1991:170). However, reduction in award variability occurred following introduction of guidelines in two of three states for low-income families, one of three for upper-income families, and in no state for middle-income families (Thoennes, Tjaden, and Pearson 1991:339–40). For a descriptive summary of state data on award variability under current guidelines, see Arnaudo 1994:88–94.

7. In the largest and most detailed study to date (Thoennes, Tjaden, and Pearson 1991), only one of three research states (the state with the lowest preguideline award levels) showed all income groups experiencing significant increases in the level of child support attributable to the introduction of mandatory guidelines; in one state no income group experienced such increases. See also Commonwealth of

Virginia 1990, which reported that the mean court child support award was 17 percent higher when the advisory guideline amount was used, even in cases in which the average parental income was lower; Vermont Agency 1989, which reported that guidelines were estimated to increase child support awards in divorce cases by an average of 23.6 percent, although the study did not report the percentage of obligor income awarded in child support. After adoption of guidelines, the weekly mean child support amount, in constant dollars, increased by 21 percent in four Ohio counties (percentage of obligor income awarded in child support not reported) (Stafford, Jackson, and Seiling 1990:376).

The only study to report a dramatic increase in child support values after the introduction of guidelines appears to be in error. Fay and Read (1991) report that the average support award increased by nearly 100 percent after the introduction of guidelines, relying on a comparison of postguidelines awards with preguideline award averages reported in Baker 1987. But Fay and Read appear to have misread Baker, who reports only a mean monthly child support award per child (1987:ii, 13–14); she does not report a mean total child support award except for one-child families. That one-child mean, updated from 1985 dollars to constant 1989 dollars, is 16 percent less than the postguidelines one-child mean reported by Fay and Read.

8. In Illinois, guidelines did not significantly increase award levels among any income group when differences in employment status of pre- and postguideline samples were taken into account (Thoennes, Tjaden, and Pearson 1991:336). A significant proportion of the increase in average child support values that researchers have noted may also result from the imposition of token, rather than zero-dollar, awards in cases of unemployed or female noncustodial parents (Bushard 1988, cited in Thoennes, Tjaden, and Pearson 1991:343, shows that a 15 percent increase in support levels in shared-custody cases after adoption of Arizona child support guidelines resulted entirely from a reduction in zero-dollar awards).

9. See Dodson and Entmacher 1994:98; Fay and Read 1991:7, 61 table 17. Divorced mothers experienced a living standard decline and fathers an improvement under California's child support guidelines (Maccoby and Mnookin 1992:160–62). Research shows disparities in living standards of noncustodial and custodial households under income-shares and Melson support formulas (Zweibel and Shillington 1994:table 4.2). When the custodial parent earns one-third of the $30,000 family income, the income-shares guidelines produce a ratio of postdivorce to predivorce scaled surplus income of 1.24 for the noncustodial household and .41 for the custodial household (Betson, Evenhouse, and Reilly 1992:12 table 3). Based on analysis of Minnesota child support cases decided under guidelines, the median income-to-needs ratio at the date of divorce was found to be 1.77 for custodial households and 1.92 for noncustodial households (Rettig, Christensen, and Dahl 1991:171).

10. Under both income-shares and Melson formulas, more than 75 percent of low-income custodial parents would have incomes below the poverty line (Zweibel and Shillington 1994:42 table 4.1). Using one estimate of family expenditures for low-income families, guidelines in fourteen states failed to produce adequate

awards; using another estimate, all guidelines fell short (Pirog-Good 1993:459). The application of Wisconsin guidelines would have provided a poverty level of living for only 42.3 percent of the case sample (Christensen, Hendrickson, and Rettig 1991:38). Eighteen state guidelines failed to offer minimum decent living standards in one middle-income scenario, twenty-one failed to do so in another, thirty-one in a third, and forty-seven for a fourth. The minimum decent standard of living was defined at 150 percent of the federal poverty level (Dodson and Entmacher 1994:97). Other researchers found that 31 percent of low-middle-income custodial parents did not attain the poverty level using both income-shares and Melson formulas (Zweibel and Shillington 1994:table 4.1).

11. The income-shares percentages were based on the study (Espenshade 1984) believed to be most reliable. For a description of how the Espenshade study was used to derive the percentages, see Williams 1994. Some income-shares guidelines have since been updated to take account of more recent data developed by the federal Office of Child Support Enforcement (Betson 1990) based on a requirement in the Family Support Act of 1988. The percentages utilized in the percentage-of-obligor-income formula were based on a review of the existing research conducted by economist Jacques van der Gaag (1982). But according to one of the formula's authors, given the "enormous" range of estimates, this economic data provided "only a starting point for determining the percentages" (Garfinkel 1992:89).

12. As of 1994, Hawaii, Montana, and West Virginia utilized a poverty-prevention (i.e., Melson-type) formula (Williams 1994:7).

13. Both the income-shares and Melson formulas include self-support reserve features (Williams 1994:305 table 4). The English and Australian child support formulas also provide for a self-support reserve (see J. Thomas Oldham, "New Methods to Update Child Support," in this volume).

14. Based on 1980–86 Current Population Survey (CPS) data, the proportion of total expenditure on two children was 35 percent in a two-parent family and 53 percent in a one-parent family (see Betson 1990); based on 1972–73 data, the proportion of income expended on children in a two-child family was 27 percent in a two-parent family and 53 percent in a one-parent family (Lazear and Michael 1988). But see U.S. Department of Agriculture 1992:10, which concludes that "expenses on a child in single-parent households are slightly higher than those in two-parent households, probably because of economies of scale."

15. For detailed discussions of the limitations of household equivalence scales, see Blackorby and Donaldson 1991; Deaton and Muellbauer 1986; Lewbel 1989; Nelson 1993.

16. While experts generally estimate that no more than 10 percent of divorce actions involve formal adjudication (Galanter 1974), recent research suggests that the rate of formal adjudication may vary substantially from one state to the next. Compare Maccoby and Mnookin 1992:159 (reporting formal adjudication of approximately 1.5 percent in California sample of divorce actions involving minor children) with Brinig and Alexeev 1993:294 table II (reporting that 5.38 percent of sample divorce actions in Wisconsin and 10.13 percent in Virginia went to trial).

17. Legal representation was significantly correlated with the value of child support awards at all income levels (Thoennes, Tjaden, and Pearson 1991:340–41

table 10). One group of researchers, for example, found that the parties' attitudes toward the divorce were a factor "of some significance" in determining child support outcomes. Custodial parents who were reluctant to end marriages and/or whose spouses were impatient to do so obtained significantly better child support awards than did the group mean. Divorcing couples consistently express concern about legal fees and sometimes settle to avoid additional expense (Melli, Erlanger, and Chambliss 1988:1155–56, 1168–71). See also Teachman 1990:697 table 3, reporting, based on data from the National Longitudinal Study of the high school class of 1972, that "both the capacity to negotiate and motivation are at work determining the likelihood and size of [child support] awards."

18. According to U.S. Bureau of the Census 1995a:11–12 table f, 34.6 percent of custodial mothers who had not been awarded child support reported that they "did not pursue a child support award"; 13.9 percent reported that they "did not want child support"; 20.5 percent reported that they were "unable to locate the other parent"; and 16.1 percent reported that the "other parent [was] unable to pay."

19. See Goode 1993:152–57, summarizing research on the relationship between socioeconomic class and divorce rates; U.S. Bureau of the Census 1991, reporting that 21 percent of families with children that experienced the loss of the father from the household during a two-year survey period were already poor, a poverty rate double that of U.S. married-couple households generally; U.S. Bureau of the Census 1992:21 table 1, reporting that divorce is approximately twice as likely among sample couples with incomes below the poverty line as among others; Conger, Elder, and Lorenz 1990, reporting that instability in husband's work, a drop in family income, and a low ratio of family income to family needs increases the risk of divorce; Norton and Moorman 1987, reporting an inverse relationship between educational attainment and divorce rates.

20. See, e.g., Phillips and Garfinkel 1993:234 table 2, showing that 41 percent of never-married nonresident fathers with tax records were poor in the year before the support action, compared to 19 percent of divorced nonresident fathers.

21. See, e.g., Hernandez 1993:374–75 table A-9.1; Danziger and Danziger 1993:66–67 table 4. The ability of one parent alone to keep a family out of poverty has declined with particular rapidity since 1980, and young, poorly educated workers—who have higher-than-average rates of nonmarital childbearing and divorce—have been particularly hard hit. See, e.g., DeParle 1994:A18, describing recent census data; Haveman and Buron 1993. Among workers between ages eighteen and twenty-five and men without high school diplomas, the percentage earning a lower-than-poverty-level wage more than doubled between 1979 and 1992 (U.S. Bureau of the Census 1994). The declining ability of one parent of either sex to keep his or her children out of poverty ensures that single-parent households will continue to be far more vulnerable to poverty than will married-couple households. See Haveman and Buron 1993:151 table 2, showing that in 1988, nearly 15 percent of all children under age six, 26 percent of such children in father-only homes, and 51.1 percent of such children in mother-only homes could not have escaped poverty even if adults in the family were earning at full capacity levels.

22. A reduction of 20 percent in the overall children's poverty rate is roughly equivalent to an 80 percent reduction in the post-1969 increase in that rate.

23. The support obligation necessary to achieve equalization of living standards was calculated using the U.S. poverty thresholds for families of varying size and determining the support obligation necessary to achieve equal income-to-poverty-level needs ratios.

24. See, e.g., Beller and Graham 1993:51 (concluding that when "fathers . . . less willing or less able to pay [are] brought reluctantly into the system by reforms in the child support enforcement program [the likely result is] a decline in the proportion of awards collected"); Bartfeld and Meyer 1994:230 (reporting a significant inverse relationship in the sample of paternity cases between the percentage of income awarded in child support and the likelihood of compliance); Danziger and Nichols-Casebolt 1990 (same).

25. Experts agree that high tax rates create significant negative payment and work incentives (see, e.g., Graetz 1983:273), but there is no consensus on the magnitude of the effect. Using "plausible" labor supply elasticities, economist David Betson calculated the labor supply effect of switching from a continuity-of-expenditure child support formula to an equal-outcomes model; with a $30,000 family income, two-thirds produced by the noncustodial parent, the net effect was a reduction in total income of about 11 percent (1993:17). Betson concluded that children were still better off under an equal-outcomes model than a continuity-of-expenditure formula, but he did not attempt to calculate the effect of nonpayment and income concealment.

26. In 1994 only 10 percent of married couples, 5 percent of male householders, and 12 percent of female householders had three or more children under the age of eighteen living at home (U.S. Bureau of the Census 1995b: 63 table 74).

27. The mean total money income of custodial mothers surveyed for the 1991 Child Support Report, for example, was $18,133, while the mean total child support received by this group was $3,011 (U.S. Bureau of the Census 1991:19 table 2).

28. Calculated by the same methodology as in the A case.

29. The economic analysis commissioned by the federal Office of Child Support Enforcement (OCSE) "creates the appearance of scientific, objective 'truth'" and is "given heightened validity by virtue of OCSE's involvement" (Polikoff 1987:27–28).

30. A memorandum explaining New York's continuity-of-expenditure-type guideline, for example, describes the primary purpose of child support as "the maintenance of the child's standard of living"—a goal that this guideline type could not possibly meet (New York Laws 1989). See also Principles of the Law of Family Dissolution (ALI 1997:§§ 3.03(1) and 3.05) (describing the "most important" goal of child support as "ensur[ing] that the child share equitably in the incomes of both parents" and adopting income-shares guideline methodology).

31. This rate is consistent with the maximum advocated by a distinguished English commentator. See Eekelaar 1994, suggesting that the English maintenance-requirement child support percentage be reduced from 50 percent to 40 percent to reduce work disincentives. Because there is very little data on the impact of child support rates on employment and earnings, a refined estimate of the optimal maximum support rate would require substantial empirical research.

32. State-by-state paternity establishment rates range from less than 10 percent

to more than 50 percent (Nichols-Casebolt and Garfinkel 1991:88 table 1); see also Roberts 1994 (summarizing enforcement problems and prospects).

33. At the state level, however, income withholding has not always been found to have a positive effect (Pearson, Thoennes, and Anhalt 1993:233–34).

34. For comparisons of the poverty status of U.S. children with their counterparts in other industrialized countries, see, e.g., Danziger and Danziger 1993:68–70; G. Duncan et al. 1993; Nichols-Casebolt and Krysik 1997; Smeeding 1988–89.

REFERENCES

Adams, Charles F., Jr., David Landsbergen, and Larry Cobler. 1992. Welfare Reform and Paternity Establishment: A Social Experiment. *Journal of Policy Analysis and Management* 11:665–87.

American Bar Association. 1993. *America's Children at Risk: A National Agenda for Legal Action.* Washington, DC: ABA Presidential Working Group on the Unmet Legal Needs of Children and Their Families.

American Law Institute. 1997. Principles of the Law of Family Dissolution: Analysis and Recommendations. Philadelphia: Executive Office, ALI.

Arnaudo, David. 1994. Deviation from State Child Support Guidelines. In *Child Support Guidelines: The Next Generation,* ed. Margaret Campbell Haynes. Washington, DC: U.S. Department of Health and Human Services, Administration for Children and Families, Office of Child Support Enforcement.

Baker, Barbara. 1987. *Family Equity at Issue: A Study of the Economic Consequences of Divorce on Women and Children.* Anchorage: [Alaska Women's Commission].

Bane, Mary Jo. 1986. Household Composition and Poverty. In *Fighting Poverty: What Works and What Doesn't,* ed. Sheldon H. Danziger and Daniel H. Weinberg. Cambridge, MA: Harvard University Press.

Bartfeld, Juda, and Daniel R. Meyer. 1994. Are There Really Deadbeat Dads? The Relationship between Ability to Pay, Enforcement, and Compliance in Nonmarital Child Support Cases. *Social Service Review* 68:219–35.

Beller, Andrea H., and John W. Graham. 1993. *Small Change: The Economics of Child Support.* New Haven: Yale University Press.

Betson, David M. 1990. *Alternative Estimates of the Cost of Children from the 1980–86 Consumer Expenditure Survey.* Special Report no. 51, December. Madison, WI: Institute for Research on Poverty.

Betson, David M., Eirik Evenhouse, and Siobhan Reilly. 1992. Trade-Offs Implicit in Child Support Guidelines. *Journal of Policy Analysis and Management* 11:1–20.

Blackorby, Charles, and David Donaldson. 1991. Adult-Equivalence Scales, Interpersonal Comparisons of Well-Being, and Applied Welfare Economics. In *Interpersonal Comparisons of Well-Being,* ed. Jon Elster and J. E. Roemer. New York: Cambridge University Press.

Brinig, Margaret F., and Michael V. Alexeev. 1993. Trading at Divorce: Preferences, Legal Rules, and Transaction Costs. *Ohio State Journal on Dispute Resolution* 8:279–98.

Bumpass, Larry L., and J. A. Sweet. 1990. Children's Experience in Single Parent Families: Implications of Cohabitation and Marital Transitions. *Family Planning Perspectives* 21:256–60.

Bushard, P. 1988. Time Series Assessment of Child Support Guidelines: Support Awards in Shared Custody Divorces. Ph.D. diss., Arizona State University.

Cassetty, Judith, and G. K. Sprinkle. 1987. The ELS (Equivalent Living Standards) Model for Child Support Awards. In *Essentials of Child Support Guidelines Development: Economic Issues and Policy Considerations.* Washington, DC: Women's Legal Defense Fund.

Cherlin, Andrew J. 1981. *Marriage, Divorce, Remarriage.* Cambridge, MA: Harvard University Press.

———. 1988. The Weakening Link between Marriage and the Care of Children. *Family Planning Perspectives* 20:302–6.

Christensen, Donna Hendrickson, and Kathryn D. Rettig. 1991. Standards for Adequacy of Child Support Awards. *Journal of Divorce and Remarriage* 16:19–45.

Clark, Homer H. 1968. *The Law of Domestic Relations in the United States.* 1st ed. St. Paul, MN: West Publishing.

Commonwealth of Virginia Department of Social Services. 1990. *The Impact of Child Support Guidelines on the Level of Child Support Awards in Virginia.* Senate Document no. 4. Richmond: Commonwealth of Virginia.

Conger, Rand D., Glen H. Elder Jr., and Frederick O. Lorenz. 1990. Linking Economic Hardship to Marital Quality and Instability. *Journal of Marriage and the Family* 52:643–56.

Czapanskiy, Karen. 1987. Foreword to *Essentials of Child Support Guideline Development: Economic Issues and Policy.* Washington, DC: Women's Legal Defense Fund.

Danziger, Sandra K., and Sheldon Danziger. 1993. Child Poverty and Public Policy: Toward a Comprehensive Antipoverty Agenda. *Daedalus* 122:57–84.

Danziger, Sandra K., and Ann Nichols-Casebolt. 1990. Child Support in Paternity Cases. *Social Service Review* 64:458–74.

Deaton, Angus S., and John Muellbauer. 1986. On Measuring Child Costs: With Applications to Poor Countries. *Journal of Political Economy* 94:720–44.

DeParle, Jason. 1994. Sharp Increase along the Borders of Poverty. *New York Times,* 31 March, A18.

Dodson, G. Diane, and Joan Entmacher. 1994. Children's Standards of Living under Child Support Guidelines: Women's Legal Defense Fund Report Card on State Child Support Guidelines Executive Summary. In *Child Support Guidelines: The Next Generation,* ed. Margaret Campbell Haynes. Washington, DC: U.S. Department of Health and Human Services, Administration for Children and Families, Office of Child Support Enforcement.

Duncan, Greg J., Bjorn Gustafsson, Richard Hauser, Günther Schmauss, Hans

Messinger, Ruud Muffels, Brian Nolan, and Jean-Claude Ray. 1993. Poverty Dynamics in Eight Countries. *Journal of Population Economics* 6:215–34.

Duncan, Greg J., and Saul D. Hoffman. 1985. A Reconsideration of the Economic Consequences of Marital Dissolution. *Demography* 22:485–97.

Duncan, Greg J., and Willard Rodgers. 1987. Single Parent Families: Are Their Problems Transitory or Persistent? *Family Planning Perspectives* 19:171–78.

———. 1988. Longitudinal Aspects of Childhood Poverty. *Journal of Marriage and the Family* 50:1007–21.

Duncan, S. Wayne. 1994. Economic Impact of Divorce on Children's Development: Current Findings and Policy Implications. *Journal of Clinical Child Psychology* 23:444–57.

Eden, Philip, Judith Cassetty, and William T. Terrell. 1987. In the Best Interests of Children: A Simplified Model for Equalizing the Living Standards of Parental Households. In *Essentials of Child Support Guidelines Development: Economic Issues and Policy Considerations.* Washington, DC: Women's Legal Defense Fund.

Edin, Kathryn. 1995. Single Mothers and Child Support—The Possibilities and Limits of Child Support Policy. *Children and Youth Services Review* 17:203–30.

Eekelaar, John. 1994. Third Thoughts on Child Support. *Family Law* 24:99–102.

Ellwood, David T., and Lawrence H. Summers. 1986. Poverty in America: Is Welfare the Answer or the Problem? In *Fighting Poverty: What Works and What Doesn't,* ed. Sheldon H. Danziger and Daniel H. Weinberg. Cambridge, MA: Harvard University Press.

Erlanger, Howard S., Elizabeth Chambliss, and Marygold S. Melli. 1987. Participation and Flexibility in Informal Processes: Cautions from the Divorce Context. *Law and Society Review* 21:585–604.

Espenshade, Thomas J. 1984. *Investing in Children: New Estimates of Parental Expenditures.* Washington, DC: Urban Institute Press.

Fay, Ginny, and Emily Read. 1991. *Child Support in Alaska: An Evaluation of the Effectiveness and Impact of Alaska's Child Support Guidelines.* Anchorage: Alaska Women's Commission.

Fletcher, Cynthia Needles. 1989. A Comparison of Incomes and Expenditures of Male-Headed Households Paying Child Support and Female-Headed Households Receiving Child Support. *Family Relations* 38:412–17.

Galanter, Marc. 1974. Why the Haves Come Out Ahead: Speculations on the Limits of Legal Change. *Law and Society Review* 9:95–160.

Garfinkel, Irwin. 1992. *Assuring Child Support.* New York: Russell Sage Foundation.

Garfinkel, Irwin, and Marygold S. Melli. 1990. The Use of Normative Standards in Family Law Decisions: Developing Mathematical Standards for Child Support. *Family Law Quarterly* 24:157–78.

Garfinkel, Irwin, Daniel R. Meyer, and Gary D. Sandefur. 1992. The Effects of Alternative Child Support Systems on Blacks, Hispanics, and Non-Hispanic Whites. *Social Service Review* 66:505–23.

Garfinkel, Irwin, Donald Oellerich, and Philip K. Robins. 1991. Child Support Guidelines: Will They Make a Difference? *Journal of Family Issues* 12:404–29.

Garfinkel, Irwin, and Philip K. Robins. 1994. Child Support Enforcement Tools and Outcomes. In *Child Support and Child Well-Being,* ed. Irwin Garfinkel, Sara S. McLanahan, and Philip K. Robins. Washington, DC: Urban Institute Press.

Garrison, Marsha. 1991. Good Intentions Gone Awry: The Impact of New York's Equitable Distribution Law on Divorce Outcomes. *Brooklyn Law Review* 57:621–754.

———. 1996. How Do Judges Decide Divorce Cases? An Empirical Analysis of Discretionary Decision Making. *North Carolina Law Review* 74:401–527.

Goode, William J. 1993. *World Changes in Divorce Patterns.* New Haven: Yale University Press.

Graetz, Michael J. 1983. To Praise the Estate Tax, Not to Bury It. *Yale Law Journal* 93:259–86.

Grimm, Claire B., and Janice T. Munsterman. 1991. *Child Support Guidelines: A Compendium.* Arlington, VA: National Center for State Courts.

Haskins, Ron, Andrew W. Dobelstein, John S. Akin, and Brad J. Schwartz. 1985. *Estimates of National Child Support Collection Potential and the Income Security of Female Headed Families: Report to Office of Child Support Enforcement.* Chapel Hill: University of North Carolina, Bush Institute for Child and Family Policy.

Haveman, Robert H., and Lawrence Buron. 1993. Escaping Poverty through Work—The Problem of Low Earning Capacity in the United States, 1973–88. *Review of Income and Wealth* 39(2):141–57.

Haveman, Robert H., and Barbara Wolfe. 1994. *Succeeding Generations: On the Effects of Investments in Children.* New York: Russell Sage Foundation.

Hernandez, Donald J. 1993. *America's Children: Resources from Family, Government, and the Economy.* New York: Russell Sage Foundation.

Jacob, Herbert. 1992. The Elusive Shadow of the Law. *Law and Society Review* 26:565–90.

Jencks, Christopher. 1992. *Rethinking Social Policy.* Cambridge, MA: Harvard University Press.

Katz, Michael B. 1989. *The Undeserving Poor.* New York: Pantheon Press.

Lazear, Edward P., and Robert T. Michael. 1988. *Allocation of Income within the Household.* Chicago: University of Chicago Press.

Leahy, Peter J., Terry F. Buss, and James M. Quane. 1995. Time on Welfare—Why Do People Enter and Leave the System? *American Journal of Economics and Society* 54:33–46.

Legler, Paul. 1996. The Coming Revolution in Child Support Policy: Implications of the 1996 Welfare Act. *Family Law Quarterly* 30:519–63.

Levy, Frank. 1987. *Dollars and Dreams: The Changing American Income Distribution.* New York: Norton.

Lewbel, Arthur. 1989. Household Equivalence Scales and Welfare Comparisons. *Journal of Public Economics* 39:377–91.

Lieberman, Joseph I. 1986. *Child Support in America.* New Haven: Yale University Press.

Maccoby, Eleanor E., and Robert H. Mnookin. 1992. *Dividing the Child: Social and Legal Dilemmas of Custody.* Cambridge, MA: Harvard University Press.

McLanahan, Sara S. 1992. Intergenerational Consequences of Divorce: The United States Perspective. In *Economic Consequences of Divorce: The International Perspective,* ed. Lenore Weitzman and Mavis Maclean. New York: Oxford University Press.

McLanahan, Sara S., et al. 1991. The Role of Mother-Only Families in Reproducing Poverty. In *Children in Poverty: Child Development and Public Policy,* ed. Aletha C. Huston. New York: Cambridge University Press.

McLanahan, Sara S., and Gary Sandefur. 1994. *Growing Up with a Single Parent: What Helps, What Hurts.* Cambridge, MA: Harvard University Press.

McLindon, James B. 1987. Separate but Unequal: The Economic Disaster of Divorce for Women and Children. *Family Law Quarterly* 21:351–409.

Melli, Marygold S., Howard S. Erlanger, and Elizabeth Chambliss. 1988. The Process of Negotiation: An Exploratory Investigation in the Context of No-Fault Divorce. *Rutgers Law Review* 40:1133–72.

Melli, Marygold S., and Judi Bartfeld. 1991. Use of the Wisconsin Percentage-of-Income Standard to Set Child Support: Experience in Twenty Counties. *Wisconsin Journal of Family Law* 11:60–68.

Michalopoulos, Charles, and Irwin Garfinkel. 1989. *Reducing Welfare Dependence and Poverty of Single Mothers by Means of Earnings and Child Support.* Discussion Paper. Madison, WI: Institute for Research on Poverty.

Murphy, Jane C. 1993. Access to Legal Remedies: The Crisis in Family Law. *BYU Journal of Public Law* 8:123–43.

Nelson, Julie A. 1993. Household Equivalence Scales: Theory versus Policy? *Journal of Labor Economics* 11:471–93.

New York Laws, Chapter 567, Governor's Approval Memorandum. 1989. *New York Legislative Annual,* 250.

New York Times. 1995. Welfare: Who Gets It? How Much Does It Cost? 23 March, A23.

Nichols-Casebolt, Ann. 1992. The Economic Impact of Reforms on Poverty Status. In *Child Support Assurance: Design Issues, Expected Impacts, and Political Barriers as Seen from Wisconsin,* ed. Irwin Garfinkel, Sara S. McLanahan, and Philip K. Robins. Washington, DC: Urban Institute Press.

Nichols-Casebolt, Ann, and Irwin Garfinkel. 1991. Trends in Paternity Adjudications and Child Support Awards. *Social Science Quarterly* 72:83–97.

Nichols-Casebolt, Ann, Irwin Garfinkel, and Patrick Wong. 1988. Reforming Wisconsin's Child Support System. In *State Policy Choices: The Wisconsin Experience,* ed. Sheldon H. Danziger and John F. Witte. Madison: University of Wisconsin Press.

Nichols-Casebolt, Ann, and J. Krysik. 1997. The Economic Well-being of Never and Ever-Married Single Mothers and Families: A Cross-National Comparison. *Journal of Social Service Research* 23:19–40.

Norton, Arthur J., and Jeanne E. Moorman. 1987. Current Trends in Marriage and Divorce among American Women. *Journal of Marriage and the Family* 49:3–14.

Pearson, Jessica. 1993. Ten Myths about Family Law. *Family Law Quarterly* 27:279–99.

Pearson, Jessica, Nancy Thoennes, and Jean Anhalt. 1993. Child Support in the United States: The Experience in Colorado. *Family and Conciliation Courts Review* 31:226–43.

Penkrot, Joseph L. 1989. Can AFDC Parents Pay Child Support? *Journal of Policy Analysis and Management* 8:104–10.

Phillips, Elizabeth, and Irwin Garfinkel. 1993. Income Growth among Nonresident Fathers: Evidence from Wisconsin. *Demography* 30:227–41.

Pirog-Good, Maureen A. 1993. Child Support Guidelines and the Economic Well-Being of Children in the United States. *Family Relations* 42:453–62.

Pirog-Good, Maureen A., and Lydia Amerson. 1997. The Long Arm of Justice: The Potential for Seizing the Assets of Child Support Obligors. *Family Relations* 46:47–54.

Polikoff, Nancy D. 1987. Looking for Policy Choices within an Economic Methodology: A Critique of the Income Shares Model. In *Essentials of Child Support Guideline Development: Economic Issues and Policy.* Washington, DC: Women's Legal Defense Fund.

Ray, Marilyn L. 1994. *New York State Child Support Standards Act Evaluation Project Report.* 1993. New York State Commission on Child Support.

Rettig, Kathryn D., Donna Hendrickson Christensen, and Carla M. Dahl. 1991. Impact of Child Support Guidelines on the Economic Well-Being of Children. *Family Relations* 40:167–75.

Roberts, Paula. 1994. Child Support Orders: Problems with Enforcement. In *The Future of Children: Children and Divorce* 4:101–20.

Sarat, Austin, and W. L. F. Felstiner. 1989. Lawyers and Legal Consciousness: Law Talk in the Divorce Lawyer's Office. *Yale Law Journal* 98:1663–88.

Sawhill, Isabel V. 1983. Developing Normative Standards for Child Support Payments. In *The Parental Child Support Obligation: Research, Practice, and Social Policy,* ed. Judith Cassetty. Lexington, MA: Lexington Books.

Smeeding, Timothy M. 1988–89. Poverty, Affluence, and the Income Costs of Children: Cross-National Evidence from the Luxembourg Income Study (LIS). *Journal of Post-Keynesian Economics* 11:222–39.

Smith, Marilyn Ray, and John Laramore. 1987. Massachusetts' Child Support Guidelines: A Model for Development. In *Essentials of Child Support Guideline Development: Economic Issues and Policy Considerations.* Washington, DC: Women's Legal Defense Fund.

Sorensen, Elaine. 1995. The Benefits of Increased Child Support Enforcement. In *Welfare Reform: An Analysis of the Issues,* ed. Isabel V. Sawhill. Washington, DC: Urban Institute Press.

———. 1997. A National Profile of Nonresident Fathers and Their Ability to Pay Child Support. *Journal of Marriage and the Family* 59:785–97.

Stafford, Kathryn, Golden Jackson, and Sharon Seiling. 1990. The Effects of

Child Support Guidelines: An Analysis of the Evidence in Court Records. *Lifestyles: Family and Economic Issues* 11:361–81.

Takas, Marianne. 1994. Addressing Subsequent Families in Child Support Guidelines. In *Child Support Guidelines: The Next Generation,* ed. Margaret Campbell Haynes. Washington, DC: U.S. Department of Health and Human Services, Administration for Children and Families, Office of Child Support Enforcement.

Teachman, Jay D. 1990. Socioeconomic Resources of Parents and Award of Child Support in the United States: Some Exploratory Models. *Journal of Marriage and the Family* 52:689–99.

Thoennes, Nancy, Patricia Tjaden, and Jessica Pearson. 1991. The Impact of Child Support Guidelines on Award Adequacy, Award Variability, and Case Processing Efficiency. *Family Law Quarterly* 25:325–45.

Tsakloglou, Panos. 1991. Estimation and Comparison of Two Simple Models of Equivalence Scales for the Cost of Children. *Economic Journal* 101:343–57.

U.S. Bureau of the Census. 1980. *Child Support and Alimony: 1978.* Washington DC: U.S. Government Printing Office.

———. 1991. *Family Disruption and Economic Hardship: The Short-Run Picture for Children.* Current Population Reports, series P-70, no. 23. Washington, DC: U.S. Government Printing Office.

———. 1992. *When Households Continue, Discontinue, and Form.* Current Population Reports, series P-23, no. 180. Washington, DC: U.S. Government Printing Office.

———. 1993. *Statistical Abstract of the United States: 1993.* Washington, DC: U.S. Government Printing Office.

———. 1994. *The Earnings Ladder—Who's at the Bottom? Who's at the Top?* Statistical Brief 94, 3. March. Washington, DC: U.S. Government Printing Office.

———. 1995a. *Child Support for Custodial Mothers and Fathers: 1991.* Washington, DC: U.S. Government Printing Office.

———. 1995b. *Statistical Abstract of the United States: 1995.* Washington, DC: U.S. Government Printing Office.

U.S. Department of Agriculture, Family Economics Research Group. 1992. *Expenditures on a Child by Families.* Washington, DC: U.S. Government Printing Office.

U.S. Department of Labor, Bureau of Labor Statistics. 1968. *Revised Equivalence Scale for Estimating Equivalent Incomes or Budget Costs by Family Type.* No. 1570-2.

van der Gaag, Jacques. 1982. On Measuring the Cost of Children. *Children and Youth Services Review* 4:77–109.

Vermont Agency of Human Services. 1989. *In Support of Our Children: A Survey of Child Support Orders and Divorced Parents in Vermont.* Montpelier.

Weitzman, Lenore J. 1985. *The Divorce Revolution: The Unexpected Social and Economic Consequences for Women and Children in America.* New York: Free Press.

White, Kenneth R., and R. Thomas Stone Jr. 1976. A Study of Alimony and Child

Support Rulings with Some Recommendations. *Family Law Quarterly* 10:75–91.

Williams, Robert G. 1987a. *Development of Guidelines for Child Support Orders: Advisory Panel Recommendations and Final Report II.* Washington, DC: U.S. Department of Health and Human Services, Office of Child Support Enforcement.

———. 1987b. Guidelines for Setting Levels of Child Support Orders. *Family Law Quarterly* 21:281–324.

———. 1994. An Overview of Child Support Guidelines in the United States. In *Child Support Guidelines: The Next Generation,* ed. Margaret Campbell Haynes. Washington, DC: U.S. Department of Health and Human Services, Administration for Children and Families, Office of Child Support Enforcement.

Wilson, Barbara Foley, and Sally Cuningham Clarke. 1992. Remarriages: A Demographic Profile. *Journal of Family Issues* 13:123–41.

Yee, Lucy M. 1979. What Really Happens in Child Support Cases: An Empirical Study of Establishment and Enforcement of Child Support Orders in the Denver District Court. *Denver Law Journal* 57:21–68.

Zweibel, Ellen B., and Richard Shillington. 1994. *Child Support Policy: Income Tax Treatment and Child Support Guidelines.* Policy Research Center on Children, Youth and Families.

The Impact of Welfare Reform on the Child Support Enforcement System

Paul K. Legler

The welfare reform legislation passed in 1996 (the Personal Responsibility and Work Opportunity Reconciliation Act, PRWORA)[1] marks the advent of the most sweeping change in welfare policy since the Social Security Act was passed more than sixty years ago. The act ended the federal entitlement to Aid to Families with Dependent Children (AFDC) and replaced it with block grants to states, thereby shifting the major responsibility for helping poor families to state and local governments. The federal government will no longer guarantee a cash assistance safety net for children, and the new welfare law requires states to impose time limits on welfare.

Almost lost within the debate about welfare policy were sweeping new child support enforcement reform provisions. These reforms are crucial because time-limited welfare means that the receipt of child support for poor single-parent families will become even more important. This chapter outlines the changes.

The need for child support reform and its history have already been described in this book's chapters by June Carbone and Marsha Garrison. Three facts that emerge from this history are striking. First, the total picture is bleak, and millions of children are not receiving the support they deserve. Second, the gap from the inadequacy of awards ($7.0 billion) is as large as the gap from the failure to collect what is owed ($7.2 billion) (Sorensen 1995b). Third, and perhaps most important, the largest part of the gap ($19.6 billion) results from failure to obtain child support awards. Paternity has been established in about half of these cases. Since the lack of paternity establishment is the chief reason for a lack of awards, improving paternity establishment is crucial to closing the collection gap (U.S. Department of Health and Human Services 1994).

Against this background, child support enforcement was incorporated in the PRWORA.

Paternity Establishment

Catalysts for Change

The changes in paternity establishment law mandated by PRWORA are the result of three developments over the past decade: a change in social perspective, in-hospital paternity establishment, and advancements in genetic testing.

The first and perhaps the major catalyst for change in paternity law has been the change in social perspective on the importance of paternity establishment. As policymakers began to pay attention to the mushrooming number of out-of-wedlock births (which increased by 75 percent in the 1980s), there was a growing focus on the poverty often associated with single parenthood (U.S. Department of Health and Human Services 1994). Establishing paternity was seen as a way to alleviate some poverty because doing so opened the door to the possible receipt of child support. A rising body of evidence showed that most unwed fathers could pay some support for their children (Pirog-Good and Good 1995; Legler and Ellwood 1993; Haskins et al. 1985; Lerman 1990; Garfinkel and Oellerich 1989; Phillips and Garfinkel 1993; Meyer 1995). Even in cases of out-of-wedlock births to teen mothers, most fathers were not teens but older males with some income (Landry and Forrest 1995; Lindberg et al. 1997). Most important, even when fathers had low incomes at the time of the birth of the child, their incomes tended subsequently to rise relatively rapidly, increasing their ability to pay support. Furthermore, evidence showed that paternity establishment was cost-effective, even for welfare cases (U.S. Department of Health and Human Services 1985).

Single-parenthood was also linked to a number of negative social consequences (McLanahan and Sandefur 1994; McLanahan 1995; Eaton 1994). Establishing paternity was seen as a way to help alleviate some of the problems associated with single-parenthood and to begin to make emotional as well as financial links to fathers.

The second catalyst for the change in paternity establishment procedure has been the research by Esther Wattenberg indicating that out-of-wedlock births were often the result of established relationships, not casual ones, and that the mothers almost always knew the identity and location of the father. Significantly, Wattenberg found that two-thirds of unmarried fathers went to the hospital at the time of the birth, and some 80 percent of such fathers took care of the baby in some way in the year following the birth. Thus, the critical time to establish paternity was at the time of the birth at the hospital, when many fathers show a clear desire to acknowledge their connection to the child (Wattenberg, Brewer, and

Resnick 1991). But as time passes, contact falls off, interest fades, and the chances for successful paternity establishment decline rapidly (McLanahan, Monson, and Brown 1992). The Omnibus Budget Reconciliation Act of 1993 (OBRA 1993)[2] required all states to adopt in-hospital, voluntary, paternity establishment programs at that critical time. Initial results have already showed astounding success (U.S. Department of Health and Human Services 1997).

The third catalyst for the change in the paternity establishment process was the advances in scientific testing for paternity, especially the use of DNA testing, which made the identification of fathers a near certainty and suggested that fathers could be readily identified (Bias, Meyers, and Murphy 1983; Blumberg 1983; Pena and Chakraborty 1994), particularly if the legal processes were changed to make it easier to obtain genetic tests (Washington State Office of Support Enforcement 1991; Adams, Landsbergen, and Cobler 1992).

Changes in Voluntary Acknowledgment of Paternity under PRWORA

The new welfare law imposes a number of requirements to expand the scope of existing in-hospital paternity establishment programs and make them more uniform. First, a signed voluntary acknowledgment of paternity establishes paternity without any further legal action (absent a challenge under narrow circumstances).

Second, the father's name can be included on the birth record only if the baby's parents have signed a voluntary acknowledgment. This requirement provides an inducement for fathers and mothers to sign acknowledgments of paternity and provides uniform legal consequences arising from having the father's name on the birth certificate.

Changes in the Paternity Establishment Process

The act requires states to streamline their processes for paternity establishment. The key to streamlining is obtaining the genetic test up front and as quickly as possible. Once the test is completed, the paternity issue is usually resolved because the results will either exclude the father or result in a very high probability (usually above 99 percent) of paternity. Most fathers admit paternity when faced with such test results, so the vast majority of cases can then be resolved by obtaining a signed acknowledgment.

To create this simplified process, the child support agency must be able to administratively order a genetic test. States must also have procedures that require parties in contested paternity proceedings to submit to genetic tests[3] if the request is supported by a sworn statement setting forth facts establishing a reasonable possibility of the requisite sexual contact between the parties. In addition, the act requires the state agency to pay costs of genetic tests and to obtain additional testing if an original test result is contested, on advance payment by the contestant.

For those cases where the alleged father still seeks to contest the matter after a genetic test, the process is further streamlined, and the incentive for delay is removed. Evidentiary rules are simplified in that the results of genetic tests meeting certain criteria are admissible, states must have procedures for entering temporary orders for support if there is clear and convincing evidence of paternity, and jury trials for paternity cases are eliminated.

As a result of these changes and ones from 1993 that created a presumption of paternity based on genetic test results, the vast majority of routine child support enforcement cases will be processed and an order of paternity quickly and simply entered through the child support agency's administrative steps without requiring any significant court involvement.

Changes in the Cooperation Determination

Another change in the paternity establishment process under PRWORA involves required paternity cooperation. AFDC recipients had always been required to assign their right to support and "cooperate" in establishing paternity and securing support.

PRWORA gives states broad flexibility in welfare cases to define what constitutes "cooperation," to define "good cause" for noncooperation, to determine the penalty for noncooperation (but not less than 25 percent of the family grant), and to determine which agency, (welfare or child support), makes the good-cause determination.[4]

It remains to be seen whether such a broad grant of discretion raises a new set of problems. Although most states are likely to adopt reasonable policies, some jurisdictions could use this authority to adopt punitive requirements that result in large numbers of women being found ineligible in an attempt to save welfare dollars. States could also use this flexibility to remove the difficult cases from their welfare rolls to meet paternity establishment standards.[5] In addition, stricter cooperation requirements are likely to increase the number of good-cause claims for domestic violence.

Collecting Support

The Vision

The vision for child support enforcement that guided legislative developments is that support payments should be automatic and inescapable, "like death or taxes" (Legler and Ellwood 1993). This vision is reflected in three key elements that interact and support each other: (1) the ability to locate individuals and assets; (2) the capacity to work cases in volume using computers, automation, and information technology; and (3) the ability to take action automatically, preferably administratively, without reliance on a complaint-driven process.

(1) Access to Information

There has been a growing recognition that access to information is a prerequisite to effective child support enforcement. Unpaid child support obligations can be collected only from two sources: a current income stream or accumulated assets. To tap into either source, information regarding the obligor is essential: Where is the obligor located? Is the obligor working, and if so, where? What is the obligor's income? Are there other sources of income? Does the obligor have bank accounts, other liquid assets, or other assets subject to seizure?

The act greatly enhances child support agencies' ability to obtain information. The law sets up a national system to track the employment of delinquent obligors so that child support collections can more closely mimic tax collection. Withholding child support directly from wages has been required for all child support orders since 1994 (exceptions are made in cases of good cause or if the parties agree to an alternative). In 1995, 56 percent of all collections, more than $6 billion, came through wage withholding (U.S. Department of Health and Human Services 1995).

The major obstacle preventing a higher use of wage withholding for collections has been job turnover (Gordon 1991). Unlike the tax system, there has been no standard requirement that the child support obligation be reported or that withholding begin at the time of hire. By the time the child support agency found out about an obligor's new employment, four to six months of child support often had been lost and the employee had moved on to another job.

Beginning in October 1997, PRWORA required all employers to report new hires to a designated state agency within twenty days of employment.[6] The information is first matched with a state registry of child support orders to find obligors within the state and is then forwarded to a national directory of new hires to be matched against the federal case registry of child support orders. The national directory and federal case registry functions as part of the existing Federal Parent Locator Service (FPLS), thereby greatly expanding the information-matching capacity of the FPLS, which could already access information from a variety of federal data sources such as the Social Security system, the Internal Revenue Service, the Department of Defense, the Veterans Administration, and the

National Personnel Records Center. This program revolutionized interstate enforcement because it dramatically improved the capacity to trace delinquent parents across state lines. About one-third of child support cases involve parents living in different states, so the potential target was huge. Moreover, PRWORA mandated that all states adopt the Uniform Interstate Family Support Act (UIFSA). Under UIFSA, state agencies can send income-withholding orders directly across state lines to employers. Thus, within days of starting work in another state, noncustodial parents could have their income attached and the children could begin receiving child support. After nine months, the national directory of new hires had located one million delinquent parents, contributing to the $13.4 billion collected, an increase of 68 percent from child support collections in 1992 (White House Press Release 1998).

Section 325 of PRWORA also significantly expands access to information by providing that state child support agencies must have access to two important categories of records. The first category includes a vast array of state and local government-agency records (vital statistics, tax and revenue records, property titles, occupational and professional licenses, and others). The second category includes certain records held by private entities, including customer records of public utilities and cable television companies and information (including assets and liabilities) on individuals who owe support held by financial institutions.[7]

Access to records must be automated for certain databases, and specified state records must use Social Security numbers to allow for computerized matching of records. Finally, states must enter into agreements with financial institutions doing business in the states to develop and operate a data-match system in which the financial institutions provide names, addresses, and Social Security numbers for all account holders who owe past-due child support. This information provides a simple and effective way to collect child support through a process that matches lists of delinquent obligors against lists of account holders. When a match is made, the IV-D (child support enforcement) agency verifies whether the past-due support is still owed. If so, the agency issues a levy on the account and the financial institution forwards the amount of the past-due obligation to the agency.

With this broad access to information under the act, it should be possible to find a delinquent obligor anywhere in the country, with few exceptions. (Private attorneys can refer clients to the IV-D agency for this and other location functions.) The vast majority of obligors have some record that allows child support agencies to find them—for example, driver's licenses, bank accounts, automobile registrations, or utility or cable-television services. Delinquent obligors will be able to run but will no longer be able to hide.

(2) Mass Case Processing

A major problem with the child support system historically is that cases are usually processed individually as an outgrowth of the traditional judicial model for child support enforcement. Action depended on a complainant taking the necessary legal steps, and generally either a prosecutor or an individual's attorney must raise the issue in court. Unfortunately, as the number of single parents skyrocketed, this system was very slow to adjust to the increased demands, and most cases languished. The system worked for wealthier parents who could afford to hire lawyers, but many more parents could not afford legal help. Legal aid for the poor could never meet more than a fraction of the need, and few local prosecutors made child support enforcement for welfare cases a high priority.

Obligee parents clamored for help and turned in ever-increasing numbers to the government. The caseload of IV-D agencies skyrocketed and forced these agencies to rethink the way they handled child support enforcement. Over the past decade, a growing number of child support professionals realized that the demand for enforcement services could only be met through mass case processing, which requires that case information and payment records be computerized (U.S. Government Accounting Office 1992). These records are then matched against other databases, such as state unemployment-compensation records, workers' compensation records, or bank account records. Once a match is made, the computer automatically prints out a wage assignment (for income) or levy (for bank accounts) notice, puts it in an envelope, affixes a stamp, and mails the notice, all without human intervention (Tarr 1994).

(3) Liens

Mass case processing involves two steps: (1) matching of lists of delinquent obligors with assets or income records, which requires access to information; and (2) an efficient means of capturing the assets or income necessary to meet the child support obligation, which requires the use of automatic wage assignments (for income) and liens (for assets).

Many delinquent obligors have assets that could be seized and applied toward unpaid child support obligations.[8] But to seize these assets efficiently, liens need to be processed automatically and in volume. Although liens have been required in child support cases for more than a decade, liens were rarely used because caseworkers had to prepare individual liens and seek judicial approval. Taking the strategy behind the use of tax liens, proponents of administrative liens saw them as the "sleeping giant" for child support collectors that could move the collection from retail to wholesale.

Under the old law, unpaid support payments became a judgment by operation of law, but PRWORA introduced two crucial changes: it provided that liens on unpaid child support obligations must arise by operation of law and that the liens must be imposed administratively. The effect of these combined requirements is that child support agencies can issue liens based on any unpaid child support obligation without having to return to court to obtain a judgment or lien prior to garnishment or attachment. The lien can then be used as the basis for tax-refund offsets; license revocation; levy and seizure of bank accounts; and seizure of government benefits, lottery winnings, and other assets not otherwise exempt by law. States are given flexibility to fashion due process requirements as long as the states do not require judicial issuance of the lien (Motz and Baida 1986).

The bank-match system is an example of how mass case processing works. Under PRWORA, financial institutions must encumber or surrender assets held by obligors in response to a notice of lien or levy. Thus, any bank account money can be identified and seized quickly. Liens can also be used to collect child support across state lines. States must accord full faith and credit to liens arising in other states, without registration of the underlying order. Furthermore, states are required to administratively enforce interstate cases by responding to requests for assistance from other states. These provisions effectively allow a state to issue liens administratively and send them to neighboring states, which will then run computer matches against their information sources to determine if there are assets (most likely bank accounts) that can be seized easily and quickly.

Central Registries and Centralized Collections

PRWORA imposed two state requirements that facilitate mass case processing: (1) central state registries of child support orders, and (2) centralized collection and disbursement units.

Central state registries maintain current records of all child support orders: the registries are required to contain all new and modified orders, and states must maintain and update payment records. The registry must also be able to extract data for matching with other databases. This state-registry requirement is designed to end the current system of fragmented state records wherein it is nearly impossible to determine what action has been taken by multiple caseworkers or courts within a state. A basic extract of the information in the state case registry (name, Social Security number, and case identifier) will be sent to a federal case registry implemented on 1 October 1998 for matching IV-D cases against the national directory of new hires and other FPLS data sources.

The state child support registries also work in conjunction with the required state "centralized collection and disbursement unit." Delivery of child support payments to custodial parents and children currently varies tremendously from state to state. Payments can be collected and disbursed through clerks of court or central child support agencies. The process may also differ depending on whether custodial parents receive child support services through public agencies.

More states are moving toward centralized collection and disbursement units, using a single central automated unit to handle processing child support payments (Policy Studies Inc. 1991). As of mid-1998, about two-thirds of all states had computer systems that were either certified or ready to be certified as being in compliance with the federal mandate (Quinn 1998). The potential advantages include efficiency, better customer service, improved enforcement, and simplicity for employers since they only have to transfer one payment to one place for all their income-withholding orders.

Proactive Enforcement

One of the goals for child support enforcement reform was to make enforcement much more proactive in that enforcement action occurs automatically whenever a payment is missed. Child support cases were too often handled on a complaint-driven basis in which the IV-D agency only took action when custodial parents pressured it to do so. The roots of child support enforcement show why it has been such a complaint-driven process: enforcement was viewed as a private matter, except where welfare dollars were involved, best left to state court discretion (Hunter 1983). The result of that legacy is the adversarial, judicial nature of support proceedings, broad court discretion and involvement, and the lack of self-starting payment mechanisms (Schuele 1988).

States are moving toward more administrative, less court dependent child support systems. At least eighteen states have some type of administrative process for establishing or enforcing child support obligations (Williams 1993). The accumulated experience of these states demonstrates that administrative process can potentially speed adjudication, reduce cost, preserve or even enhance due process, improve access to the adjudicatory process, reduce fragmentation of case processing, and free up court time by relieving the court system of routine child support matters.

This trend toward adoption of administrative process for child support matters is likely to continue and will generally lead to improved child support enforcement. Still, the fundamental issue for child support enforcement is not administrative process versus judicial process. There are many types of administrative process and quasi-judicial systems and, as John Eekelaar notes in "Child Support as Distributive and Commutative Justice: The United Kingdom Experience" (in this volume), various alternatives work in different circumstances. The crucial determination is whether the process, whatever it is, ensures that the child support payments reach the child quickly, efficiently, and in all cases. To accomplish that goal, the real key is to build the process around the routine cases rather than the exceptional ones.

The PRWORA child support provisions are built on that key concept. They do not mandate that all states adopt full administrative-process systems. Instead, PRWORA provides that states must have certain "expedited procedures" for handling routine cases that allow the state child support agency to take routine enforcement steps without the necessity of obtaining an order from any other judicial or administrative tribunal. This distinction is important: child support agencies will have sufficient administrative authority to process the vast majority of cases without requiring prior court intervention, yet states can maintain limited court-based processes for the collection of support when necessary for exceptional cases.[9] States also retain the authority to determine the due process requirements for these expedited processes as long as states do not require prior orders from judicial or administrative tribunals. Even with mass case processing, some cases—such as when the obligor is self-employed—will still need to be handled on an individual basis. In these cases, obligees can still bring motions for contempt, job search orders, and so forth before the court. No nonwelfare obligee is forced to be in the IV-D system, so private attorneys can still handle child support cases externally.

These expedited processes work in conjunction with the central registries and centralized collection and disbursement, so that for IV-D cases, any delay or failure to make payment should automatically trigger enforcement actions. This is broad new authority for child support agencies in many states, and when fully implemented it should revolutionize the collection process.

There can be little doubt that these changes toward greater child support agency authority, expedited procedures, mass case processing, and proactive enforcement will send repercussions throughout the judicial system. When these changes are fully implemented, the child support enforcement system will have moved from one that was primarily self-initiated, adversarial, judicially based, and discretionary to one that is proactive, less adversarial, highly administrative, and based on rule. Fewer cases will be enforced through the traditional court system. Yet few people will mourn the passing of the old regime. Its legacy is a record of enforcement that let the "deadbeats" off and left most children with only a fraction of the child support they deserved.

Interstate and Other Enforcement Issues

As the U.S. Commission on Interstate Child Support reported, some of the most difficult cases involve families that reside in different states: there are variations in laws governing such essential functions as the enforcement of support, service of process, and jurisdiction (U.S. Commission 1992). According to a recent U.S. Government Accounting Office (GAO) report (1992), although interstate cases are as likely as in-state cases to have awards in place, the chance of receiving a payment is much less. This problem is significant because interstate cases represent about 30 percent of all child support awards yet yield only 7 percent of all public collections (GAO 1989:2).

In developing reforms for an increasingly mobile society, there was a strong consensus that the need for a stronger federal role in interstate location and enforcement had grown. One key part of the expanded federal role is the new-hire program and expanded FPLS; the second is mandating uniform procedures for interstate cases. Under the act, all states are required to adopt UIFSA, a uniform state law approved by the National Conference of Commissioners on Uniform State Laws in 1992. UIFSA replaces a previous uniform act, the Uniform Reciprocal Enforcement of Support Act. UIFSA should dramatically improve parents' ability to obtain child support across state lines because it imposes uniform requirements, procedures, and evidentiary rules for interstate cases.[10]

Another prominent enforcement remedy required under the act is the authority to revoke drivers, professional, occupational, and recreational licenses—a remedy especially useful in forcing self-employed obligors to comply. All states must use such authority, but they have discretion to determine the due process for doing so. Preliminary reports from a number of states indicate that license revocation can significantly boost collections.[11] Enforcement is also strengthened by the act's numerous other changes, including courts' authority to impose work requirements, international enforcement, and denial of passports (Dixon 1993; Chambers 1979; Dehart 1994).

Modifications of Awards, Distribution, and Pass-Through

PRWORA allows a state to choose one of three routes to update child support awards: (1) to do review and adjustment against the guidelines under existing law;[12] (2) to do a cost-of-living adjustment;[13] or (3) to conduct an automated review.[14] Notice and standards of proof are specified in the statute.[15] States are required to do review and adjustment only if a party (or the state, in the case of a welfare recipient) requests one.[16]

Modification of awards is one area where the new legislation falls short. It does nothing to insure that all awards are periodically updated.[17] PRWORA places the burden of requesting review on the parent, usually a custodial mother, but many mothers will not make such requests because they do not understand the process or do not want to rock the boat (Caliber Associates 1992). Closing the gap caused by failure to update awards is perhaps the principal remaining task left in reforming child support (Mincy 1995; Mincy and Sorensen 1994; Bartfeld and Garfinkel 1994; Meyer, Bartfeld, and Kost 1993).

Another provision of PRWORA entails some good news for those recipients who leave welfare. Previous law provided for payment first of arrears to the state. The new "family first" distribution policy provides that families who have left welfare must receive any child support arrears. This change will result in substantial child support flowing to families that have left welfare, a group that is overwhelmingly poor. In an era of block grants and time-limited welfare, the receipt of child support for this group is especially significant. However, people receiving welfare are negatively affected by one change under PRWORA. Under the block-grant changes to AFDC, states are no longer required to provide a fifty-dollar pass-through of child support to cash assistance recipients.

Conclusion

PRWORA's child support policy changes are revolutionary. Paternity establishment will be an increased focus of attention, and paternity establishment rates will continue to rise. Tougher enforcement of child support obligations will be the rule. The system will change from one where payment is often discretionary to one where payment is compelled and automatic. Collections should soar as a result. Indeed, positive results are already in evidence because states began implementing many of the required changes in anticipation of their passage (White House Press Release 1998).

Improved child support enforcement will increase the financial security of millions of custodial parents and their children (Sorensen 1995a; Garfinkel and McLanahan 1994). It will enable low- and middle-income families to have more financially secure lives. It will keep some poor families from falling onto the welfare rolls, help them leave if they are on welfare, and keep families from returning to welfare once they have left (Meyer 1991; Sandfort and Hill 1996; Luttrell 1996). Evidence suggests that the receipt of child support also has other positive nonfinancial impacts for families and children (Nixon 1997), including a positive impact on academic achievement (Knox 1996).

Still, as Marsha Garrison, Irwin Garfinkel, and Martha Albertson Fineman point out elsewhere in this volume, collecting child support is not a silver bullet for the problem of poverty in single-parent families. Alone, doing so will have a modest impact on poverty rates and welfare costs.[18] States should not expect changes in child support policy to substitute for cuts in welfare expenditures. Child support should be considered as part of a package of supports[19] that can play an important role in reducing poverty and increasing the financial security of children in single-parent families.

NOTES

Paul K. Legler is the Assistant Commissioner, Office of Child Support Enforcement, U.S. Department of Health and Human Services, Washington, D.C. The views expressed are the author's own and do not necessarily represent the views of the U.S. Department of Health and Human Services or the U.S. government.

1. Pub. L. 104–193, 110 Stat. 2105 (1996).

2. Pub. L. 103–66, 107 Stat. 312 (1993).

3. Subject to good-cause exceptions or unless otherwise barred by state law. States are not required to order genetic tests in cases where the mother is married and a "stranger to the marriage" seeks to establish paternity (Smith 1989).

4. The act shifts the responsibility for determining cooperation from the IV-A (welfare) agency to the IV-D (child support agency) (PRWORA § 332). This shift is designed to streamline the process and place the determination with the same agency that is establishing paternity. According to some studies, one of the reasons identified for the difficulties in paternity establishment is the poor interface and lack of cooperation between IV-A and IV-D agencies (Nichols-Casebolt 1992; Adams, Landsbergen, and Hecht 1994).

5. Under §§ 341 and 452(g) of the Social Security Act, states are required to meet paternity establishment standards by showing improvement each year until they reach 90 percent. See 42 U.S.C. § 652. This incentive to remove difficult cases is mitigated, however, by the fact that many of these cases remain Medicaid cases and hence are mandatory IV-D cases.

6. This reporting requirement was patterned on a program the state of Washington pioneered in 1990 that required employers to report new hires directly to the child support agency, using W-4 information. Completion of the W-4 form, which contains the employee's name and address, is already required at the time of hire; the form is not normally sent anywhere but is simply filed in the employer's records. Once received by the child support enforcement agency, the information was matched against child support records. If a delinquent obligor was found, the state would immediately implement a wage-withholding order. Subsequent experience in other states confirmed that the program dramatically increased collections, allowed some families to leave welfare entirely, and saved the states millions of dollars.

An example of the benefits of the new-hire program was demonstrated in the commonwealth of Massachusetts, which reported that in the first year of operation of the new hire/automated wage assignment system, employers reported more than one million new hires. Processing this new information required the efforts of only eleven full-time state employees and cost $300,000. Massachusetts used the new-hire information to locate 13,500 obligors who were delinquent in paying child support and increased payments in its wage-assignment cases by $33.2 million annually. Moreover, the increased child support from these automated wage assignment programs helped 1,872 Massachusetts families to move off welfare rolls, for an additional taxpayer savings of $21.6 million. This information also enabled the state to detect fraud and abuse in other government-benefit programs, saving taxpayers an estimated $15.9 million annually. All told, the new hire/automated wage assignment system was estimated to be worth $70.7 million per year (Massachusetts Department of Revenue 1994).

7. Information from credit histories can be used to establish and modify child support orders as well as to enforce orders. Under existing law, information about an obligor's credit history can be used only to enforce an existing child support order and cannot be used to establish or modify an order (PRWORA §§ 325, 352, 372).

8. It is estimated that by age thirty-five, 48.5 percent of absent fathers have savings and/or stocks. Between ages twenty and thirty-five, the value of the holdings averaged $980 to $7,246. Also between ages twenty and thirty-five, 34.5 percent of absent fathers had equity in other assets, with the average value of the holdings ranging from $1,560 to $9,691 (Pirog-Good and Amerson 1995).

9. The required expedited procedures under the act include ordering genetic tests; subpoenaing information or requiring entities in the state to provide employment information (and imposing penalties or sanctions for failure to respond to subpoenas); accessing certain records; changing payees in cases of assignment; ordering income withholding; intercepting or seizing periodic or lump-sum payments (including unemployment compensation, workers' compensation, other state benefits, judgments, settlements, and lotteries); attaching and seizing assets of the obligor held in financial institutions; attaching public and private retirement funds; imposing liens (and, in appropriate cases, forcing the sale of property and the distribution of proceeds); and increasing the amount of the monthly payment to cover amounts for arrearages (PRWORA § 325).

10. Under UIFSA, all states will have long-arm statutes, there will be only one controlling order, states can modify orders only if they have jurisdiction under the act, choice of law is specified, there is direct income withholding between states, and other procedures and evidentiary rules will be uniform (UIFSA §§ 205, 206, 611, 303, 501).

11. Estimates based on various state data indicated that a national requirement for license revocation would increase total child support collections by $2.5 billion over ten years (Office of the Assistant Secretary for Planning and Evaluation 1994).

12. "Review and adjustment" of awards, also called review and modification or updating, is a process of reviewing the guidelines factors (primarily income) at a

new point in time and applying the child support guidelines to redetermine the appropriate child support award. For a discussion of review and adjustment issues and case law, see J. Thomas Oldham, "New Methods to Update Child Support," in this volume.

13. Cost-of-living adjustments (COLAs) use a consumer price index to periodically update the award amount. COLAs are arguably better than making no adjustment, but experience shows that they have their own set of shortcomings. (Minnesota is the only state to have regular COLA. Minn. Stat. Ann. § 518.641 [1993]). First, unless it is automatically applied to all cases, the COLA process puts the burden on the obligee to initiate the change. As a result, the process is often not initiated because the obligee does not want to rock the boat or is unaware of the process. The modification requirements under the act would duplicate and perpetuate this problem, since modification is only required on request. Second, COLAs are at best a very rough way of capturing increases in the obligor's income, because the obligor's income may go up faster or slower than the rate of inflation. Some evidence suggests that in typical cases the COLA will result in a lower award than a review and adjustment based on actual income. A comparison between the average increases in modified order amounts and increases that would have resulted from COLAs varied in a four-sites study from 67 percent increases for modification versus 41 percent for a COLA adjustment in Colorado to 141 percent for modification versus 30 percent for a COLA adjustment in Illinois (Caliber Associates 1992). Conversely, for low-income obligors, the COLA increase may be greater than the actual increase in income.

14. The automated-adjustment option allows the state to review against tax or other records and make an adjustment only if that limited review shows that a change in the award amount is warranted. This method will be facilitated by the increased access to information in the act. Still, this method of review and adjustment is highly dependent on the adequacy of the information reviewed, and experience will be necessary to determine if this procedure results in adequate awards or if a more comprehensive review is necessary.

15. If either COLAs or automated reviews are chosen, the state must provide notice and opportunity to allow the parties to contest the adjustment and have the review made against the guidelines. Review and adjustments under these three options are only required on request of the parties or, in welfare cases, at the request of either the state agency or the parents. These three-year reviews and adjustments do not require proof of a change in circumstances. States must give notice to parents every three years of the right to request a review. Adjustments outside the three-year cycle can be made but require a showing of a substantial change in circumstances (PRWORA § 351).

16. This is one area where the PRWORA takes a step backward, because review is no longer mandatory in welfare cases. If not mandated, some child support agencies may not periodically review these cases, and, therefore, when recipients leave the transitional assistance program, they are likely to have inadequate child support awards (unless the recipients take the initiative to request reviews). While it may be in the best interest of the state to request a review every three years for

AFDC cases, this responsibility often falls on county child support offices. Since review and modification is labor intensive and county offices do not see a direct benefit to them of such reviews, it is probable that reviews will not be done in all welfare cases. (However, PRWORA makes review and adjustment less labor intensive if the state chooses an automated review process, which may mitigate some of the incentive for county offices not to conduct reviews.)

17. According to one study, $7.0 billion of the collection gap results from inadequate awards (Sorensen 1995a). The proposed Work and Responsibility Act of 1994 would have expanded modification by requiring states to review and, if necessary, modify all child support awards in the state central registry every three years. Since all new orders are to be put in the central registry, all cases eventually would have been updated every three years, with the exception that parents could opt out of modification if both agreed (WRA § 652). States also would have been required to adopt expedited procedures so that awards could be modified administratively according to the guidelines (WRA § 636). Such a process, if it had been adopted, would close a significant portion of the gap in collections because of the inadequacy of awards. Garfinkel, Oellerich, and Robins (1991) estimated the impact of applying guidelines to all awards, including awards from prior years, and projected increases of about 70 percent for divorced mothers, 44 percent for separated mothers, 25 percent for never-married mothers, and 100 percent for married mothers. About one-third of these gains would accrue from updating past awards for increases in (male) earnings.

18. Increased child support collections will decrease the costs of welfare and help some families leave the welfare rolls, although the decrease will probably be less than many people expect. Sorensen estimates that if the child support system were perfect, AFDC participation would drop by 400,000 units, welfare costs (i.e., AFDC, food stamps, and Medicaid) would fall by $4 billion, or 13 percent of the cost of providing welfare benefits to custodial families (Sorensen 1995b).

19. The best source of support would be an adequate-paying job in the private sector. Additional supports could include expanded education and training opportunities, expanded health insurance, a more sizable earned-income-tax credit, a refundable child-tax credit, expanded child-care assistance, and a higher minimum wage. It is worth noting that the Clinton administration has made substantial progress in most of these areas. Additionally, policymakers could experiment with insured child support payments that would set a minimum amount that the custodial parent would receive (Ellwood 1988; Garfinkel, "The Limits of Private Child Support and the Role of an Assured Benefit," in this volume).

REFERENCES

Adams, Charles F., Jr., David Landsbergen, and Larry Cobler. 1992. Welfare Reform and Paternity Establishment: A Social Experiment. *Policy Analysis and Management* 11:665–87.

Adams, Charles F., Jr., David Landsbergen, and Daniel Hecht. 1994. Organizational Impediments to Paternity Establishment and Child Support. *Social Science Review* 68:109–26.

Bartfeld, Judi, and Irwin Garfinkel. 1994. *Utilization and Effects of Payments on Percentage-Expressed Child Support Orders.* Madison, WI: Institute for Research on Poverty.

Bias, Wilma, Deborah Meyers, and Edmond Murphy. 1983. Theoretical Underpinning of Paternity Testing. In *Inclusion Probabilities in Parentage Testing.* Arlington, VA: American Association of Blood Banks.

Blumberg, Patricia Bundschuh. 1983. Human Leukocyte Antigen Testing: Technology Versus Policy in Cases of Disputed Parentage. *Vanderbilt Law Review* 36:1587–1613.

Caliber Associates. 1992. *Cross-Sites Final Report.* Fairfax, VA: Caliber Associates.

Chambers, David L. 1979. *Making Fathers Pay: The Enforcement of Child Support.* Chicago: University of Chicago Press.

Crenshaw, Albert. 1997. A Struggling IRS Collects Its Fair Share of Problems: Computer Dilemma, Critics Tax Agency. *Washington Post,* 14 April, A1.

Dehart, Gloria Folger. 1994. Comity, Conventions, and the Constitution: State and Federal Initiatives in International Child Support Enforcement. *Family Law Quarterly* 28:89–115.

Dixon, Jennifer. 1993. Parents Who Fail to Pay Child Support Are Being Put to Work in Wisconsin. *Buffalo News,* 23 June, A3.

Eaton, William J. 1994. Shalala Revives "Murphy Brown" Pregnancy Issue. *Los Angeles Times,* 15 July, A1.

Ellwood, David T. 1988. *Poor Support: Poverty in the American Family.* New York: Basic Books.

Garfinkel, Irwin, and Sara S. McLanahan. 1994. Single Mother Families, Economic Security, and Government Policy. In *Confronting Poverty: Prescriptions for Change,* ed. Sheldon Danziger, Gary D. Sandefur, and Daniel H. Weinberg. New York: Russell Sage Foundation.

Garfinkel, Irwin, and Donald Oellerich. 1989. Noncustodial Fathers' Ability to Pay Child Support. *Demography* 26:219–33.

Garfinkel, Irwin, Donald Oellerich, and Philip K. Robins. 1991. Child Support Guidelines: Will They Make a Difference? *Journal of Family Issues* 12:404–29.

Gordon, Ann. 1991. Implementation of the Income Withholding and Medical Enforcement Provisions of the 1984 Child Support Enforcement Amendments. Paper presented at the Conference on Child Support and Child Welfare, Washington, DC.

Haskins, Ron, J. Brad Schwartz, John S. Akin, and Andrew W. Dobelstein. 1985. How Much Child Support Can Absent Parents Pay? *Policy Studies Journal* 14:201–22.

Hunter, Nan D. 1983. Child Support Law and Policy: The Systematic Imposition of Costs on Women. *Harvard Women's Law Journal* 6:1–27.

Knox, Virginia. 1996. The Effects of Child Support Payments on Developmental Outcomes for Elementary School-Age Children. *Journal of Human Resources* 31:816–40.

Landry, David J., and Jacqueline Darroch Forrest. 1995. How Old Are U.S. Fathers? *Family Planning Perspectives* 27 (4): 159–61, 165.

Legler Paul K., and David T. Ellwood. 1993. Getting Serious about Paternity. Unpublished report to the Ford Foundation. Malcolm Wiener Center for Social Policy, Harvard University.

Lerman, Robert. 1990. Fatherhood, Child Support and Earnings: A Report on the Links between Family Responsibility and Job Market Outcomes. Washington, DC: American University.

Lindberg, Laura Duberstein, Freya I. Sonenstein, Leighton Ku, and Gladys Martinez. 1997. Age Differences between Minors Who Give Birth and Their Adult Partners. *Family Planning Perspectives* 29:61–66.

Luttrell, Carol Ann. 1996. Child Support and the Transition from Welfare to Work: Massachusetts Evidence. Paper presented at the Association of Public Policy Analysis and Management Conference, Pittsburgh, PA.

Massachusetts Department of Revenue 1994. Massachusetts New Hire/Automated Wage Assignment System. Cambridge, MA: Massachusetts Department of Revenue.

McLanahan, Sara S. 1995. The Consequences of Nonmarital Childbearing for Women, Children and Society. In *Report to Congress on out-of-Wedlock Childbearing.* Washington, DC: U.S. Department of Health and Human Services.

McLanahan, Sara S., Renee Monson, and Pat Brown. 1992. Paternity Establishment for AFDC Mothers: Three Wisconsin Counties. In *Studies of the Circumstances of Mothers and Fathers.* Special Report 56B. Madison, WI: Institute for Research on Poverty.

McLanahan, Sara S., and Gary Sandefur. 1994. *Growing Up with a Single Parent: What Hurts, What Helps.* Cambridge, MA: Harvard University Press.

Meyer, Daniel R. 1991. Child Support and Welfare Dynamics: Evidence from Wisconsin. Madison, WI: Institute for Research on Poverty.

———. 1995. Supporting Children Born outside of Marriage: Do Child Support Awards Keep Pace with Changes in Father's Income? *Social Science Quarterly* 76:577–93.

Meyer, Daniel R., Judi Bartfeld, and Kate Kost. 1993. *Fixed, Percentage-Expressed, and Hybrid Child Support Orders in Wisconsin.* Madison, WI: Institute for Research on Poverty.

Mincy, Ron. 1995. *Reforming Income Maintenance and Family Support Systems to Strengthen Fragile Families.* Washington, DC: U.S. Commission on Child and Family Welfare.

Mincy, Ron, and Elaine Sorensen. 1994. *Child Support Reform: Moving the Debate beyond Deadbeat Dads.* Washington, DC: Urban Institute Press.

Motz, Diana Gribbon, and Andrew H. Baida. 1986. The Due Process Rights of Postjudgment Debtors and Child Support Obligors. *Maryland Law Review* 45:61–90.

Nichols-Casebolt, Ann. 1992. *Paternity Establishment in Arizona: A Case Study of the Process and Its Outcomes.* Tempe: Arizona State University Press.

Nixon, Lucia. 1997. The Effect of Child Support Enforcement on Marital Dissolution. *Journal of Human Resources* 32:159–81.

Office of the Assistant Secretary for Planning and Evaluation. 1994. *Cost Estimates for the Work and Responsibility Act of 1994.* Washington, DC: U.S. Department of Health and Human Services.

Pena, S. D., and Ranajit Chakraborty. 1994. Paternity Testing in the DNA Era. *Trends in Genetics* 10:204–9.

Phillips, Elizabeth, and Irwin Garfinkel. 1993. Income Growth among Nonresident Fathers: Evidence from Wisconsin. *Demography* 30:227–41.

Pirog-Good, Maureen A., and Lydia Amerson. 1995. *Making Waves by Seizing Assets: Shifting the Uneven Tides of Poverty in Favor of Children.* Bloomington: Indiana University School of Public and Environmental Affairs.

Pirog-Good, Maureen A., and David H. Good. 1995. Child Support Enforcement for Teenage Fathers: Problems and Prospects. *Journal of Policy Analysis and Management* 14:25–42.

Policy Studies Inc. 1991. *Implementing a Child Support Payment Center.* Denver, CO: Policy Studies Inc.

Quinn, Jane Bryant. 1998. Despite '96 Law, Collecting Child Support Can Be Tough. *Baltimore Sun,* 15 June, 7C.

Sandfort, Jodi R., and Martha S. Hill. 1996. Assisting Young, Unmarried Mothers to Become Self-Sufficient: The Effects of Different Types of Early Economic Support. *Journal of Marriage and the Family* 58:311–26.

Schuele, Donna. 1988. Origins and Development of the Law of Parental Child Support. *Journal of Family Law* 27:807–41.

Smith, Marilyn Ray. 1989. Paternity Litigation Involving Presumed versus Putative Fathers: Conflicting Rights and Results. Paper presented at the ABA's Third National Child Support Conference. Updated version available from Massachusetts Department of Revenue, Child Support Division, Cambridge, MA.

Sorensen, Elaine. 1995a. *Dispelling the Myths about the Benefits of Increased Child Support Enforcement.* Washington, DC: Urban Institute.

———. 1995b (1994). *Non-Custodial Fathers: Can They Afford to Pay More Child Support?* Washington, DC: Urban Institute.

Tarr, Amy. 1994. *Child Support Enforcement in Massachusetts: A Study in Reengineering.* Boston, MA: ABA

U.S. Commission on Interstate Child Support Enforcement. 1992. *Supporting Our Children: A Blueprint for Reform.* Washington, DC: U.S. Commission.

U.S. Department of Health and Human Services. 1985. *Costs and Benefits of Paternity Establishment.* Washington, DC: U.S. Department of Health and Human Services, Center for Health and Social Services Research, Office of Child Support Enforcement.

———. 1994. *Background Papers on Welfare Reform: Child Support Enforcement. Policy Information Center.* Report 5777, ASPE-HHS. Washington, DC: U.S. Department of Health and Human Services.

———. 1995. *Twentieth Annual Report to Congress.* Washington, DC: U.S. Department of Health and Human Services, Office of Child Support Enforcement.

———. 1997. *Preliminary Data on in-Hospital Paternity Programs.* March. Washington, DC: U.S. Department of Health and Human Services.

U.S. Government Accounting Office. 1989. *Interstate Child Support: Case Data Limitations, Enforcement Problems, Views on Improvements Needed.* Washington, DC: U.S. Government Accounting Office.

———. 1992. *Interstate Child Support: Mothers Report Receiving Less Support from out-of-State Fathers.* Washington, DC: U.S. Government Accounting Office.

Washington State Office of Support Enforcement. 1991. *Paternity Acknowledgment Program, Program Summary.* Olympia: Washington State Office of Support Enforcement.

Wattenberg, Esther, Rose Brewer, and Michael Resnick. 1991. *A Study of Paternity Decisions of Young Unmarried Parents.* Final report submitted to the Ford Foundation. Minneapolis: University of Minnesota, Center for Urban and Regional Affairs.

White House Press Release. 1998. President Hails Child Support Progress and Signs Tough Penalties for Deadbeat Parents. *M2 Communications,* 26 June.

Williams, Victoria. 1993. *A Comparative Analysis of Minnesota's Administrative Process.* Denver, CO: Policy Studies Inc.

Part II

The Current Social Structure and Its Relevance to Reform

Child Support and Child Access: Experiences of Divorced and Nonmarital Families

Judith A. Seltzer

Child support reform focuses attention on parents' financial responsibilities to children. Altering financial ties to children may also affect other aspects of parents' involvement with children. Parents who pay child support are more likely to visit children than those who do not pay support (Seltzer 1991; Furstenberg et al. 1983). By making child support orders more universal and enforcing these obligations, recent reforms may increase visits between nonresident parents and children. Stricter enforcement of child support responsibilities is likely to increase contact between parents who would otherwise avoid each other to limit disagreements. Encouraging both parents to remain involved in children's lives, even when the parents are no longer a couple, may have the unintended effect of exposing children to high levels of conflict that may counter the benefits of higher child support.

Reforms to the child support system may have different effects for children born in nonmarital relationships than those whose parents divorce (McLanahan et al. 1994). Parents of children born outside of marriage face paternity adjudication as an additional step in the establishment of child support orders. The establishment of paternity may be an uncomplicated and friendly arrangement, as when the parents are living together (see, for example, Pearson and Thoennes 1995). However, in cases where one or both parents prefer to end the relationship, establishing paternity is likely to be stressful and filled with conflict between parents and between parents and administrative agencies and courts. A major focus of child support reform in the Family Support Act as well as the 1996 Welfare Reform Act has been to increase the percentage of nonmarital births for which paternity is established.

Nearly a third of U.S. children are born to unmarried parents. This high and rising percentage points to the importance of considering the consequences of child support reforms for nonmarital families as well as for divorced families (Ventura et al. 1998). Despite the demographic and administrative significance of children born outside of marriage for anticipating the potential effects on families of child support reform, past research emphasizes the experiences of divorced families (Seltzer 1994). The lack of attention to families of children born outside of marriage reflects that earlier studies included too few children born outside of marriage to support multivariate statistical analysis (for example, the National Survey of Children; Furstenberg et al. 1983). More recent studies use court-based samples, which are a valuable source of information about parents who are divorcing but cannot adequately represent parents whose children were born outside of marriage, because such a low percentage of the latter enter the court system (for example, Stanford Child Custody Study; Maccoby and Mnookin 1992; Arizona Noncustodial Parent Project; Braver et al. 1993). Finally, even the Child Support Supplement to the Current Population Survey (CSS-CPS) conducted by the U.S. Bureau of the Census includes limited information about the child support and visiting patterns of nonmarital families, because for many years the survey has identified nonmarital families as those in which the mother was "never married" at the time of interview (Scoon-Rogers and Lester 1995). More than one-fifth of nonmarital births occur to previously married women; thus, the CPS does not correctly classify a significant minority of nonmarital families (Bumpass 1996).

This chapter examines the effects of child support payments on contact between nonresident fathers and children using data from a large national survey of parents who divorced or who bore their children out of wedlock. The focus on nonresident fathers reflects that for the vast majority of children who live apart from a parent, the father is the nonresident parent (Scoon-Rogers and Lester 1995; Nord and Zill 1996). The first section of the chapter elaborates reasons for expecting an effect of child support on fathers' time with children. The second section describes the new longitudinal data used to examine the association between child support and nonresident fathers' contact with children. The third section reports results from an investigation of two questions: How does fathers' contact with children change over time? Do fathers who pay more child support see their children more frequently? The investigation pays particular attention to differences between children born in marriage and those whose parents were not married to each other. The last section of the chapter considers implications of the answers to these questions for child support policy.

Effects of Child Support on Fathers' Time with Children

Just as parents who live with their children look after them by spending time with them and spending money on them, nonresident parents may invest both time and money in their children. Parents who live with children may give up time with their children but compensate by spending more money on them, as when parents work longer hours to pay for new school clothes. Compared to nonresident fathers who pay less child support, those who pay more support may not be able to see their children as frequently because paying more support requires the father to work more. Paying support and spending time with children may also be negatively related if fathers spend money on child support that would otherwise pay for travel expenses for children's visits or for things the children need when they stay overnight in the nonresident father's home.

Despite these explanations for a potential negative effect of child support on nonresident fathers' time with children, previous research generally shows a positive relationship between child support and visiting (Furstenberg et al. 1983; Seltzer 1991; Seltzer, Schaeffer, and Charng 1989; Seltzer, McLanahan, and Hanson 1998; McLanahan et al. 1994). Similarly, families that report problems with paying or collecting child support are also likely to report problems with visiting (Pearson and Anhalt 1994; Bay et al. 1993). These findings are consistent with economic theory, which suggests that nonresident fathers will use visits to keep track of how the children's mothers spend child support contributions (Weiss and Willis 1985). Child support may increase contact between nonresident fathers and children if the act of paying child support alters nonresident fathers' and resident mothers' attitudes about fathers' right to spend time with the children. Fathers who pay support may see their children more frequently to fulfill the role of "good father." Mothers who receive support regularly may also view fathers' claims for time with children as more legitimate than do mothers who do not receive regular child support.

Another interpretation of the positive association between child support and visiting observed in previous studies is that both activities are the result of some third factor, such as parents' commitment to children, parents' ability to cooperate with each other about child rearing, or fathers' socioeconomic status. Evidence of continuity in family relationships and in children's behavior before and after separation support interpretations of the association between paying support and visiting as spurious (Koch and Lowery 1984; Block, Block, and Gjerde 1988; Cherlin et al. 1991). To the extent that nonresident parents pay child support and spend time with their children because of their affection for the children (or another characteristic of the parents or the family), child support enforcement is unlikely to increase the amount of time that nonresident parents spend with children.

A way to adjudicate between claims that child support payments and visiting are causally related and claims that the association between payments and visits is explained by other family characteristics is to observe families over time. Most previous studies have examined the association between child support payments and visiting using measures observed at a single time. As a result, the causal association between payments and visits is ambiguous. Longitudinal data allow an assessment of the effects of child support payments at an earlier time on subsequent visitation. In addition, longitudinal data can be used to take account of other, stable characteristics of fathers or families that might explain both child support payments and visiting. Observing child support and visiting patterns over time may provide a different picture of the possible effects of child support and visiting than is available from cross-sectional (one-time, snapshot) studies. For example, an investigation of young parents found that when families are followed over time, changes in a nonresident father's visits with children are unrelated to changes in how much child support he pays (Veum 1993).[1] The research reported in this chapter builds on previous work by examining the effects of child support payments at an earlier time on the frequency of subsequent visits between nonresident fathers and children.

The Data: National Survey of Families and Households

The National Survey of Families and Households (NSFH) provides information about child support and visiting behavior for divorced and nonmarital families. The first wave of the survey was conducted with a cross section of adults in U.S. households in 1987–88. The sample includes oversamples of single-parent families, families with stepchildren, cohabiting and recently married couples, and some minority groups. The response rate at the first wave was 74 percent. A follow-up survey of original respondents was conducted in 1992–94, with a response rate for original respondents of about 82 percent. Sampling weights are available to adjust for differential probabilities of sample selection and nonresponse (Sweet, Bumpass, and Call 1988; Sweet and Bumpass 1996).

This chapter uses data from interviews with 645 women who were resident mothers in 1987–88 and who were reinterviewed in 1992–94.[2] At the first interview, mothers were asked questions about fathers' contact with a randomly selected minor child. Cases selected were those in which this child was still under age eighteen at the second interview. The unit of analysis was a family as represented by the mother's report. The sample was about evenly split between families in which the parents were divorced and those in which the child was born outside of marriage. The NSFH includes information about both formal and informal child support payments on behalf of the randomly selected child and that child's siblings, including contributions from parents without child support orders. As a result, the survey is especially valuable for studying families of children born out of wedlock, because these families are much less likely than divorced families to have child support orders (Beller and Graham 1993). Questions about child support and contact between fathers and children all refer to behavior in the year before the interview.

By restricting the analysis to families that were already separated in 1987–88, the data show the frequency of visits between nonresident fathers and children from long-term separated families. At the first interview, about half of the families had been separated for four years. By the second interview, half had been separated for about ten years. Children were under twelve years old at the first interview and between five and seventeen years old by the second interview.

Relying on the mothers' reports has both advantages and disadvantages. Resident mothers are easier to locate and to interview than nonresident fathers. Samples of nonresident fathers in most national surveys are biased by high nonparticipation rates (Seltzer and Brandreth 1995; Sorensen 1995; Cherlin et al. 1983; Schaeffer, Seltzer, and Dykema 1998). In addition to the advantage of better sample coverage for resident mothers than for nonresident fathers, resident mothers report more accurately about child support, at least in the aggregate, than do nonresident fathers (Schaeffer, Seltzer, and Klawitter 1991). Conversely, a mother may not know about all of a father's contributions to child support, as when the father pays money to a third party for such things as children's medical expenses and clothes or when the mother receives Aid for Families with Dependent Children and the father pays support to the welfare agency.

Results

Nonresident Fathers' Disengagement from Children

Figure 1 shows substantial declines in contact between the two interviews both for divorced fathers and fathers of children born out of wedlock. Overall, about 77 percent of fathers had seen their children in the year before the first interview, but this percentage declined to 66 percent by the second interview. The percentage of all fathers who saw their children at least weekly shows a similar decline, from 34 percent to 25 percent between the two interviews (total percentages not shown). Only the percentage of all fathers who paid any child support remained relatively constant, at about 50 percent.

Whether parents were married when their child was born has a big effect on whether the father is in touch with the child and pays child support. As in previous research, those who were married are much more

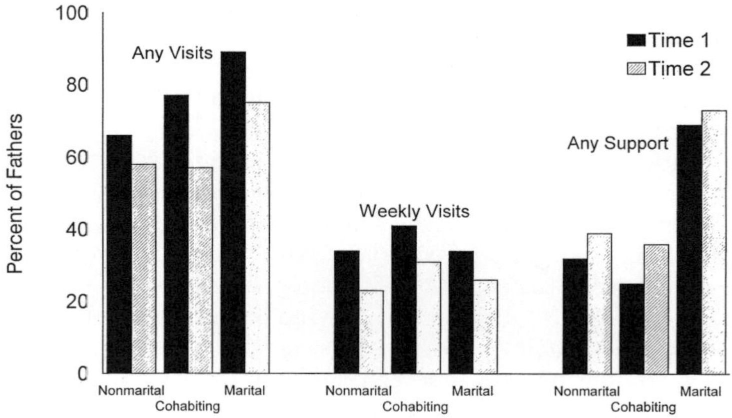

Fig. 1. Nonresident father's involvement by union status at child's birth. (Data from National Survey of Families and Households, 1987–88 and 1992–94, child living with single mother in 1987–88.)

likely to see their children after separation than fathers of children born out of wedlock (Seltzer 1991; King 1994). Higher levels of contact among previously married fathers may result from the bonds fathers establish with children when they live together. However, fathers of children born in cohabiting relationships have patterns of contact that are more similar to those of fathers who were unmarried and did not live with the child's mother than to fathers who were previously married. Among all fathers of children born outside of marriage, about 58 percent had contact with their children at the second interview. When nonmarital fathers were identified as the child's legal father through paternity establishment, they were more likely to have contact with their children than those for whom paternity was not established. However, the difference between the two groups is statistically significant only at the second interview. (Data not shown.)

Differences across parents' marital status in whether the father paid any child support are also large. The higher probability of paying child support among previously married men may reflect their greater economic resources. Among fathers of children born outside of marriage, those with legal paternity were more likely to pay at least some child support than those without legal paternity. (Data not shown.) The more secure economic circumstances of fathers for whom legal paternity is established relative to those without paternity may account for this difference as well.

The picture of marital status differences in contact disappears when one considers whether the father saw his child at least weekly, although there is a clear pattern of decline in weekly contact between the two interviews. Nevertheless, children of divorce were slightly more likely than children born out of wedlock either to be living with their father at the second interview or to have lived with him in the year before that interview (12 percent compared to 8 percent, respectively). The difference just misses statistical significance at conventional levels ($F = 3.12, p = .08$; not shown). That children move between their parents' homes is consistent with Eleanor E. Maccoby and Robert H. Mnookin's (1992) finding of changing residence patterns in the early period after divorce. Among those with any contact, nonresident fathers of children born in marriage are also much more likely than those whose children were born out of wedlock to have their children for overnight visits (74 percent versus 47 percent). (Data not shown.) The NSFH unfortunately does not include information about overnight visits at time 1, thus preventing an examination of changes over time in this type of contact for marital and nonmarital families.

Another way to evaluate the extent of nonresident fathers' disengagement from children is to compare contact between fathers and children who have been separated for a short time to those who have been separated for longer periods. Figure 2 shows the frequency of contact between fathers and children by the number of years separated.[3] Eighty-four percent of fathers separated for less than two years had seen their children in the year before the interview, compared to between 64 and 76 percent of fathers separated for eight to ten years. The big decline in contact occurred in the first few years after divorce (compare those separated for two years or less to those separated between three and four years). Psychological studies of children whose parents divorce mark the first year or two after separation as a critical transition point in parents' and children's adjustment to their new circumstances (Hetherington, Cox, and Cox 1982).

The level of contact remains fairly stable across longer durations of separation, as represented by the observations at time 2. Nonresident fathers who are likely to remain involved with their children may establish these patterns early in the postseparation period. By the time they have been separated for ten to twelve years, those who still spend time with their children are probably those who were originally more committed to staying involved with children. These fathers may arrange other aspects of their lives to facilitate continued contact. Longitudinal data, which show changes over time in an individual father's contact, provide more insight into this pattern than do the cross-sectional data used in this figure.

Aggregate statistics showing substantial disengagement of nonresident fathers from their children mask variability in families' experiences (Furstenberg and Harris 1992). Following the same families over time

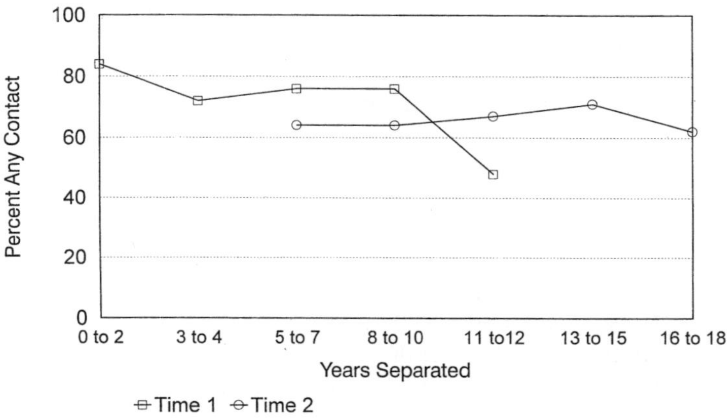

Fig. 2. Nonresident father's contact with children. (Data from National Survey of Families and Households, 1987–88 and 1992–94, child living with single mother in 1987–88.)

allows the distinction between fathers who lose touch with their children and those in which fathers and children reestablish ties. The NSFH data show that about 41 percent of fathers saw their children less frequently by the time of the second interview than when they were originally observed about six years earlier. Among those with any contact at the first interview, 53 percent of fathers have less contact and 21 percent have more contact at time 2. Fathers of children born outside of marriage are less likely to reduce their contact over time, because such a high percentage had already lost touch with their children by the first interview.

Some fathers and children reestablish contact with each other as time passes. Just over a quarter of fathers who did not see their children at time 1 had reestablished contact by time 2. Figure 3 shows that fathers in nonmarital families were more likely to regain contact than fathers from maritally separated families. However, the difference between the two groups is not statistically significant, primarily because the sample size is so small. The results in figure 3 are based on the 137 nonresident fathers in this sample who had no contact with their child at time 1. Fathers and sons were more likely to recontact each other than fathers and daughters (32 percent versus 19 percent, F = 3.18, $p = .08$). There are also substantial age differences in whether children and fathers reestablish contact. During children's late childhood and early adolescence, children and

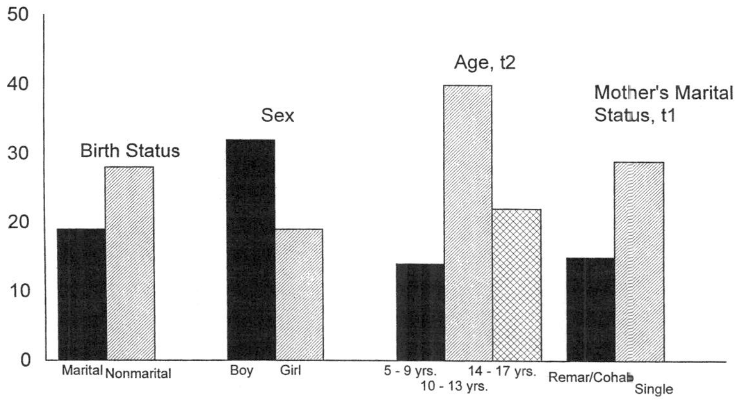

Fig. 3. Nonresident father reestablished contact with child. (Data from National Survey of Families and Households, 1987–88 and 1992–94, child living with single mother and child had no contact with father in 1987–88.)

fathers are more likely to recontact each other than when children are either younger or older. As children grow up, they have more independence and freedom to see their father without relying on either of their parents to organize visits. The pattern of reinitiating contact when children are older is consistent with Frank F. Furstenberg and Kathleen Mullan Harris's (1992) findings from a study of children whose parents were maritally separated. When there were stepfathers in the children's homes, fathers were less likely to have reestablished contact, perhaps because of conflict or ambiguity about each father's responsibility to the children (see, for example, Seltzer and Bianchi 1988). The difference between single mothers and those who were married or cohabiting, however, is not statistically significant.

Although a substantial minority of fathers and children reestablish contact with each other after separation, the overall picture is still one of significant disengagement. Among families in which contact was reinitiated between the two interviews, frequency of visits varied substantially, but the modal frequency was for fathers to see their children several times a year. Notwithstanding the small sample size, this pattern of low and unstable levels of contact may be altered by more rigorous child support enforcement. The next section considers the relationship between child support payments and fathers' contact with children.

Effects of Child Support on Father's Contact with Children

Compared to fathers who do not pay child support, fathers who pay see their children more frequently. Figure 4 shows the cross-sectional association between child support payments and whether the father saw his child at least weekly at each interview. Both child support payments and frequency of visits describe behavior in the year before the interviews, as noted previously. At each interview, fathers who paid any support had significantly more frequent contact with their children. The amount of child support that fathers pay is less closely related to visiting. The absence of a monotonic association between amount of support paid and frequent visits is particularly apparent at time 2, because fathers who both contribute more child support and spend more time with children do so in the context of shared residence (i.e., joint physical placement). Fathers whose children live with them for substantial parts of the year are not included in the time 2 data for this figure.[4]

The longitudinal design of the NSFH allows a direct investigation of whether child support payments affect subsequent contact between fathers and children. Fathers who paid at least some child support at time 1 were more likely to live with their children around the time of the second interview, although the difference between those who paid and those who did not is not statistically significant at conventional levels (11 percent versus 8 percent, $F = 2.15$, $p = .14$). Among the vast majority of families in which children still lived with their mother at the second interview, fathers who paid support at time 1 were about twice as likely as fathers who did not pay support at time 1 to see their children at least weekly at time 2 (23 percent versus 12 percent, $F = 11.6$, $p < .001$). This relationship is similar regardless of whether parents were married to each other when their child was born. Finally, fathers were more likely to have weekly contact with their children at time 2 when they had paid a high proportion of their child support orders at the earlier interview. Fathers who paid at least half of what they owed were much more likely to see their children frequently than fathers who did not comply with their child support orders, even among those who paid at least some support, although the latter difference is not statistically significant at conventional levels. (Tables not shown.)

These findings suggest that compared to fathers who do not pay child support, fathers who pay at least some support are more likely to maintain close contact with their children, even in the context of declining involvement. Arguments that child support payments explain fathers' continued involvement with children require information about other characteristics of fathers and families that may account for both higher payments and more frequent visits. Figure 5 summarizes the results of a multivariate

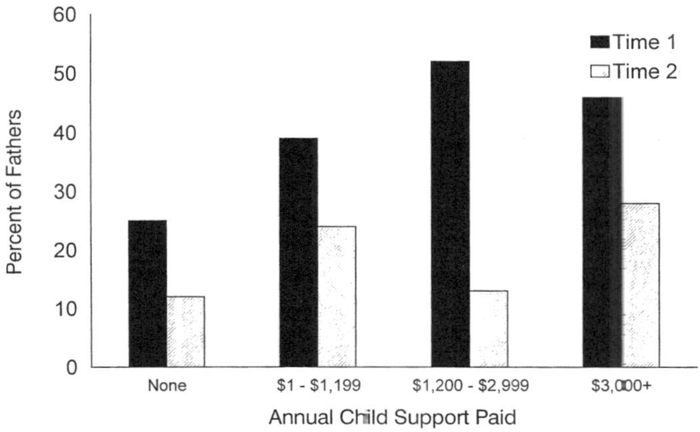

Fig. 4. Nonresident father saw child at least weekly by child support paid. (Data from National Survey of Families and Households, 1987–88 and 1992–94, child living with single mother in 1987–88.)

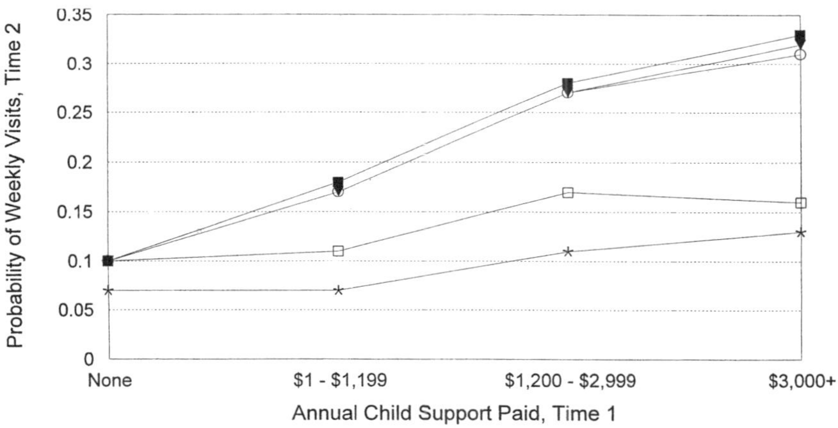

Fig. 5. Predicted probability of weekly visits at time 2 by child support at time 1. (Data from National Survey of Families and Households, 1987–88 and 1992–94, child living with single mother in 1987–88. Models described in the text.)

analysis of the effects of child support payments at time 1 on the frequency of nonresident fathers' visits with children at the second interview. The analysis is restricted to families in which the children lived with their mother at both interviews.[5]

The figure shows the predicted probabilities that the father has at least weekly contact by the amount of child support paid at time 1, adjusting statistically for other differences across families.[6] Each consecutive model includes more statistical controls. The zero-order model includes only child support paid at time 1 to illustrate the gross association between visits and payments. Models 1–4 adjust for characteristics of children and their families that might explain an effect of child support payments on frequency of visits.

Model 1 adjusts for race, child's sex, whether the child was born in a marriage, parents' education, parents' marital status at time 1, and years separated by time 1. Model 2 adjusts for the model 1 characteristics as well as for the terms of parents' legal arrangements, whether they have a formal child support order, and whether they share joint legal custody. Model 3 adds controls for these time 1 characteristics: frequency of visits, whether parents had serious disagreements, and distance between the parents' homes. The last model adjusts for all characteristics included in previous models as well as time 2 family characteristics, including whether parents are married or cohabiting with new partners, distance between the parents' homes at the second interview, and the time between the two interviews. Parents' marital status and how far away from each other they live may be both a cause and a consequence of how much time a nonresident father spends with the children. Therefore, the results of model 4 are presented for descriptive purposes only and the discussion emphasizes the results in the previous models where the interpretation of direction of causation is clearer.

Taking account of parents' education, whether the child was born in a marriage, and other background characteristics has little effect on the relationship between child support and subsequent contact with children (compare zero-order and model 1). Adding adjustments for whether the family has a child support order and whether parents share joint legal custody also does not alter the relationship between child support payments and visiting (compare model 1 and model 2). Only the introduction of statistical controls for how frequently the nonresident father and child saw each other at the earlier time, conflict between parents, and distance diminishes child support differences in weekly visits at the later interview (model 2 vs. model 3). However, when fathers paid at least $1,200 in child support, the probability of weekly visits was still greater than for fathers who paid less support. The contrasts between not paying any support and payments in the two highest categories ($1,200 to $2,999 and $3,000 +) are nearly statistically significant ($z = 1.82, p = 0.07; z = 1.56, p = 0.12$).[7] This finding shows that even after a variety of other aspects of family relationships are taken into account, child support payments still increase fathers' contact with children.

Details of the analysis not shown in figure 5 include that fathers of children born outside of marriage remain less likely than fathers of children born in marriage to see their children at least weekly, taking account of other family characteristics. The difference between fathers of children born in and outside of marriage mirrors that reported in the description of fathers' disengagement reported earlier. However, the effect of parents' marital status at the child's birth is not statistically significant in model 3, which controls statistically for both child support and contact at time 1.[8]

Parents' marital status and distance between parents' homes at the second interview along with time between interviews further diminish the association between the amount of child support paid at time 1 and subsequent contact between fathers and children. Only very high annual payments—$3,000 or more—marginally increase the probability of weekly visits, when all of the time 1 and time 2 characteristics in model 4 are taken into account.

As noted previously, compared to model 4, the adjustments in model 3 provide a more appropriate picture of the net effects of child support on fathers' later contact with children. The model 3 results show that most but not all of the association between paying child support and later visiting is explained by time 1 frequency of visits and conflict between parents. This finding differs from Jonathan R. Veum's (1993) finding that changes in visitation are completely independent of changes in child support payments. However, the effect of payments on visits is modest at best when other factors are taken into account. That child support payments have a weak effect on visits is consistent with causal interpretations of the correlation between payments and visits observed in cross-sectional studies.

Child Support Reform and Fathers' Access to Children

Once fathers and children begin to live apart, fathers disengage from both financial and time-intensive aspects of rearing children. Both fathers of children born in marriage and those whose children were born outside of marriage have less contact with their children the longer they are separated. The pattern of disengagement masks some fathers' and children's efforts to spend more time together as time passes. However, even among families that reestablish contact, most nonresident fathers and children spend little time together.

Fathers who pay child support are more likely to spend time with their children, regardless of whether the child was born in a marriage. The effect of child support payments on how frequently fathers see their children is explained only in part by fathers' contact with children at an earlier time. This finding suggests that child support may have a small direct effect on visits even after fathers' initial visiting practices have been established.

That previous visiting practices explain much of the association between child support and subsequent visits leaves unresolved the question of exactly why visits and payments are related when they are observed contemporaneously. Stronger evidence on whether payments and visits are causally related would show that payments increase visits, even after adjusting explicitly for other important characteristics of families, such as parents' commitment to children or stability of father's employment. By focusing on families that were first observed after fathers and children had already begun to live apart, the data used in this chapter cannot identify the initial conditions, such as parents' cooperation or attitudes about child rearing, that explain why some fathers spend significant time and money on children and others do not.

Nevertheless, my finding of a weak positive effect of child support on visiting is consistent with findings from other studies using different methodological approaches (McLanahan et al. 1994; Seltzer, McLanahan, and Hanson 1998). Taken together, these findings provide modest support for claims that stricter child support enforcement will increase fathers' contact with children. Higher child support payments are likely to moderately increase visits, at least once families establish the initial conditions for fathers' involvement with children after separation. For families that are already separated, the weight of arrangements in parents' new lives and the constraints of decisions made at the time of separation imply that increased child support enforcement will have only a small effect on fathers' contact with children.

The effect of strict child support enforcement on fathers' contact with children may be greater for families that separate in a social and legal environment that puts more weight on fulfilling child support responsibilities than for families that separated under a more lenient enforcement regime. The data analyzed in this chapter describe families already separated by the time of the 1988 Family Support Act. Parents who separate in the 1990s do so knowing that child support enforcement through withholding and other state and federal interventions help insure that child support will be collected. Knowledge that child support enforcement is reasonably effective may alter both mothers' and fathers' expectations about how to reallocate their child-rearing and child support responsibilities after separation. Consequently, the findings reported here are useful for understanding the effects on visiting for families that are experiencing the transition to more rigorous child support enforcement but should be applied cautiously to predictions about how child support reform is likely to affect visiting among newly separated parents and children.

Strict child support enforcement may increase a father's expectations about spending time with children in the early period after his relationship with the child's mother dissolves. When parents' relationship with each other dissolves, they must negotiate child-rearing arrangements at the same time they reorganize other aspects of their lives—for example, where they live, employment, relationships with new partners. If fathers expect to pay child support, they may organize other aspects of their lives to spend more time with their children. Fathers who face stricter child support enforcement may prefer to have children live with them instead of with the mothers.

Mothers may be more willing to facilitate fathers' involvement with children when the fathers pay child support. Alternatively, child support enforcement may reduce fathers' time with children by changing the balance of power in parents' negotiations about visitation. This situation might result if mothers observe that they can rely on the child support system to collect payments effectively. If child support payments are guaranteed, mothers have less need to trade time with the children for fathers' child support payments. Understanding the relationship between child support and visiting requires information about family relationships when parents are still married (or in a nonmarital relationship), before their relationship dissolves. Only by studying what happens as parents separate and as fathers—and mothers—establish new child-rearing practices can more light be shed on how stronger child support enforcement will affect fathers' access to children.

NOTES

This research was supported by a grant from the National Institute of Child Health and Human Development (HD24571). Support also came from the Center for Demography and Ecology at the University of Wisconsin. The National Survey of Families and Households was funded by the Center for Population Research of NICHD and by NIA. I am grateful to Julia Gray for her programming assistance and to Maria Cancian and the editors for their helpful suggestions. Opinions expressed are my own.

1. Nord and Zill (1996) also use longitudinal data to examine the relationship between child support and visiting. Unfortunately, the data they use, from the Survey of Income and Program Participation, include only information about visiting

for families with agreements about child support (i.e., child support orders). This restriction limits the value of the data for understanding the experience of nonmarital families, because they are much less likely than divorced families to have child support orders (Beller and Graham 1993).

2. This includes children who moved to live with their fathers in the year before the time 2 interview or who were living with their fathers at time 2.

3. Contact at time 2 includes either visits or living with the father.

4. Fathers with whom children spend a substantial number of overnights are excluded because information on the amount of their child support is not available. These fathers probably make most of their child support contribution by paying directly for children's expenses rather than by transferring money to the children's mothers.

5. Amount of child support paid at time 1 has no effect on whether the child lived with the father at time 2, controlling for parents' education, whether the child was born in a marriage, race, the child's sex, parents' marital status at time 1, whether the parents have a formal child support order, whether they have joint legal custody, frequency of visits at time 1, and conflict between the parents at time 1.

6. Predictions use parameter estimates from ordered probit regressions. All variables other than child support payments are evaluated at the sample mean. Frequency of visits is a six-category variable ranging from no visits to visits more than once a week. Child support is a series of categorical variables to take account of potential nonlinearities in the effect of payments on visits. The categories are as shown in figure 5. Number of cases is 508.

7. The coefficients for the effects of child support payments on visits for the two highest categories of child support payments are close in magnitude. When they are constrained to be equal, the coefficient for payments of $1,200 or more is statistically significant at conventional levels ($z = 2.11, p < 0.05$).

8. I also examined whether child support payments have a different effect on visits for families of children born out of wedlock relative to those in which parents were married at their child's birth. Although the coefficients for within-group models differ somewhat, showing larger positive effects of payments among previously married families, the test for interactions suggests that payment effects do not differ significantly for these two family types.

REFERENCES

Bay, R. Curtis, Sanford L. Braver, Irwin N. Sandler, and Sharlene A. Wolchik. 1993. Child Support Non-Compliance/Visitation Interference: Empirically Disentangling the Causal Sequence. Paper presented at the annual meeting of the American Psychological Association, Toronto, ON.

Beller, Andrea H., and John W. Graham. 1993. *Small Change: The Economics of Child Support.* New Haven: Yale University Press.

Block, Jack, Jeanne H. Block, and Per F. Gjerde. 1988. Parental Functioning and the Home Environment in Families of Divorce: Prospective and Concurrent Analyses. *Journal of the American Academy of Child and Adolescent Psychiatry* 27:207–13.

Braver, Sanford L., Sharlene A. Wolchik, Irwin N. Sandler, Virgil L. Sheets, Bruce Fogas, and R. Curtis Bay. 1993. A Longitudinal Study of Noncustodial Parents: Parents without Children. *Journal of Counseling Psychology* 7 (1): 9–23.

Bumpass, Larry L. 1996. Personal Communication.

Cherlin, Andrew J., Frank F. Furstenberg Jr., P. Lindsay Chase-Lansdale, Kathleen E. Kiernan, Philip K. Robins, Donna Ruane Morrison, and Julien O. Teitler. 1991. Longitudinal Studies of Effects of Divorce on Children in Great Britain and the United States. *Science* 252: 1386–89.

Cherlin, Andrew J., Jeanne Griffith, and James McCarthy. 1983. A Note on Maritally-Disrupted Men's Reports on Child Support in the June 1980 Current Population Survey. *Demography* 20:385–89.

Furstenberg, Frank F., and Kathleen Mullan Harris. 1992. The Disappearing American Father? Divorce and the Waning Significance of Biological Parenthood. In *The Changing American Family: Sociological and Demographic Perspectives,* ed. Scott J. South and Stewart E. Tolnay. Boulder, CO: Westview Press.

Furstenberg, Frank F., Christine Winquist Nord, James L. Peterson, and Nicholas Zill. 1983. The Life Course of Children of Divorce. *American Sociological Review* 48:695–701.

Garfinkel, Irwin, Daniel R. Meyer, and Sara S. McLanahan. 1998. A Brief History of Child Support Policies in the United States. In *Fathers under Fire: The Revolution in Child Support Enforcement,* ed. Irwin Garfinkel, Sara S. McLanahan, Daniel R. Meyer, and Judith A. Seltzer. New York: Russell Sage Foundation.

Hetherington, E. Mavis, Martha Cox, and Roger Cox. 1982. Effects of Divorce on Parents and Children. In *Nontraditional Families: Parenting and Child Development,* ed. Michael E. Lamb. Hillsdale, NJ: Erlbaum.

King, Valarie. 1994. Variation in the Consequences of Nonresident Father Involvement for Children's Well-Being. *Journal of Marriage and the Family* 56 (4): 963–72.

Koch, Mary Ann P., and Carol R. Lowery. 1984. Visitation and the Noncustodial Father. *Journal of Divorce* 8:47–65.

Maccoby, Eleanor E., and Robert H. Mnookin. 1992. *Dividing the Child: Social and Legal Dilemmas of Custody.* Cambridge, MA: Harvard University Press.

McLanahan, Sara S., Judith A. Seltzer, Thomas L. Hanson, and Elizabeth Thomson. 1994. Child Support Enforcement and Child Well-Being: Greater Security or Greater Conflict? In *Child Support and Child Well-Being,* ed. Irwin Garfinkel, Sara S. McLanahan, and Philip K. Robins. Washington DC: Urban Institute Press.

Nord, Christine Winquist, and Nicholas Zill. 1996. *Non-Custodial Parents' Participation in Their Children's Lives: Evidence from the Survey of Income and Program Participation.* Vol. 1: *Summary of SIPP Analysis.* August. Final report prepared for the Office of Human Services Policy, Office of the Assistant Secretary for Planning and Evaluation. Washington, DC: U.S. Department of Health and Human Services.

Pearson, Jessica, and Jean Anhalt. 1994. Examining the Connection between Child Access and Child Support. *Family and Conciliation Courts Review* 32 (1): 93–109.

Pearson, Jessica, and Nancy Thoennes. 1995. The Child Support Improvement Project: Paternity Establishment. September. Final report submitted to the Division of Child Support Enforcement, Colorado Department of Social Services and Denver Division of Child Support. Denver, CO: Denver Department of Social Services.

Schaeffer, Nora Cate, Judith A. Seltzer, and Jennifer Dykema. 1998. *Methodological and Theoretical Issues in Studying Nonresident Fathers: A Selective Review.* National Center on Fathers and Families Working Paper no. WP-02. Philadelphia: University of Pennsylvania.

Schaeffer, Nora Cate, Judith A. Seltzer, and Marieka M. Klawitter. 1991. Estimating Nonresponse and Response Bias: Resident and Nonresident Parents' Reports about Child Support. *Sociological Methods and Research* 20:30–59.

Scoon-Rogers, Lydia, and Gordon H. Lester. 1995. *Child Support for Custodial Mothers and Fathers: 1991.* U.S. Bureau of the Census, Current Population Reports, series P60-187. Washington, DC: U.S. Government Printing Office.

Seltzer, Judith A. 1991. Relationships between Fathers and Children Who Live Apart. *Journal of Marriage and the Family* 53:79–101.

———. 1994. Consequences of Marital Dissolution for Children. *Annual Review of Sociology* 20:235–66.

Seltzer, Judith A., and Suzanne M. Bianchi. 1988. Children's Contact with Absent Parents. *Journal of Marriage and the Family* 50:663–77.

Seltzer, Judith A., and Yvonne Brandreth. 1995. What Fathers Say about Involvement with Children after Separation. In *Fatherhood: Contemporary Theory, Research, and Social Policy,* ed. William Marsiglio. Thousand Oaks, CA: Sage Publications.

Seltzer, Judith A., Sara S. McLanahan, and Thomas L. Hanson. 1998. Will Child Support Enforcement Increase Father-Child Contact and Parental Conflict after Separation? In *Fathers under Fire: The Revolution in Child Support Enforcement,* ed. Irwin Garfinkel, Sara S. McLanahan, Daniel R. Meyer, and Judith A. Seltzer. New York: Russell Sage Foundation.

Seltzer, Judith A., Nora Cate Schaeffer, and Hong-Wen Charng. 1989. Family Ties after Divorce: The Relationship between Visiting and Paying Child Support. *Journal of Marriage and the Family* 51:1013–32.

Sonenstein, Freya Lund, Pamela Holcomb, and Kristin Seefeldt. 1994. Promising Approaches to Improving Paternity Establishment Rates at the Local Level. In *Child Support and Child Well-Being,* ed. Irwin Garfinkel, Sara S. McLanahan, and Philip K. Robins. Washington, DC: Urban Institute Press.

Sorensen, Elaine. 1995. A National Profile of Noncustodial Fathers and Their Ability to Pay Child Support. Unpublished manuscript. Urban Institute, Washington, DC.

Sweet, James A., and Larry L. Bumpass. 1996. *The National Survey of Families and Households—Waves 1 and 2: Data Description and Documentation.* Madison, WI: Center for Demography and Ecology, University of Wisconsin-Madison.

Sweet, James, Larry Bumpass, and Vaughn Call. 1988. *The Design and Content of the National Survey of Families and Households.* NSFH Working Paper no. 1. Madison: Center for Demography and Ecology, University of Wisconsin, Madison.

Ventura, Stephanie J., Joyce A. Martin, Sally C. Curtin, and T. J. Mathews. 1998. *Report of Final Natality Statistics, 1996.* Monthly Vital Statistics Report 46 (11, supplement). Hyattsville, MD: National Center for Health Statistics.

Veum, Jonathan R. 1993. The Relationship between Child Support and Visitation: Evidence from Longitudinal Data. *Social Science Research* 22:229–44.

Weiss, Yoram, and Robert J. Willis. 1985. Children as Collective Goods and Divorce Settlements. *Journal of Labor Economics* 3:268–92.

Williams, Robert G., Jane C. Venohr, Dawn E. Baxter, and Lisa M. Fitzgerald. 1995. Massachusetts Paternity Acknowledgment Program: Implementation Analysis and Program Results. Report submitted to Child Support Enforcement Division, Massachusetts Department of Revenue, May.

Fathers and the Child Support System

Daniel R. Meyer

Child support research has focused almost exclusively on the most common cases—those that involve children who live with their mothers—and usually has taken the mother's perspective.[1] Little attention has been paid to how the child support system works from the father's perspective.

This chapter provides some information on fathers and child support. The chapter begins with a review of the way the system works for fathers in the usual situation when children live with their mother and then looks at how the system works for fathers in a small but growing number of cases in which children live with their fathers or spend a significant proportion of time with each parent. It examines outcomes for each of these situations—children living with their mothers, their fathers, and both parents—examining whether the nonresident parent is ordered to pay child support, the amount ordered, and the amount paid in various living arrangements. The discussion draws on both national and state data, particularly from the state of Wisconsin, which has a data set that enables researchers to examine issues that could not be examined with existing national data. Each section includes information on fathers who had nonmarital children, although the bulk of the empirical research reviewed focuses on divorced fathers. The chapter closes with a discussion of the effects of child support on fathers' economic well-being.

Child Support When Children Do Not Live with Their Fathers

We know the most about the way the child support system works in the most common situation—when the resident parent is the mother. The prevalence of mother custody is confirmed by data from studies in four states from the 1980s on the frequency of different custody arrangements after divorce. Remarkably, the prevalence of arrangements was found to be identical in studies from Wisconsin (Seltzer 1990) and Michigan (Fox and Kelly 1995): physical custody was awarded solely to the mother in 89 percent of the cases, to the father in 9 percent, and jointly to both parents in 2 percent. In Minnesota, the percentage with shared physical custody was slightly higher (6 percent), with a corresponding decrease in mother custody (81 percent) (Christensen, Dahl, and Rettig 1990). In California in the mid-1980s, custody was awarded to mothers in 67 percent of the cases, to fathers in 9 percent, and to both parents in 20 percent (Maccoby and Mnookin 1992).

Are Fathers Ordered to Pay Child Support?

A variety of studies have examined the extent to which fathers are ordered to pay child support and the characteristics of those who were or were not ordered to do so. In the most recent national data, 49 percent of resident mothers were owed cash child support in 1991, and 56 percent had child support orders (U.S. Bureau of the Census 1995). (Some mothers have child support orders that provide health insurance but not cash.)[2] The characteristic that most significantly determines the likelihood of an order is whether the parents were married: child support is ordered about three-fourths of the time when the parents divorce, about half the time when the parents were married and are currently separated, and only about one-fourth of the time when the parents were not married (U.S. Bureau of the Census 1995).

Because most research examines the likelihood of gaining a support order from the mother's perspective, data showing which types of fathers are likely to be ordered to pay child support are limited. One national study found a child support order in 82 percent of divorces and the probability of being ordered to pay child support higher for fathers who were married longer, had young children, had fewer children, and had higher income (Teachman 1990).

Court records in various states show the same pattern as the national data. In recent divorces, there is almost always a child support order when the mother receives sole physical custody of the children. For example, child support was ordered when mothers were awarded sole physical custody in 98 percent of Wisconsin divorces between 1990 and 1993 (Meyer and Hu 1996:20) and in 94 percent of California divorces during the mid-1980s (Maccoby and Mnookin 1992:117).

There is more variance in child support orders in nonmarital cases. If paternity is not legally established, no formal child support order can be issued. The percentage of nonmarital births in which paternity has been adjudicated has increased (Nichols-Casebolt and Garfinkel 1991), but states (and even counties within states) vary in the degree to which they establish paternity (Maniha 1992; Sonenstein, Holcomb, and Seefeldt 1994). In many instances, a child support order is issued whenever paternity is legally established; it is one of the main purposes of formally establishing paternity.[3] For example, in Wisconsin between 1980 and 1986, 79 percent of the cases in which paternity was established had child support orders (Danziger and Nichols-Casebolt 1990:463), increasing to more than 95 percent during 1990–93 (Meyer and Hu 1996:20).[4]

Recent legislation directed at increasing the likelihood of child support orders has sought to make it easier to establish paternity and may be having some effect: between 1979 and 1991, the percentage of never-married women with orders increased from 11 to 25 percent, presumably reflecting an increased likelihood of establishing paternity (U.S. Bureau of the Census 1995:6). Among divorced, separated, and remarried women, there were only small changes in the likelihood of an order.

How Much Are Fathers Supposed to Pay?

The most recent national data, from 1991, show that the average order for fathers ordered to pay child support was $3,375 (U.S. Bureau of the Census 1995:10). The average child support order declined from $4,042 in 1978 (1991 dollars) to $3,160 by 1985 (1991 dollars), which led to a reexamination of the way child support orders were determined. Prior to the 1980s, orders were determined case by case, based primarily on an estimate of how much money the resident mother needed to care for the children. The 1984 Child Support Amendments required each state to develop guidelines for use in establishing child support orders, and today nearly all states require nonresident parents to share the same percentage of their income with their children that they would have had the family stayed together.

Average child support orders increased from $3,160 in 1985 to $3,616 in 1989, but they did not again reach the 1978 average of $4,042. Furthermore, the average order declined between 1989 and 1991 from $3,616 to $3,375 (all figures in 1991 dollars). There are several reasons for the general lack of increase: one was a shift in caseload composition toward those with lower orders: although dollar amounts within some categories were increasing, the average order was reduced because of increases in the number of orders received among groups that have typically had lower orders (Beller and Graham 1993). Another reason for the decline was that mothers have higher earnings (Robins 1992): in most states, the mother's earnings are figured into the guideline formula, and a higher mother's income typically leads to a lower order. Even in states in which the mother's income is not directly a part of the formula, mothers with higher incomes tend to have somewhat lower orders (Cancian and Meyer 1996). Finally, the earnings of many men, particularly those with only a high-school education or less, have not kept pace with inflation (Acs and Danziger 1993), leading to lower average orders.

Although the level of child support is supposedly now set according to state guidelines, standard orders do not necessarily result for two reasons: first, the state child support guidelines vary so that the amounts are very different across states for identical fathers (see, for example, Pirog-Good 1993); second, guidelines may not be used to set orders, although comprehensive national information is lacking.

The average dollar amount of child support orders is easier to analyze than the typical percentage of the father's income that is required to be paid, because national data on the income of nonresident fathers are problematic[5] and state-level research is somewhat limited. In California in the preguideline mid-1980s, child support orders in divorces in which the mother received sole physical custody averaged about 10 percent of the father's gross income when there was one child, and 17–18 percent when there were two children (Maccoby and Mnookin 1992:121). Some research suggests that the larger effect of guidelines is not on the amount of the average order but on increasing the "rationality" of orders. For example, Daniel R. Meyer et al. (1996) show that orders, considered as a percentage of the father's income, varied significantly before guidelines were introduced but were much more consistent afterward. By the late 1980s about half of all nonresident fathers in Wisconsin with one child were ordered to pay 17 percent of their gross income, the amount required by the guidelines (Meyer et al. 1996:14).

Which types of fathers are ordered to pay higher amounts? In the preguideline policy regime, low-income fathers were asked to pay a higher percentage of their income than middle- and upper-income fathers (Cancian and Meyer 1996; Christensen, Dahl, and Rettig 1990; Meyer 1997). Most research on the amount of orders has been conducted from the mother's perspective, but the U.S. Bureau of the Census (1995) reports that order amounts are higher for divorced mothers (and thus divorced fathers) than for never-married mothers. In one of the few national studies that provides data on fathers, Jay D. Teachman (1990) found that orders were higher for divorced fathers when they had higher incomes, when there were more children, and when they had been married longer. State studies also show that, among divorces in the mid-1980s and early 1990s, orders are higher when fathers have more income and when there are more children (Maccoby and Mnookin 1992; Cancian and Meyer 1996). This finding reflects the fact that guidelines require fathers with higher incomes and more children to pay more—although not necessarily a higher percentage of income.

Does the amount of support ordered change over time? A study of Wisconsin paternity cases in the 1980s found that while amounts did change in about half the cases, the changes were unrelated to income changes among fathers (Meyer 1995). In response to the concern that support orders were not keeping pace with inflation or with changing circumstances, the 1988 Family Support Act required that child support offices review cases every three years to determine if the order amounts were still appropriate. Several states conducted pilot tests of this policy, and the results were quite consistent across states (see Kost et al. 1996): in each project, only 10–15 percent of the orders were revised, with a substantially higher percentage of revisions in Aid to Families with Dependent Children (AFDC) cases, where recipients were not given a choice about pursuing a revision. Revised orders increased substantially, by about a hundred dollars per month.

How Much Do Fathers Pay?

Again, almost all the research on the level of payments is from the mother's perspective. In the national data for 1991, mothers reported receiving an average of $3,011. Amounts were higher for divorced mothers ($3,623) than for never-married mothers ($1,534) (U.S. Bureau of the Census 1995:19). Fairly consistently over time, about half of mothers with orders report receiving the full amount due, about one-quarter report receiving nothing, and about one-quarter report receiving partial payments. Fathers who pay report that they pay about 15 percent of their income; fathers in the lowest income group report that they pay 28 percent of their income, compared to 10 percent for fathers in the highest income group (Sorensen 1995:792).

Fathers report paying substantially higher amounts than mothers report receiving. Using national data, Judith A. Seltzer and Yvonne Brandreth (1995:179) found that 77 percent of fathers claimed that they had paid some money in the previous year, whereas only 46 percent of mothers said that they had received money. In a sample of Arizona divorce cases, two-thirds of fathers said that they paid the full amount due, whereas fewer than half the mothers said that they received the full amount. Only 4 percent of fathers said that they owed something but paid nothing, but 13 to 16 percent of mothers said that they received nothing (Braver, Fitzpatrick, and Bay 1991:182). These differences in reporting between mothers and fathers persisted over time (Braver et al. 1993).

A variety of empirical research describes the types of fathers who pay more or who pay a higher percentage of what is due.[6] Fathers of marital children report paying more child support than fathers of nonmarital children (Seltzer 1991). In a recent summary of the research on compliance with child support orders, Meyer and Judi Bartfeld (1996) hypothesize that compliance is related to a father's ability to pay, to the strength of family ties between the father and his former partner and children, to the economic needs of mothers and children, and to the policy environment. The research shows that fathers with jobs and with higher incomes pay more. A related finding is that fathers whose orders are very high relative to their incomes tend to pay a lower percentage of their child support orders. Some researchers have found that family ties have little effect (Meyer and Bartfeld 1996; Meyer, forthcoming), whereas others have found a significant effect, with payments and strong family ties going together (for further discussion, see Seltzer, "Child Support and Child Access: Experiences of Divorced and Nonmarital Families," in this volume). Researchers have found only limited support for the proposition that compliance is higher when the mother's family is in greater need. The policy environment also has an effect on payments; for example, when child support is withheld from the father's income, compliance with child support orders is higher (see, for example, Beller and Graham 1993; Garfinkel and Klawitter 1990) for both divorce and paternity cases (Bartfeld and Meyer 1994; Meyer and Bartfeld 1996; Meyer, forthcoming). Similarly, child support receipts are higher in states in which liens against the nonresident parent's property can be placed in the event of nonpayment (Beller and Graham 1993). A recent examination of child support in Wisconsin (Lin 1997) has found that when fathers have discretion about whether they will pay (that is, they are not subject to a withholding order), those who think their orders are fair pay more support.

Although research has focused on whether fathers make payments when ordered to do so, some fathers report paying child support without formal orders. In national data, about one-quarter of divorced or separated fathers report making informal payments, averaging about one hundred dollars per month (Seltzer 1994:246). Interviews with mothers in four cities suggest that about 20 percent received some informal financial support from low-income fathers and that another 30 percent received nonmonetary support (Edin 1995:209). Fathers also report providing informal and in-kind support (Haskins 1988; Stier and Tienda 1993; Sullivan 1993). When resident parents receive cash welfare, they must sign over their child support to the government, which generally shares part with the family and uses the rest to offset welfare costs.[7] Thus fathers of children receiving AFDC have less incentive to pay child support through formal means, although little is known about the extent of their informal payments.

Little empirical research has examined payment patterns over time. Some national research has found that fathers who have been separated longer pay less (Garfinkel and Robins 1994; Furstenberg and Harris 1993; Seltzer 1991). A California study (Peters et al. 1993:725) found substantial changes in compliance rates over time among divorce cases. For example, of thirty-two fathers who paid no child support eighteen months after the divorce petition was filed, about half were paying one year later. In contrast, one-third of 151 fathers who paid in full were no longer doing so one year later. In another study, Meyer and Bartfeld (1998:15) examined five years of payments among Wisconsin divorce and paternity cases. Among those fathers who made no payment in one year, about one-fourth made some payment in the next year. Compliance rates changed for three-fifths of the fathers during the five years. Of the remaining two-fifths, 26 percent paid in full during each year, 8 percent paid nothing, and 6 percent paid partial amounts in each year.

Child Support When Children Live with Their Fathers

There has been much less research on child support outcomes when children live with their fathers. Father custody is far less common than mother custody, although father-only families grew nationally by 42 percent over the 1980s, whereas mother-only families increased by 15 percent (Garasky and Meyer 1996:387). This increase occurred among blacks, whites, and Hispanics and in every state.

In contrast, state data from Wisconsin show that father-custody after divorce remained roughly constant over the 1980s at about 10 percent (Cancian and Meyer 1998). The potential contradiction of increases in the share of single fathers awarded custody after divorce may occur because fathers with custody are becoming less likely to remarry or because more children who live with their mothers after divorce are subsequently moving to live with their fathers.

A few empirical studies have examined factors associated with the custody decision at divorce. Father custody is more likely among boys and older children and is less likely when the mother has a college degree (Cancian and Meyer 1998; Christensen, Dahl, and Rettig 1990; Fox and Kelly 1995; Maccoby and Mnookin 1992; Seltzer 1990). The findings regarding the father's income are inconsistent: Greer Litton Fox and Robert F. Kelly (1995) found father custody to be less likely when the father had higher income, whereas Seltzer (1990) and Donna Hendrickson Christensen, Carla M. Dahl, and Kathryn D. Rettig (1990) found it to be more likely. Maria Cancian and Meyer (1998) find that father custody is less likely when there is high total income and when the mother has a higher share of total income. Some legal factors have also been found to be important: father custody is more likely when the father is the plaintiff (Cancian and Meyer 1998; Christensen, Dahl, and Rettig 1990; Fox and Kelly 1995) and when he has a lawyer but the mother does not (Cancian and Meyer 1998).[8]

Are Fathers Supposed to Receive Child Support?

For the first time, in 1992 the Current Population Survey—Child Support Supplement asked child support questions of fathers as well as mothers (U.S. Bureau of the Census 1995). These data show that nearly 60 percent of the 1.6 million resident fathers did not have child support orders, and another 28 percent had child support orders but were due no payments during 1991. In contrast, 44 percent of resident mothers lacked orders, and only 7 percent had orders but were not due payments during 1991. One reason for this difference is apparently parental preference: more than one-third of fathers without orders reported that they "did not want child support," compared to 14 percent of mothers without orders (U.S. Bureau of the Census 1995:5, 12).

As with resident mothers, there are substantial differences in the likelihood of child support orders for fathers of different marital status. About 30 percent of men who were divorced or remarried were owed support during 1991, but only 13 percent of those who had not been married had child support owed to them. Whites were more likely to be owed child support than were African Americans—43 percent to 27 percent (U.S. Bureau of the Census 1995:16).

Data from individual states show a similar discrepancy. In recent divorces in Minnesota, Wisconsin, and California and in data from the four-state Child Custody and Child Support Project (CCCSP), there are child support orders only about one-third of the time that fathers receive physical custody but more than 80 percent of the time when mothers receive physical custody (Christensen, Dahl, and Rettig 1990:390; Maccoby and Mnookin 1992:117; Meyer 1996:94; Pearson and Thoennes 1988:324). Little is known about the types of fathers who are awarded child support.[9] J. Thomas Oldham (1994) notes several potential reasons that fathers may receive orders less frequently than mothers: judges may be reluctant to require mothers to pay; resident fathers tend to have higher incomes than nonresident mothers and so might have less need of child support; some might feel that it is not the mother's role to provide for the family after divorce; and mothers might agree to give up custody in exchange for not having to pay child support. In the empirical research,

Eleanor E. Maccoby and Robert H. Mnookin (1992) found that the fathers who were awarded physical custody in California and who earned less than the mothers almost always had orders, but there were only thirteen cases to analyze. In Wisconsin divorces in which the father has received sole physical custody, Meyer has found the existence of a support order is unrelated to the father's income, and there is no trend toward a greater or lesser likelihood of support orders between 1985 and 1993. Orders are much more likely when the mother has higher income and are somewhat more likely when the father is younger than thirty, there is at least one child younger than thirteen, and there are fewer than three children.[10]

How Much Are Fathers Supposed to Receive?

Although the national data from 1991 show that child support orders were about twice as common among custodial mothers as custodial fathers, order amounts were relatively similar for both groups. Fathers were supposed to receive $2,727 per year, 81 percent of the $3,375 that mothers were owed. As with mothers, the average masks a great deal of diversity in order amounts: 13 percent of fathers were to receive less than $1,000 per year, and 11 percent were to receive $5,000 or more (U.S. Bureau of the Census 1995:29).

State data also show that custodial fathers have lower orders. In Minnesota in 1986, the median order for fathers with custody was $1,800 per year, compared to $3,600 for mothers (Christensen, Dahl, and Rettig 1990:391). Similarly, in Wisconsin in the late 1980s, about one-third of the father's orders were below $1,200 per year, another third were $1,200–$2,399 per year, and the remainder were $2,400 and above; orders are significantly higher when mothers have physical custody (Meyer 1996:94).

Current guidelines vary according to the income of the nonresident parent (higher incomes yield higher orders) and the number of children (more children bring higher orders). As a result, resident fathers would be expected to have lower average orders than resident mothers, because nonresident mothers typically have lower earnings than nonresident fathers and fathers generally have custody of fewer children. Lower orders may, therefore, reflect use of the child support guidelines rather than a gender differential. There are no national data, but data from Wisconsin divorces between 1990 and 1993 suggest that the differences are not solely related to the use of the guidelines. Even when fathers were supposed to receive child support, orders were consistent with the guideline-required amount about 24 percent of the time, compared to about 75 percent among mothers (Meyer and Hu 1996:11). Meyer's analyses of child support orders among Wisconsin-resident fathers suggest that these fathers have higher orders when mothers have higher incomes and when the fathers have custody of more children.[11]

How does the child support system work when the resident parent earns more than the nonresident parent (common when children live with their fathers)? Oldham (1994) argues that policy needs to be more specific regarding the level of orders; he also points out that, in the absence of clear policy, similar situations will be treated very differently, more cases will be litigated, and court-system costs will be higher.

How Much Do Fathers Receive?

National data show that fathers who have child support orders receive a lower percentage of these orders than do mothers: in 1991 37 percent received nothing (compared to 24 percent of mothers) and 43 percent received the full payment (compared to 52 percent of mothers). Because both orders and the rate of payment are lower when children live with their fathers, the average 1991 amount received by fathers was $1,442, compared to $2,298 for mothers (U.S. Bureau of the Census 1995:10).

The only state data on payment come from Wisconsin and also show higher rates of noncompliance: almost half the fathers with orders receive nothing, compared to about one-fourth of the mothers. Similarly, only about one-fourth of the fathers with orders receive the full amount owed, compared to about 40 percent of mothers with orders (Meyer 1996:95). More research on this topic is needed.

Child Support When Children Live with Both Parents

Little is known about child support in families in which parents share physical custody. There are no national data on child support in shared-custody cases, so this discussion relies on state studies.[12] The vast majority of children still live with their mothers, but shared physical custody appears to be increasing. One national study estimated the prevalence of joint custody at 13 percent, although the term was imprecisely defined (Donnelly and Finkelhor 1993:58). State studies also show increases. The number of Wisconsin divorces with equal shared custody increased from 1–2 percent in 1981–83 to 6–7 percent in 1989–91. In addition, the proportion of cases with unequal shared custody (one parent has responsibility 30–49 percent of the time and the other parent has custody 50–70 percent of the time) also increased, from 2.5 percent in 1987 to 7.5 percent in 1991. In these unequal-shared-custody cases, the mother had more time than the father in 85 percent of cases (Cancian and Meyer 1998:150).

In a national study, shared physical custody was associated with higher income, higher education, being nonwhite, and living in a large city (Donnelly and Finkelhor 1993). A Wisconsin study of equal shared physical custody found it was more likely when the father or mother had high income or when the mother had higher income and was also more likely in the mid-1980s than the early 1980s (Seltzer 1990). Another study of both equal and unequal shared custody in Wisconsin found that shared custody was more likely when total income is higher and when there are only boys (Cancian and Meyer 1998). A California study reported that shared physical custody was also more likely when the father had higher income, but the mother's income was unrelated to the custody outcome (Maccoby and Mnookin 1992).

Is Child Support Supposed to Be Paid? By Whom?

Jessica Pearson and Nancy Thoennes (1988:324), analyzing CCCSP data, reported that about half of the families in which parents shared physical custody had child support orders, presumably for the father to pay the mother, compared to more than 90 percent of cases in which the mother had sole physical and legal custody. Among shared-custody cases in California, fathers were required to pay child support 67 percent of the time, and mothers were required to pay 1 percent of the time (Maccoby and Mnookin 1992:117).

What factors are related to which parent is asked to pay? Child support guidelines are gender neutral; whether there is an order is based on who has the child for more time, and, in some cases, on the relative income level of the parents (Melli and Brown 1994). Thus, because fathers tend to have higher incomes than mothers, fathers are more likely to be ordered to pay; and in cases of unequal shared physical custody, because mothers tend to have the children for longer periods than fathers, fathers are more likely to be ordered to pay (Maccoby and Mnookin 1992; Melli and Brown 1994).

What factors are related to whether there is a child support order? In the CCCSP, child support orders were more likely when there were more children or when the father had a high income and the mother a low one (Pearson and Thoennes 1988). Even though half of the parents did not have orders, the lack of orders was not reported as a significant problem, perhaps because in those cases the parent who had the child for a longer period had high income.

The existence of a support order may also depend on whether children have exactly equal time with both parents or substantial but unequal time with both parents. Marygold S. Melli and Patricia R. Brown (1992:25, 28), using data from Wisconsin, found that only 32 percent of the equal-shared-physical-custody cases had child support orders, compared to 72 percent of the unequal-shared-physical-custody cases.

Some of the variation in the prevalence of child support orders is related to state guidelines. For example, in Wisconsin in 1992 the guidelines were silent on the subject of child support when parents had equal time with their children, leaving it to the court's discretion (Melli and Brown 1994:24). Other states may have a guideline for both equal-time cases and unequal-time cases or may leave the amounts to the court's discretion (Czapanskiy 1994:45).

How Much Is Supposed to Be Paid?

Little is known about the level of orders in shared-physical-custody cases. Data from the CCCSP reveal that order amounts are smaller than when mothers had sole physical custody, but the difference is not statistically significant (Pearson and Thoennes 1988:321). However, California data show that order amounts for one child constitute, on average, about 6 percent of the father's income in cases with shared physical custody, compared to 10 percent among sole-custody cases (Maccoby and Mnookin 1992:121). A lower order may be appropriate: if children live with both parents for a substantial portion of time, child-related costs are borne by both parents, and the amount of child support expected might be less (see Melli and Brown 1994 for a discussion of these issues). Indeed, the guidelines in many states direct that orders should be lower in cases with shared physical custody (Czapanskiy 1994).

How Much Is Paid?

Compliance was quite high among shared-physical-custody cases with child support orders in the CCCSP; almost three-fourths of the parents owed support reported that they received full or nearly full payments, although only half received all payments on time (Pearson and Thoennes 1988:329).

Effect of the Child Support System on the Economic Well-Being of Fathers

While most of the empirical research conducted on child support has focused on when fathers are supposed to pay child support, some research has examined whether child support orders and payments affect a father's earnings. Microeconomic theory suggests that child support should affect a father's earnings in several ways. If a father believes that a child support order will not change, he may work more in response to an order so that he has more income. If, however, he believes that his order will increase if he works more, any effect on increased earnings may be small or nonexistent. If the child support order is tied to his earnings, so that he is required to pay a given percentage of every dollar of earnings, theory predicts ambiguous effects on his labor supply. Two empirical studies of the effects of orders (Del Boca and Flinn 1994; Klawitter 1994) generally found that child support orders (of either type) have little effect on fathers' work behavior. Another study (Lerman 1993), however, found that the amount of child support paid in one year is positively associated with earnings in the next year, which may reflect fathers' decisions to work more.

Research shows that there is a great deal of diversity in the economic status of nonresident fathers (Garfinkel, McLanahan, and Hanson 1998; Meyer 1998). Whereas some fathers are poor (particularly nonwhite fathers and fathers of nonmarital children), few fathers are pushed into poverty by the child support they pay. For example, Ann Nichols-Casebolt (1986:879) found that full collection of a percentage-of-income standard among white divorced fathers would increase their poverty level from 4.8 percent to 6.3 percent; among nonwhite fathers, the percentage would rise from 26.1 percent to 35.0 percent. Elaine Sorensen (1995:790) found that between 8.0 and 14.1 percent of fathers are poor before paying child support. An additional 1.1–1.2 percent of fathers become poor after paying child support, and 3.2–3.8 percent of fathers would become poor if they paid "potential child support." Similarly, Meyer (1997:82) estimated that the poverty rate of fathers is increased by about one percentage point through payment of current child support.

Although quantitative research indicates that few fathers fall into poverty because of child support, some ethnographic research suggests differently, particularly for nonwhite men who father children outside of marriage and who live in the inner city. In several studies, fathers report or imply that they are providing as much child support as could be expected (see, for example, W. Johnson 1995; E. Johnson and Doolittle 1998; Sullivan 1993). Indeed, quantitative research from Wisconsin found that about half of the fathers who were not paying child support had incomes below the poverty level for a family of one (Bartfeld and Meyer 1994:227).[13] Nonpaying divorced fathers, however, had substantially higher incomes (Meyer and Bartfeld 1996; Meyer, forthcoming). Paying child support clearly diminishes a father's economic well-being, but it may bring him nonmonetary rewards and generally benefits his children financially and perhaps in other ways (Garfinkel, McLanahan, and Robins 1994).

The effects of the child support system when fathers have custody have not been investigated to a great extent. Father-only families tend to be much less economically vulnerable than mother-only families: poverty rates are about 18 percent, compared to 45 percent for mother-only families (Meyer and Garasky 1993:80). Nevertheless, the poverty rate of father-only families is about twice that of husband-wife families (Bianchi 1995; Meyer and Garasky 1993:80), so the economic well-being of father-only families should not be neglected. Because fathers receive little child support when they have physical custody, such support has little effect on their economic well-being. For example, national data show that the average income among custodial fathers in 1991 was more than $28,000, and the amount of child support received, averaged over all custodial fathers, was about $400 (U.S. Bureau of the Census 1995:16, 21).

Among families with shared physical custody, there is so little research on child support that it is difficult to draw conclusions about child support's effects on fathers. However, the sketchy data discussed earlier in this chapter show that child support orders are less frequent, and child support consequently has a smaller effect.

Summary and Conclusion

This chapter has examined the way the child support system works for fathers. While most children live with their mothers when their parents do not live together, the number of children living with fathers or with each parent for a substantial portion of time is growing.

When a father does not have custody, the child support system could have large effects on his economic well-being. A substantial majority of divorced fathers are ordered to pay child support, and the proportion of fathers of nonmarital children who are ordered to pay support, while much lower, is increasing. The level of child support ordered typically increases with the number of children and with the father's income. The most persuasive evidence is that, in general, child support does not impoverish fathers, particularly divorced fathers. Individual fathers may face unfair situations, but this review of the literature suggests no reasons to redo dramatically general child support policy to favor fathers. Nevertheless, the economic status of many fathers, particularly those of nonmarital children, is weak, suggesting that policymakers consider not merely the most efficient way to collect what is owed but also ways to increase the earning capacity of some nonresident fathers.

The little extant evidence suggests that the system works very differently when fathers receive physical custody of their children than when mothers receive custody. Fathers are much less likely to have child support orders: those orders are likely to be lower, and smaller proportions are paid. Little is also known about how the child support system works when children spend significant amounts of time with both their fathers and mothers. Child support policy needs to address what should happen in these less-common situations when fathers share physical custody or have sole custody.

To the extent that the child support system treats fathers and mothers differently, are these outcomes a problem that public policy needs to address? Three factors could be considered in evaluating this question. First, are the lower child support orders and payments when fathers have physical custody merely a function of nonresident mothers' lower ability to pay, or do these orders reflect the possibility that child support rules are not followed when fathers get physical custody? Second, do fathers lack child support orders because they do not want them or because the court is reluctant to require a nonresident mother to pay, given that she has already been deprived of physical custody? Third, even if fathers are less likely to choose to receive child support, does doing so affect children? Some research is beginning to find that child support has positive effects on children above and beyond the financial assistance it provides (Garfinkel, McLanahan, and Robins 1994). If so, society may want to place limits on a father's ability to refuse child support. Social-science research has yet to address these issues.

NOTES

This research was supported in part by the U.S. Department of Health and Human Services, Office of the Assistant Secretary for Planning and Evaluation, through the Institute for Research on Poverty. Some of the data used in this research were collected through a contract between the Wisconsin Department of Health and Social Services and the Institute for Research on Poverty. Opinions expressed are those of the author and not necessarily those of the sponsoring institutions.

1. In part, this focus has occurred because of an overriding concern about children's well-being: because the children typically live with the mother, research has focused on mothers and children. But the focus on mothers has also occurred for pragmatic reasons. The primary national data set used to study child support issues, the Current Population Survey—Child Support Supplement, initially asked mothers about the characteristics of nonresident fathers. But the accuracy of responses to these questions was seriously questioned, and the questions were dropped. Finally, attempts to focus on fathers in large national data sets have been plagued by difficulties in getting fathers to state that they have children living elsewhere. When men are asked about the number of children they have fathered who do not live with them, the total is a much smaller number than when women are

asked about the number of children who live with them whose father is not present. This difficulty in identifying nonresident fathers holds in the National Survey of Families and Households (Seltzer and Brandreth 1995), the National Longitudinal Survey of Youth (Veum 1993), the Survey of Income and Program Participation (Sorensen 1995), and the Current Population Survey (Cherlin, Griffith, and McCarthy 1983).

2. The difference in numbers may also be related to the timing of the question: women who received their first order between January 1992 and April 1992, when they were interviewed, would have said they had an order but were not owed any cash support in calendar year 1991.

3. The recent trend has been toward decoupling the paternity establishment process from the child support process. Thus, many fathers are now encouraged to voluntarily acknowledge paternity at the time of the child's birth, and a child support action may or may not occur later. For a discussion of related issues, see Wattenberg 1993.

4. Many of these orders are fixed-percentage orders (where the child support order states that the father is to pay a particular percentage of his income); thus, nothing is owed if the father has no income.

5. For a discussion of these difficulties, see Garfinkel, McLanahan, and Hanson 1998; Meyer 1997; Sorensen 1997.

6. For examples of research on the dollar amount paid, see Beller and Graham 1993; Braver, Fitzpatrick, and Bay 1991; Danziger and Nichols-Casebolt 1990; Hill 1992; Sonenstein and Calhoun 1990; Teachman 1991. For examples of research on the percentage of the order that is paid (compliance), see Bartfeld and Meyer 1994; Braver, Fitzpatrick, and Bay 1991; Meyer and Bartfeld 1996; Meyer, forthcoming; Peters et al. 1993.

7. Prior to 1984, no child support was shared with the family. Between 1984 and 1996, the first fifty dollars per month of child support paid was shared with families receiving Aid to Families with Dependent Children (AFDC). The 1996 welfare reform legislation replaced the AFDC program with programs designed by the states: states may now determine how much child support collected on behalf of welfare recipients will be shared with families.

8. Teachman and Polonko (1990) conducted a latent-class model and found that their data suggest two main types of divorce outcomes: a common outcome (mother receives sole physical custody, father has visitation, child support is ordered), and all other outcomes—a conceptualization that treats father-custody cases as identical to mother-custody cases without child support orders, making it impossible to identify factors associated with father custody. The authors found that the presence of young children increases the probability of the common outcome (which is consistent with the other studies), as do the father's earnings at divorce (a finding roughly consistent with that of Fox and Kelly [1995]).

In discussions about factors related to custody, I have not included information from a four-state Child Custody and Child Support Project (CCCSP) (Pearson and Thoennes 1988, 1990) because the authors' sample included cases in which custody was contested and comprised cases collected for different purposes.

Pearson and Thoennes (1990) also found that shared-custody cases showed the highest levels of income and education for both mothers and fathers.

9. Greif and DeMaris (1991) examined fathers with custody who responded to a magazine survey. They found that fathers with lower incomes in general and lower income than their wives were more likely to have child support orders. Because the representativeness of the survey respondents is unknown, it is impossible to know how generally applicable these findings are.

10. Author's calculations, unpublished, from a probit analysis of 334 cases.

11. Author's calculations, unpublished. These results are consistent across several models, including both a multivariate analysis of order amounts among those who have orders and a tobit analysis of order amounts (in which those without orders are included as having orders of zero).

12. The survey that provides the national child support data (Current Population Survey—Child Support Supplement) does not differentiate between legal and physical custody and thus does not provide information on child support when there is shared physical custody.

13. In this study, income was taken from tax records. If fathers with the lowest incomes are least likely to file taxes, then the economic status of nonpaying fathers may be even worse.

REFERENCES

Acs, Gregory, and Sheldon Danziger. 1993. Educational Attainment, Industrial Structure, and Male Earnings through the 1980s. *Journal of Human Resources* 28:618–48.

Bartfeld, Judi, and Daniel R. Meyer. 1994. Are There Really Dead-Beat Dads? The Relationship between Enforcement, Ability to Pay, and Compliance in Nonmarital Child Support Cases. *Social Service Review* 68 (2): 219–35.

Beller, Andrea H., and John W. Graham. 1993. *Small Change: The Economics of Child Support.* New Haven: Yale University Press.

Bianchi, Suzanne M. 1995. The Changing Demographic and Socioeconomic Characteristics of Single Parent Families. *Marriage and Family Review* 20:71–97.

Braver, Sanford L., Pamela J. Fitzpatrick, and R. Curtis Bay. 1991. Noncustodial Parent's Report of Child Support Payments. *Family Relations* 40:180–85.

Braver, Sanford L., Sharlene A. Wolchik, Irwin N. Sandler, Virgin L. Sheets, Bruce Fogas, and R. Curtis Bay. 1993. A Longitudinal Study of Noncustodial Parents: Parents without Children. *Journal of Family Psychology* 7 (1): 9–23.

Buehler, Cheryl, and Jean M. Gerard. 1995. Divorce Law in the United States: A Focus on Child Custody. *Family Relations* 44:439–58.

Cancian, Maria, and Daniel R. Meyer. 1996. Changing Policy, Changing Practice: Mothers' Incomes and Child Support Orders. *Journal of Marriage and the Family* 58:618–27.

———. 1998. Who Gets Custody? *Demography* 35:147–57.

Cherlin, Andrew J., Jeanne Griffith, and James McCarthy. 1983. A Note on Maritally-Disrupted Men's Reports of Child Support in the June 1980 Current Population Survey. *Demography* 20:385–89.

Christensen, Donna Hendrickson, Carla M. Dahl, and Kathryn D. Rettig. 1990. Noncustodial Mothers and Child Support: Examining the Larger Context. *Family Relations* 39:388–94.

Czapanskiy, Karen. 1994. Child Support, Visitation, Shared Custody and Split Custody. In *Child Support Guidelines: The Next Generation,* ed. Margaret Campbell Haynes. Washington, DC: U.S. Department of Health and Human Services.

Danziger, Sandra K., and Ann Nichols-Casebolt. 1990. Child Support in Paternity Cases. *Social Service Review* 64 (3): 458–74.

Del Boca, Daniela, and Christopher J. Flinn. 1994. *Welfare Effects of Fixed and Percentage-Expressed Child Support Awards.* Discussion Paper no. 1041-94. Madison, WI: Institute for Research on Poverty.

Donnelly, Denise, and David Finkelhor. 1993. Who Has Joint Custody? Class Differences in the Determination of Custody Arrangements. *Family Relations* 42:57–60.

Edin, Kathryn. 1995. Single Mothers and Child Support: The Possibilities and Limits of Child Support Policy. *Children and Youth Services Review* 17 (1–2): 203–30.

Emery, Robert E., E. Mavis Hetherington, and Lisabeth F. Dilalla. 1984. Divorce, Children, and Social Policy. In *Child Development Research and Social Policy,* ed. Harold W. Stevenson and Alberta E. Siegel, vol. 1. Chicago: University of Chicago Press.

Fox, Greer Litton, and Robert F. Kelly. 1995. Determinants of Child Custody Arrangements at Divorce. *Journal of Marriage and the Family* 57:693–708.

Freeman, Richard, and Jane Waldfogel. 1998. Does Child Support Enforcement Policy Affect Male Labor Supply? In *Fathers under Fire: The Revolution in Child Support Enforcement,* ed. Irwin Garfinkel, Sara S. McLanahan, Daniel R. Meyer, and Judith A. Seltzer. New York: Russell Sage Foundation.

Furstenberg, Frank F., Jr. 1988. Good Dads—Bad Dads: Two Faces of Fatherhood. In *The Changing American Family and Public Policy,* ed. Andrew J. Cherlin. Washington, DC: Urban Institute Press.

Furstenberg, Frank F., Jr., and Kathleen Mullan Harris. 1993. When and Why Fathers Matter: Impacts of Father Involvement on the Children of Adolescent Mothers. In *Young Unwed Fathers: Changing Roles and Emerging Policies,* ed. Robert I. Lerman and Theodora J. Ooms. Philadelphia: Temple University Press.

Garasky, Steven, and Daniel R. Meyer. 1996. Reconsidering the Increase in Father-Only Families. *Demography* 33 385–93.

Garfinkel, Irwin, and Marieka M. Klawitter. 1990. The Effect of Routine Income Withholding on Child Support Collections. *Journal of Policy Analysis and Management* 9:155–77.

Garfinkel, Irwin, Sara S. McLanahan, and Thomas L. Hanson. 1998. A Patchwork Portrait of Nonresident Fathers. In *Fathers under Fire: The Revolution in Child Support Enforcement,* ed. Irwin Garfinkel, Sara S. McLanahan, Daniel R. Meyer, and Judith A. Seltzer. New York: Russell Sage Foundation.

Garfinkel, Irwin, Sara S. McLanahan, and Philip K. Robins, eds. 1994. *Child Support and Child Well-Being.* Washington, DC: Urban Institute Press.

Garfinkel, Irwin, and Philip K. Robins. 1994. The Relationship between Child Support Enforcement Tools and Child Support Outcomes. In *Child Support and Child Well-Being,* ed. Irwin Garfinkel, Sara S. McLanahan, and Philip K. Robins. Washington, DC: Urban Institute Press.

Garrison, Marsha. 1996. The Goals and Limits of Child Support Policy. Manuscript.

Greif, Geoffrey L., and Alfred DeMaris. 1991. When a Single Custodial Father Receives Child Support. *American Journal of Family Therapy* 19 (2): 167–76.

Haskins, Ron. 1988. Child Support: A Father's View. In *Child Support: From Debt Collection to Social Policy,* ed. Alfred J. Kahn and Sheila B. Kamerman. Newbury Park, CA: Sage Publications.

Hill, Martha S. 1992. The Role of Economic Resources and Remarriage in Financial Assistance for Children of Divorce. *Journal of Family Issues* 13:158–78.

Johnson, Earl S., and Fred Doolittle. 1998. Low-Income Parents and the Parents' Fair Share Program: An Early Qualitative Look at Improving the Ability and Desire of Low-Income Noncustodial Parents to Pay Child Support. In *Fathers under Fire: The Revolution in Child Support Enforcement,* ed. Irwin Garfinkel, Sara S. McLanahan, Daniel R. Meyer, and Judith A. Seltzer. New York: Russell Sage Foundation.

Johnson, Waldo. 1995. Contextual Factors Affecting Child Support Provision among Urban, Poor Young African-American Males. Paper presented at conference on "The Effects of Child Support Enforcement on Non-Resident Fathers," Princeton, NJ.

Kelly, Joan B. 1994. The Determination of Child Custody. *Future of Children* 4 (spring): 121–42.

Klawitter, Marieka M. 1994. Child Support Awards and the Earnings of Divorced Noncustodial Fathers. *Social Service Review* 68:351–68.

Kost, Kathleen A., Daniel R. Meyer, Thomas Corbett, and Patricia R. Brown. 1996. Revising Old Child Support Orders: The Wisconsin Experience. *Family Relations* 45:19–26.

Lerman, Robert I. 1993. Employment Patterns of Unwed Fathers and Public Policy. In *Young Unwed Fathers: Changing Roles and Emerging Policies,* ed. Robert I. Lerman and Theodora J. Ooms. Philadelphia: Temple University Press.

Lin, I-Fen. 1997. "Perceptions of Fairness and Compliance with Child Support Obligations." Ph.D. diss., University of Wisconsin, Madison.

Maccoby, Eleanor E., and Robert H. Mnookin. 1992. *Dividing the Child: Social and Legal Dilemmas of Custody.* Cambridge, MA: Harvard University Press.

Maniha, John K. 1992. *New Data on State Performance in the Establishment of Paternity: Is It Valid and What Use Can Be Made of It?* Special Report 56a. Madison, WI: Institute for Research on Poverty.

Mason, Mary Ann. 1994. *From Father's Property to Children's Rights: The History of Child Custody in the United States.* New York: Columbia University Press.

Melli, Marygold S., and Patricia R. Brown. 1992. *Child Support in Shared Physical Custody in Wisconsin: Present Guidelines and Possible Alternatives.* Report to the Wisconsin Department of Health and Social Services. Madison, WI: Institute for Research on Poverty.

———. 1994. The Economics of Shared Custody: Developing an Equitable Formula for Dual Residence. *Houston Law Review* 31:543–84.

Meyer, Daniel R. 1995. Supporting Children Born outside of Marriage: Do Child Support Awards Keep Pace with Changes in Fathers' Incomes? *Social Science Quarterly* 76 (3): 577–93.

———. 1996. The Economic Vulnerability of Midlife Single Parents. In *The Parental Experience in Midlife,* ed. Carol D. Ryff and Marsha Mailick Seltzer. Chicago: University of Chicago Press.

———. 1998. The Effect of Child Support Reforms on the Economic Status of Nonresident Fathers. In *Fathers under Fire: The Revolution in Child Support Enforcement,* ed. Irwin Garfinkel, Sara S. McLanahan, Daniel R. Meyer, and Judith A. Seltzer. New York: Russell Sage Foundation.

———. Forthcoming. Compliance with Child Support Orders in Paternity and Divorce Cases. In *The Postdivorce Family,* ed. Paul R. Amato and Ross A. Thompson.

Meyer, Daniel R., and Judi Bartfeld. 1996. Compliance with Child Support Orders in Divorce Cases. *Journal of Marriage and the Family* 58:201–12.

———. 1998. Patterns of Child Support Compliance in Wisconsin. *Journal of Marriage and the Family* 60:309–18.

Meyer, Daniel R., Judi Bartfeld, Irwin Garfinkel, and Patricia Brown. 1996. Child Support Reform: Lessons from Wisconsin. *Family Relations* 45:11–18.

Meyer, Daniel R., and Steven Garasky. 1993. Custodial Fathers: Myths, Realities, and Child Support Policy. *Journal of Marriage and the Family* 55:73–89.

Meyer, Daniel R., and Mei-Chen Hu. 1996. *Is the Guideline Used to Set Child Support Orders in Wisconsin?* Final report to the Wisconsin Department of Health and Social Services. Madison WI: Institute for Research on Poverty.

Nichols-Casebolt, Ann. 1986. The Economic Impact of Child Support Reform on the Poverty Status of Custodial and Noncustodial Families. *Journal of Marriage and the Family* 48:875–80.

Nichols-Casebolt, Ann, and Irwin Garfinkel. 1991. Trends in Paternity Adjudications and Child Support Awards. *Social Science Quarterly* 72 (1): 83–97.

Oldham, J. Thomas. 1994. The Appropriate Child Support Award When the Noncustodial Parent Earns Less than the Custodial Parent. *Houston Law Review* 31:585–616.

Pearson, Jessica, Paul Munson, and Nancy Thoennes. 1982. Legal Change and Child Custody Awards. *Journal of Family Issues* 3:5–24.

Pearson, Jessica, and Nancy Thoennes. 1988. Supporting Children after Divorce: The Influence of Custody on Support Levels and Payments. *Family Law Quarterly* 22:319–39.

———. 1990. Custody after Divorce: Demographic and Attitudinal Patterns. *American Journal of Orthopsychiatry* 60 (2): 233–49.

Peters, H. Elizabeth, Laura M. Argys, Eleanor E. Maccoby, and Robert H. Mnookin. 1993. Enforcing Divorce Settlements: Evidence from Child Support Compliance and Award Modifications. *Demography* 30:719–35.

Pirog-Good, Maureen A. 1993. Child Support Guidelines and the Economic Well-Being of Children in the United States. *Family Relations* 42:453–62.

Robins, Philip K. 1992. Why Did Child Support Award Levels Decline from 1978 to 1985? *Journal of Human Resources* 27:362–79.

Seltzer, Judith A. 1990. Legal and Physical Custody Arrangements in Recent Divorces. *Social Science Quarterly* 71:250–66.

———. 1991. Relationships between Fathers and Children Who Live Apart: The Father's Role after Separation. *Journal of Marriage and the Family* 53:79–101.

———. 1994. Consequences of Marital Dissolution for Children. *Annual Review of Sociology* 20:235–66.

Seltzer, Judith A., and Yvonne Brandreth. 1995. What Fathers Say about Involvement with Children after Separation. In *Fatherhood: Contemporary Theory, Research, and Social Policy,* ed. William Marsiglio. Thousand Oaks, CA: Sage Publications.

Sonenstein, Freya L., and C. A. Calhoun. 1990. Determinants of Child Support: A Pilot Survey of Absent Parents. *Contemporary Policy Issues* 8:75–94.

Sonenstein, Freya L., Pamela A. Holcomb, and Kristin S. Seefeldt.1994. Promising Approaches to Improving Paternity Establishment Rates at the Local Level. In *Child Support and Child Well-Being,* ed. Irwin Garfinkel, Sara S. McLanahan, and Philip K. Robins. Washington, DC: Urban Institute Press.

Sorensen, Elaine. 1995. A National Profile of Noncustodial Fathers and Their Ability to Pay Child Support. Urban Institute, Washington, DC.

———. 1997. A National Profile of Noncustodial Fathers and Their Ability to Pay Child Support. *Journal of Marriage and the Family* 59:785–97.

Stier, Haya, and Marta Tienda. 1993. Are Men Marginal to the Family? Insights from Chicago's Inner City. In *Men, Work, and Family,* ed. Jane C. Hood. Newbury Park, CA: Sage Publications.

Sullivan, Mercer L. 1993. Young Fathers and Parenting in Two Inner-City Neighborhoods. In *Young Unwed Fathers: Changing Roles and Emerging Policies,* ed. Robert I. Lerman and Theodora J. Ooms. Philadelphia: Temple University Press.

Teachman, Jay D. 1990. Socioeconomic Resources of Parents and the Award of Child Support in the United States. *Journal of Marriage and the Family* 52:689–99.

———. 1991. Who Pays? Receipt of Child Support in the United States. *Journal of Marriage and the Family* 53:759–72.

Teachman, Jay D., and Karen Polonko. 1990. Negotiating Divorce Outcomes: Can We Identify Patterns in Divorce Settlements? *Journal of Marriage and the Family* 52:129–39.

U.S. Bureau of the Census. 1995. *Child Support for Custodial Mothers and Fathers:*

1991. Current Population Reports, series P60-187. Washington, DC: U.S. Government Printing Office.

Veum, Jonathan R. 1993. The Relationship between Child Support and Visitation: Evidence from Longitudinal Data. *Social Science Research* 22 (September): 229–44.

Wattenberg, Esther. 1993. Paternity Actions and Young Fathers. In *Young Unwed Fathers: Changing Roles and Emerging Policies,* ed. Robert I. Lerman and Theodora J. Ooms. Philadelphia: Temple University Press.

Part III

Improving the Present System

Guideline Review: The Search for an Equitable Child Support Formula

Marygold S. Melli

This chapter addresses a very important issue to the future of child support: the task of ensuring the adequacy and fairness of the numerical formulas, known as child support guidelines, that have been at the core of the child support revolution of the past decade. The guidelines have transformed the setting of child support by replacing a discretionary system of individualized child support determinations with mathematical formulas. Historically, child support decision making had been highly individualized, based on a case-by-case assessment of the child's budget and the noncustodial parent's ability to pay. The new formulas shifted the focus from individualized cases to the use of normative standards (Garfinkel and Melli 1990).

Child support guidelines were put into place by federal mandate in the Family Support Act of 1988, which required the states to develop and use mathematical formulas to set child support by October 1989. But Congress recognized at the time that this pioneering effort to change the structure of decision making in the area of child support was still in its formative stages. Therefore, Congress required the states to review the guidelines at least once every four years to ensure that they resulted in "appropriate amounts of child support" (42 USC § 667).

Neither Congress nor the federal regulations promulgated to implement the Family Support Act gave the states any guidance on the scope of the guideline review they were to undertake or on the process they were to use to accomplish the review. The federal regulations did add two specific directives (45 CFR §302.56[e] and [h]). The first was a requirement that, as a part of the reviews, the states were to consider economic data on the cost of raising children. The second requirement recognized that the effectiveness of a formula is related to the regularity of its use and directed the states to analyze case data, gathered through sampling or other methods, on deviations from the guidelines to ensure that deviations were limited.

However, the regulations provided no direction on how case sampling should be conducted or what specific issues should be addressed.

By now, states should have conducted at least one and probably two guideline reviews. The first review was to have been completed by 13 October 1993. This chapter attempts an assessment of these state guideline reviews using as criteria the progress made toward two of the federal guideline-review mandate's objectives: (1) whether the guidelines produce appropriate amounts of child support; and (2) whether the number of cases in which there is a deviation from the guidelines is limited.

The chapter concludes that the guideline reviews fall far short of what is needed to develop a structure that provides appropriate child support awards and limits deviations. The chapter recommends that the U.S. Department of Health and Human Services assume the kind of leadership role it provided in the early development of child support guidelines, when it appointed an advisory panel to assist in the process (Williams 1987). That panel devised the income-shares model that has been enormously influential in the development of child support guidelines.

This chapter's assessment is based on a detailed study of the first set of reviews conducted by the states before 13 October 1993. That study was made as part of an evaluation for the Office of Child Support Enforcement of the U.S. Department of Health and Human Services under a contract with CSR Inc. and the American Bar Association (ABA) Center on Children and the Law. The study was based on five sources of information: (1) a panel of experts composed of knowledgeable judges, attorneys, officials, administrators, representatives of advocacy groups for custodial and noncustodial parents, consultants, and academics; (2) the latest available data from the Child Support for Mothers and Fathers supplement to the 1992 Current Population Survey; (3) case-record analysis of more than 4,200 case records from twenty-one counties (200 case records per county) in eleven states;[1] (4) interviews with various participants in the child support system in each of the twenty-one study counties to obtain their views on guideline implementation and operation; and (5) reports submitted to the ABA by state child support agencies. A total of forty-nine jurisdictions provided some form of written response. The states were asked to submit information concerning the number of guideline reviews undertaken since 13 October 1989, a summary of the state's review process (for example, hearings, advisory committees, case studies, case data compilations, judicial reviews, and child-rearing cost studies), all guideline review reports, a summary of the action taken as a result of the review(s), and information about upcoming reviews. Of the forty-nine responding jurisdictions, forty-five had completed at least one review since October 1989 (ABA 1996).

The discussion in this chapter relies most heavily on the ABA's case-record analysis and the states' reports to the ABA describing guideline reviews. In attempting an assessment of state progress on guideline reviews, this chapter looks at two areas and several issues covered in the evaluation study and relates them to the two objectives that guideline review should accomplish.

An Appropriate Amount of Child Support

The Child Support Formulas and Costs of Child Raising

The federal requirement that the states review child support guidelines to ensure that they set an appropriate child support amount reflects concern about the formulas chosen by the states for use in setting child support. There is reason for such concern. As Marsha Garrison points out in "The Goals and Limits of Child Support Policy," in this volume, considerable evidence has now accumulated that the children's standards of living drop after divorce.

In response to concerns about the adequacy of child support, the federal regulations implementing the Family Support Act require the states in their mandated guideline reviews to consider economic data on the cost of raising children. The evaluation study found that a large number of the reporting states had not done so. Some states that did consider such data relied on national studies (as did the original guidelines), but others conducted a state-specific analysis of the existing studies and data relating to the cost of raising children. None apparently considered the study commissioned under a directive from Congress in the Family Support Act that required the secretary of the U.S. Department of Health and Human Services to conduct "a study of patterns of expenditures on children in 2-parent families, in single-parent families following divorce or separation, and in single-parent families in which the parents never married" (Family Support Act of 1988 §128). David Betson conducted this study, which estimated the costs of raising children in both two-parent and single-parent households. In two-parent households, the estimate, expressed as a percentage of total household expenditure, was 25 percent, 35 percent, and 40 percent for one, two, and three children, respectively. In single-parent households, Betson estimated 40 percent, 55 percent, and 60 percent for one, two, and three children, respectively (1990:57).

Some states used a process of review in which they compared awards under the state guidelines against average child-rearing costs to determine whether children's needs were being met. Some states found that their guidelines operated satisfactorily, but a few recommended increases in the percentages set in their child support guidelines because the awards produced by the guidelines did not meet average child-rearing costs.

The evaluation study did not indicate any discussion by the states of the point made by Garrison and others that the problem of postdivorce child poverty is not solely one of the failure of the economic studies to address the issue of costs in single-parent families. The problem also results—principally—from the failure of child support policy to focus on maintaining the child's standard of living (Betson, Evenhouse, and Reilly 1992; Haynes 1997:140). The current guidelines were never intended to maintain a standard of living for the child but rather to provide a continuity of expenditure by the noncustodial parent—that is, to ensure that noncustodial parents spend the same amount as they would have if the family had remained together. As Garrison explains, this marginal expenditure base for the guidelines results in lower standards of living for children unless the custodial parent's income is roughly equivalent to that of the noncustodial parent. Garrison makes a compelling argument for a reexamination in the guideline reviews of the objectives of child support policy.

Definition of Income

Federal regulations require that child support guidelines apply to all noncustodial parent income, but there is no federal definition of income. The evaluation study reported that state guideline-review committees devoted a great deal of time to income-determination issues—an indication of their importance to the child support process and also of the fact that income determination is one of the most litigated issues in child support enforcement (Morgan 1996). The importance of the issue is clear because the appropriate amount of support is affected by the income base used to compute the child support award. If the income base is too limited and too many items are excluded, the amount of child support generated is less.

In the guideline reviews compiled by the evaluation study, some states proposed definitions of income. These definitions were generally expansive and included resources such as salary and wages, commissions, bonuses, tips, rental income, estate or trust income, royalties, interest, dividends, annuities, self-employment earnings, alimony, in-kind compensation, noncash fringe benefits, and lottery winnings. Other issues addressed by state guideline-review committees were income from overtime and second jobs and gross versus net income.

The ABA case-record analysis found that more uniform treatment occurred when the guideline clearly defined income. One of the evaluation study's recommendations was that states adopt definitions that cover all income issues so that cases are treated similarly from court to court and county to county. Given the fact that one-third of child support cases are now interstate (Legler, "The Impact of Welfare Reform on the Child Support Enforcement System," in this volume), a common definition, used by all the states, should be an objective of guideline review.

Limiting Deviations from the Guidelines

The second objective specifically mentioned in the federal regulations as a subject for guideline review is that of ensuring that deviations from the guideline are limited.

Federal law provides that child support guidelines create a "rebuttable presumption" that the amount of the award resulting from application of the guideline is the correct amount (42 USC § 667[b][2]). Although the purpose of using guidelines is to treat similar cases in a similar manner, thus decreasing the variability across similar cases, the law recognizes the need for discretion to depart from the guidelines in certain situations. Therefore, the law provides that the presumption that the guideline amount is correct may be rebutted by a finding that use of the guideline is unjust or inappropriate in a particular case (45 CFR § 302.56[g]). In federal child support parlance, this departure from the guideline amount is known as a deviation.

The requirements for allowing a deviation are spelled out in the federal regulation.[2] The state must establish criteria for determining whether the guideline amount is inappropriate or unjust. These criteria must take into consideration the best interest of the child. The finding supporting the deviation then must state the amount of support as determined by the guideline and include a justification, based on the state criteria, of why the order varies from the guideline amount. This finding must be either a written finding or a specific finding in the record of the proceeding.

A recent study describes the way the states have approached the duty of establishing criteria for deviations. The study notes that most states have a list of reasons to be considered with a catchall phrase, such as "where justice so requires" or "any other factors which the court in each case determines are relevant," that allows the decision maker to exercise discretion. Twelve states have a few factors plus this catchall, and twenty-one list many factors. Twelve states have a list of reasons with no catchall, and six have only a general catchall-type criterion (Morgan 1996). The requirement that deviations be limited has been interpreted to refer to the number of deviations from the presumptive guideline amount in child support awards, not to the number of criteria that a state allows as a basis for deviation (Arnaudo 1994).

Any assessment of how successfully states limit deviations from their guidelines requires two inquiries. The first deals with the extent to which decision makers deviate from the guideline—that is, the number of times that the guideline is not used. The second looks at the identification of areas of frequent deviation for the purpose of adopting a provision in the guideline formula to cover the situation (Williams 1994). The following discussion examines both of these areas.

Amount of Deviation

The best answer to the question of how often the states do not apply their guidelines is that it is unknown. Fewer than half of the states completed case reviews as directed by the federal regulation, deviations were not always noted, and the reasons for deviations were not always available in the record reviewed. Furthermore, the bulk of the information about the use of guidelines in the evaluation study was based on the ABA's independent analysis of a sample of 4,200 case records using a problematic methodology. The case records examined included court orders, work sheets, and supplemental data on deviations, but the records did not contain reasons for deviation that had only been placed orally on the record in the proceeding without any written documentation. The evaluation study considered all support awards to be in compliance with the guideline unless there was some written documentation of a deviation. These cases were described as formal deviations. This methodology resulted in the report's somewhat misleading statement that "83 percent of the cases were considered to follow the guidelines, while 17 percent of cases were categorized as formal deviations" (ABA 1996, vol. 1:2.3.) In fact, the 83 percent of the cases considered to be guideline cases contained a significant number that did not follow the guidelines amount.

Further data analysis examined the group of guideline cases without written documentation of a deviation to determine the extent to which the amount awarded in those cases was the same as a computed guideline amount would be for the case. If the support award agreed with the computed amount or if it was within 2 percent above or below that amount, the case was regarded as in compliance with the guideline. If the support order was not within that range, it was classified as a discrepancy case. In a significant number of cases—ranging from less than 10 percent to more than 45 percent across the twenty-one counties in the data analysis—there was a discrepancy.

Surprisingly, the evaluation study did not attribute any of the discrepancies to the researcher's inability to obtain reasons not available in the written record. Instead, the study divided the reasons for these discrepancies into two groups, random or systematic. Errors, such as those in computing the guideline amount or in using the state child support amount tables, were classified as random errors. The evaluation study recommended that the states require better training and more standard case documentation to lessen the number of random discrepancies. Errors indicating an inconsistency in state policy, such as how to exercise discretion in cases of obligors with low incomes, were classified as systematic errors. The evaluation study recommended more consistent and better-developed state policies to lessen the number of systematic discrepancies.

It seems imperative that states follow these recommendations as well as others to require work sheets or other written documentation of the reasons for deviation to decrease the number of discrepancies before any truly valid analysis of deviations can be made.

The evaluation study provided an instructive analysis of the 17 percent of the cases considered formal deviations. In the vast majority of deviation cases, 83 percent, the deviation was downward, and the average amount of the decrease was 36 percent. For the 17 percent of cases with an increase, the amount of increase averaged 30 percent (ABA 1996, vol. 1:2.4, 2.5).

The most frequent reason for deviation, listed in 21 percent of the cases, was an agreement of the parties. Second households, extended or extraordinary visitation expenses, and low income of the noncustodial parent each accounted for deviations in 10 percent of the cases. In 8 percent of the cases the reason given was that the guideline amount would be unjust or inappropriate. In 4 percent of the cases, the reason was extraordinary needs of the parent (but the study did not specify which parent). Fifteen percent of the cases cited other reasons, and 13 percent gave no reason. Cases in which the mother was the obligor were more likely to have deviations, although fathers were the obligors in 93 percent of the cases. Twenty-eight percent of the cases where the mother was the obligor had deviations, compared to only 16 percent of cases with father obligors. More than 90 percent of the deviations because of low income of the noncustodial parent or because of a second household were downward deviations. In contrast, more than 20 percent of the deviations because of agreement of the parties were upward, as was the case with deviations because the amount of the award was inappropriate or unjust (ABA 1996, vol. 1:2.5, 2.6, tables 2-3 and 2-6).

Areas of Frequent Deviation

The second issue related to limiting the amount of deviation from the guidelines is to identify areas of frequent deviation for the purpose of formulating a guideline to cover it.

The following discussion looks at three child support issues that arise with sufficient frequency that the states have enough experience to develop standard ways to cover them: multiple families, extended visitation and shared custody, and health care. In its review of case records, the ABA found much more consistency when the formula covered an issue than when the matter was a reason for deviation from the formula.

Multiple Families

The evaluation study found multiple families to be one of the most common reasons for deviation. The study compilation of guideline-review documents found that most states addressed the issue of multiple families.

One of the most troublesome areas in the use of child support guidelines has been their application in multiple-family cases. The basic child support guidelines were developed to apply to situations where the obligor parent had no other children to support. However, increasingly, as divorced parents remarry and have additional children, child support awards must be determined in situations where a prior child support order exists. In that type of case, many state guidelines deduct the prior order from the income of the obligor parent used to set child support for the second family (Morgan 1996). This solution means that the children of the second marriage receive lesser child support than the children with the earlier support award. This "first family first" principle is based on the policy decision that parents of the second family knew of the prior obligation when they decided to have more children. This same value judgment is reflected in the fact that many state guidelines do not contain provisions for considering the fact that a parent has subsequent children, an issue that normally arises in the case of a modification. A significant number of states provide that costs of subsequent children are a basis for deviating from the guideline amount (Arnaudo 1994).

The evaluation study found that the states were beginning to reassess their approach to multiple families. Whether the standard approach of giving preference to prior orders when setting an award for a subsequent family is good public policy is being reexamined. Along with this reconsideration is an assessment of the current guideline approach to subsequent families in modification situations. The issues are so complex that providing for subsequent families—as a number of states have done—as an allowable deviation from the guideline support amount appears undesirable. The evaluation study recommended that states adopt mandatory formulas to consider prior support orders and subsequent obligations of both parents to ensure consistent treatment of families.

Multiple families raise another issue: whether the income of a new spouse should be considered in determining the ability to support. The

U.S. Commission on Interstate Child Support (1992) recommended that states adopt policies on whether the income of the remarried parent's spouse should affect a support obligation. The evaluation study found that most states that considered this issue in their reviews excluded it.

Shared Custody: Dual Residence and Extended Visitation

Early child support guidelines were intended to provide child support to a sole custodial parent. That sole custodian was assumed to be the parent who incurred all child-raising costs. Little attention was paid to any noncustodial parent's costs incurred when spending time with the child. However, there are a number of situations in which child-related expenditures by noncustodial parents arise, and guideline development to deal with them has been spotty and poorly conceptualized. The guideline evaluation study reported that the state guideline review teams spent a great deal of time considering the way that child support guidelines should be applied to various custody and visiting arrangements. These arrangements include ordinary visitation, extended visitation, shared custody or dual residence, and split custody.

(1) Ordinary Visitation

The evaluation study found that state reviews devoted considerable attention to the definition of normal visitation. The majority of noncustodial parents have visitation with their children.[3] Therefore, it could be assumed that the child support awards set by the guidelines have considered the costs to the noncustodial parent for visitation, and some commentators have said that the guidelines are discounted to take account of noncustodial parents' expenditures during ordinary visitation (Czapanskiy 1994:43). Some states specifically authorize a decrease or an increase in child support when visitation is more or less than traditional visitation (Melli and Brown 1994:561). However, the majority of states make no specific reference in their guidelines to accommodating any discount for visitation.

In revising their guidelines, states should determine whether the basic award is—or should be—discounted for ordinary visitation.

(2) Extended or Extraordinary Visitation

A second area in which noncustodial parents may incur costs for their children is when the visitation is for an extended period of time, such as a month. Several states have guidelines for child support reductions in these cases. These guidelines are quite specific about the number of days required before the court may excuse or reduce a child support payment

(Morgan 1996:§ 3.03[c]). In addition to specific guidelines, a number of states authorize reductions in child support under general language such as cases of extended or extraordinary visitation (Arnaudo 1994:85). Where there is no specified time as to what constitutes extended or extraordinary visitation, the court must first determine whether the amount of time involved qualifies. Finally, questions have been raised about the economics of reducing a child support award for stays as short as one week because most costs will not be reduced. Therefore, some guidelines and courts consider whether a reduction in the child support amount will result in insufficient funds in the custodial household (Morgan 1996:§ 303[d]).

The report of the guideline reviews lumped extended visitation and shared custody together for discussion purposes. That may be the proper public policy decision, but it makes it even more imperative that guideline revision consider both issues.

(3) Shared Custody

Recent studies of custody arrangements show a trend toward increased shared physical custody—that is, dual residence (Melli, Brown, and Cancian 1997). This phenomenon makes the issue of child support in cases where the child spends substantial amounts of time with both parents a matter of importance in revising guidelines. At present most states either do not mention the issue in their guidelines or provide very generally that it may be a reason for the court to deviate from the guideline amount in a particular case (Morgan 1996:§ 3.303[a], table 3-4).

One reason that the states have not made more explicit provision in their guidelines for shared time is because the issues in apportioning child support in these cases are extremely complex. They involve at least two major determinations: (1) the amount of time that a child must spend with both parents before a reduction in child support is considered, and (2) how child support should be reduced, if at all, in these cases.

The evaluation study found that the state guideline reviews generated a wide variety of responses. Because of the demonstrated complexity of the issues in this area as well as the increase in the number of cases involving shared custody, it seems particularly desirable that the states address the public policy issues involved rather than leave them to the unguided discretion of busy judges. The findings of the case-record analysis indicated that when there is guideline treatment of this issue, children in similar circumstances are treated more uniformly than when deviation is a matter of discretion.

(4) Split Custody

Split, or divided custody, is the situation where each parent has sole or primary physical custody of one or more children of the relationship. A number of state reviews considered the calculation of support in these cases. Most recommended the calculation of separate support obligations for each household. The parent with the larger obligation then pays the difference between the two obligations. Most states that have guideline provisions for split custody solve the issue in this way (Morgan 1996:§ 3.04). The evaluation study recommended that all states consider a formula provision for split custody.

Health Care

Federal law now requires that the state child support guidelines provide for the children's health care needs through health-insurance coverage or other means (45 CFR § 302.56[c]). States' responses to this mandate have been to treat it as an add-on or as a reason for the court to deviate from the presumptive amount of support. The result is great variety in the way in which these very necessary costs are handled and allocated between parents (Notar and Schmidt 1994:51).

Commentators divide health care expenses into three categories: health insurance, ordinary uninsured medical expenses, and extraordinary uninsured medical expenses (Elrod 1994:62). This discussion considers guideline development in each of these areas.

(1) Health Insurance

Because of the federal requirement specifically mentioning health insurance in connection with the mandate to cover children's health care needs, all states provide that health-insurance coverage be considered in child support orders. State provisions commonly require that health-insurance coverage be ordered if it is available to either parent through employment or another group plan at reasonable cost (Morgan 1996:§ 3.01[a]). The ABA's case-record-analysis evaluation study found that decision makers followed these directions.

Provision for payment for health-insurance premiums varies. Some states deduct it from the income of the obligor parent before calculating the amount of child support, which reduces the amount of the child support award. It is not clear how this approach works when the health insurance is provided through a group plan to which the custodial parent belongs. Most states treat the insurance premium as an add-on to the child support award. How the cost of the premium is allocated between parents varies. In some cases, it is the sole responsibility of the insured parent; in others it is prorated between the parents in proportion to their respective incomes; in others it is shared equally. Finally, in some states the premium cost is treated as a reason to deviate from the guideline amount (Morgan

1996:§ 3.01[a]). The evaluation study recommended that mandatory treatment in the guideline be considered. It found much more equitable treatment when the guideline was a specific provision.

Health insurance is so important in providing for children's health care needs that states should revisit the issue in revising their guidelines. It may be that employment-related health insurance is not a sufficiently complete answer. The U.S. Commission on Interstate Child Support (1992:140) recommended that state guidelines quantify a reasonable cost for health care so that parents could negotiate for health insurance based on knowledge of the amount that the court would order for child support. This solution may not be the answer, but more study of the issue is warranted.

(2) Ordinary Uninsured Health Care Expenses

Ordinary uninsured health care expenses have been defined as "regular medical expenses, such as check-ups, eyeglasses or medication" (Elrod 1994:63). Deductibles and copayments related to health insurance have also been included (Goldfarb 1987:144). To be an ordinary health care expense two features have been found to be necessary: first, the expense should be one that occurs with some regularity, so that it is expected, and, second, it should not exceed a certain threshold dollar amount.

Some states specifically include ordinary health care expenses in the basic child support award, often with an upper limit of a dollar amount or a percentage of the award (Morgan 1996:§ 3.01(b)[3]). But except for the fact that the guidelines specifically mention health insurance and extraordinary health expenses for special treatment, thus implying that ordinary medical expenses are included in the basic award, most states do not deal with the problem.

The evaluation study recommends that states develop guidelines to cover uninsured ordinary medical care. In so doing, the states should define what ordinary medical care includes and consider an upper limit on the cost.

(3) Extraordinary Uninsured Health Care Expenses

All states make some provision for extraordinary medical expenses. A significant number specifically authorize a deviation from the child support award set by the guideline for extraordinary health care expenses (Arnaudo 1994:87).

One difficulty with extraordinary health care expense is that it is often not an expenditure that can be predicted, planned, and incorporated into an award. By their nature, extraordinary expenses often must be dealt with after the expenditure occurs. The evaluation study took the position that a discretionary approach may be preferred for extraordinary health care expenses because individual circumstances need to be evaluated.

Finally, both extraordinary and ordinary health care expenses require some definition of what is considered a medical expense. A number of states now attempt to define the term or to list services that they consider to be medical services (Morgan 1996:§ 3.01(b)[2]). States also should define the differences between extraordinary health care costs and ordinary ones.

Conclusion

This chapter has reviewed the two objectives Congress sought to achieve with guideline review: (1) ensuring that the guidelines produce appropriate amounts of child support, and (2) limiting the cases that deviate from the guidelines.

The guideline evaluation reported in the evaluation study recommended that in the future, states conduct more thorough guideline reviews and (1) allocate sufficient resources, time, and staff to the guideline-review process; (2) conduct case surveys, using the results to improve guidelines by reducing deviations and increasing consistency; and (3) review the data about the costs of child rearing. Given the experience of the guideline reviews compiled in the study, these general recommendations seem to be inadequate. They give states very little concrete guidance on preferable approaches to guideline development and fall far short of the specific recommendations under particular topics in the report.

As mentioned earlier in this chapter, what is needed now is the kind of leadership the U.S. Department of Health and Human Services gave in the early days of child support guideline development. Instead of exhorting states to look more closely at child-rearing costs, the federal government should again lead the way and suggest formulas—perhaps a choice of formulas—that are expressly intended to maintain the child's standard of living, if possible. Garrison suggests a formula that seeks that objective in "The Goals and Limits of Child Support Policy," in this volume. The American Law Institute Project on Principles of the Law of Family Dissolution also has recommended a formula that addresses the issue of maintaining the child's standard of living (American Law Institute 1997).

On the objective of limiting deviations, the federal government should amend the regulations to require that the reasons for deviation be in writing. The case-record analysis conducted in the guideline evaluation was unable to check variations in cases where the reasons were only on the tape or in the transcript of the child support proceeding.

The federal government should also give leadership in developing guidelines for areas of frequent deviation. Three of those areas are discussed in this chapter, and the evaluation study makes several recommendations for guideline treatment of the issues. Recommended formula treatment for subjects of frequent deviation should be part of any model formula the federal government develops in response to the suggestions in this chapter.

Finally, the federal government should map out a process for guideline review that gives the states guidance on specific issues to be addressed and a recommended process to follow. The present open-ended approach wastes limited state resources and is not helpful to the progress of child support guidelines.

NOTES

1. The states were Arkansas, Delaware, Florida, Massachusetts, Minnesota, Missouri, New Hampshire, New Jersey, Pennsylvania, Washington, and Wisconsin.

2. 45 CFR § 302.56(g) provides, "A written finding or specific finding on the record of a judicial or administrative proceeding for the award of child support that the application of the guidelines established under paragraph (a) of this section would be unjust or inappropriate in a particular case shall be sufficient to rebut the presumption in that case, as determined under criteria established by the State. Such criteria must take into consideration the best interests of the child. Findings that rebut the guidelines shall state the amount of support that would have been required under the guidelines and include a justification of why the order varies from the guidelines."

3. In fact, many statutes provide that the noncustodial parent is entitled to visitation unless it would seriously endanger the child's physical, mental, moral, or emotional health (Clark 1988:812; Uniform Marriage and Divorce Act § 407, 9A Unif. L. Ann. 207).

REFERENCES

American Bar Association Center on Children and the Law. 1996. Vol. 1, *Evaluation of Child Support Guidelines: Findings and Conclusion;* Vol. 2, *Findings of State Guidelines Review, State Guideline Studies and Unstructured Interviews.* Washington, DC: CSR.

American Law Institute. 1997. *Principles of the Law of Family Dissolution: Analysis and Recommendations.* Preliminary draft no. 7. Philadelphia: Executive Office, ALI.

Arnaudo, David. 1994. Deviation from State Child Support Guidelines. In *Child Support Guidelines: The Next Generation,* ed. Margaret Campbell Haynes. Washington, DC: U.S. Department of Health and Human Services, Administration for Children and Families, Office of Child Support Enforcement.

Betson, David M. 1990. *Alternative Estimates of the Cost of Children from the 1980–86 Consumer Expenditure Survey.* Madison, WI: Institute for Research on Poverty.

Betson, David M., Eirik Evenhouse, and Siobhan Reilly. 1992. Trade-Offs Implicit in Child Support Guidelines. *Journal of Policy Analysis and Management* 11:1–20.

Clark, Homer. 1988. *The Law of Domestic Relations in the United States.* 2d ed. St. Paul, MN: West Publishing.

Czapanskiy, Karen. 1994. Child Support, Visitation, Shared Custody, and Split Custody. In *Child Support Guidelines: The Next Generation,* ed. Margaret Campbell Haynes. Washington, DC U.S. Department of Health and Human Services, Administration for Children and Families, Office of Child Support Enforcement.

Elrod, Linda. 1994. Adding to the Basic Child Support Obligation. In *Child Support Guidelines: The Next Generation,* ed. Margaret Campbell Haynes. Washington, DC: U.S. Department of Health and Human Services, Administration for Children and Families, Office of Child Support Enforcement.

Garfinkel, Irwin, and Marygold S. Melli, The Use of Normative Standards in Family Law Decisions: Developing Mathematical Standards for Child Support. *Family Law Quarterly* 24:157–78.

Goldfarb, Sally F. 1987. Child Support Guidelines and Child Care, Medical and Educational Expenses. In *Essentials of Child Support Guidelines Development: Economic Issues and Policy Considerations.* Washington, DC: Women's Legal Defense Fund.

Haynes, Margaret Campbell. 1997. Review of *Child Support Guidelines: Interpretation and Application,* by Laura Morgan. *Family Law Quarterly* 31:133–59.

Melli, Marygold S., and Patricia R. Brown. 1994. The Economics of Shared Custody: Developing an Equitable Formula for Dual Residence. *Houston Law Review* 31:543–84.

Melli, Marygold S., Patricia R. Brown, and Maria Cancian. 1997. Child Custody in a Changing World: A Study of Postdivorce Arrangements in Wisconsin. *Illinois Law Review* 1997:773–800.

Morgan, Laura. 1996. *Child Support Guidelines: Interpretation and Application.* New York: Aspen Law and Business.

Notar, Susan A., and Nicole C. Schmidt. 1994. State Child Support Guidelines Treatment of Children's Health Care Needs. In *Child Support Guidelines: The Next Generation,* ed. Margaret Campbell Haynes. Washington, DC: U.S. Department of Health and Human Services, Administration for Children and Families, Office of Child Support Enforcement.

U.S. Commission on Interstate Child Support. 1992. *Supporting Our Children: A Blueprint for Reform.* Washington, DC: U.S. Government Printing Office.

Williams, Robert G. 1987. Development of Guidelines for Child Support Orders: Advisory Panel Recommendations and Final Report. September. Washington, DC: U.S. Department of Health and Human Services, Office of Child Support Enforcement.

———. 1994. An Overview of Child Support Guidelines in the United States. In *Child Support Guidelines: The Next Generation,* ed. Margaret Campbell Haynes. Washington, DC: U.S. Department of Health and Human Services, Administration for Children and Families, Office of Child Support Enforcement.

New Methods to Update Child Support

J. Thomas Oldham

Introduction

American policymakers are giving increasing attention to the impoverishing effects of child support modification rules (Glendon 1989; Sidel 1986). In almost all American states, a parent obligated to pay child support (the obligor) makes periodic payments in an amount fixed by court order. Historically, under the "American rule" for child support modification, the amount remained fixed throughout the period of the child's minority unless a parent initiated an action and a court found that the circumstances of at least one of the parents or of the child had substantially changed since the decree was rendered.

The rule frequently required the custodial parent, usually the mother, to absorb the effects of inflation and changes in the child's needs, regardless of changes in the obligor's income. The custodial mother had to bear the cost of pursuing a new action and, in most states, prove that the child's or the obligor's circumstances had substantially changed since the date of the original order (Clark 1988:727). Further, she had to make this decision with little guidance as to the likelihood of success: she was generally ignorant of the obligor's true financial situation, and the judge's broad discretion to find that circumstances had or had not substantially changed created even more uncertainty.

These imbalances, coupled with these disincentives for seeking child support modification, contribute to the poverty of families headed by women (Lewin 1994; Robins 1992). This chapter discusses alternatives to the traditional American rule for child support modification, including several automatic adjustment mechanisms that courts could include in child support orders to avoid, in many instances, the necessity of subsequent judicial action. In addition, it summarizes how recent federal legislation has changed child support modification rules and concludes by recommending that courts allow automatic adjustment and by advancing some new ideas to help remedy the imbalances facing custodial parents without duplicating the current system's disincentives to modification.

Automatic Adjustment of Child Support Awards

Instead of expressing a child support award as a fixed amount, the award could be drafted so that the amount due automatically changes without the need for additional court action, thus obviating the need for a modification proceeding. The alternatives are discussed in this section.

A. Adjusting for Inflation

Although the rate of inflation has significantly decreased during the past decade, annual inflation rates of 3–5 percent are still common. Expressing child support awards as a fixed amount causes inflation to erode their real value over time, unless awards are modified. This erosion obviously can have substantial negative effects on the child's standard of living.[1] Although short periods during this century have been deflationary rather than inflationary, the past four decades have been periods of continuing inflation, and a period of significant deflation in the near future seems unlikely (Eden 1979).

1. American Courts' Responses to Automatic Adjustments for Inflation

a. General approval. More than any other automatic adjustment mechanism, courts have approved automatic periodic adjustment of child support to account for inflation; these automatic adjustments are called cost-of-living adjustments (COLAs) Judges generally seem to perceive COLA provisions to differ fundamentally from other adjustment procedures. COLA provisions are viewed as a means of merely retaining the real value of the initial order rather than of modifying it. These courts have been sensibly receptive to a means of trying to anticipate inflation without forcing the custodial parent to initiate a new legal action to increase support.[2]

b. Courts' concerns and qualifications. Some courts have stated that orders with COLA provisions, while less objectionable where the obligor has a steady job with regular salary increases to match inflation, are inadvisable where both parties are self-employed with significant oscillation of their incomes. Even in a period of inflation, there is no guarantee that such obligors' incomes will increase commensurately.[3] For this reason, the Washington Supreme Court has concluded that a COLA provision is unenforceable unless it provides for the possibility of an obligor's financial hardship.[4] Minnesota, a state that has adopted a COLA adjustment scheme by statute,[5] deals with this problem by giving the obligor the right to petition the court to reduce or suspend the COLA increase upon a showing that the obligor's income did not increase by the amount of inflation. Still other courts have incorporated such a limit to COLA provisions in the divorce decree.[6]

Also, unless the COLA provision sets forth the mechanics of the adjustment, the COLA can be ambiguous and lead to disputes.[7] For example, a reference to the U.S. Department of Labor's cost-of-living index would not distinguish between numerous different computations—some figures are national, while others are local.

Courts have sometimes attempted to include in decrees estimates of future annual inflation; under such decrees, child support would automatically increase each year by the amount specified. Although fixing the annual increase in orders creates certainty, doing so also increases the potential for inaccuracy and has generated a mixed judicial response.[8]

2. Analysis of Automatic Adjustment for Inflation

COLA systems have the advantage of being simpler than other automatic adjustment procedures, such as percentage-expressed orders. Although they require periodic notification to the parties of the amount of the change in the cost of living and computation of the new child support amount, the additional administrative costs are probably small and would be justified by the benefits. In Minnesota, the state office of child support enforcement calculates the change in the cost of living every two years and notifies the parties of the presumptive new order. Administrators of Minnesota's program indicated during informal discussions with the author that the program appears to be working well.[9] In the alternative, a state could promulgate one COLA annually that would govern all decrees. This COLA system would be clear, although it would still require individual computation of the amount of the change in each support award. If either of these two systems is perceived as burdensome by state employees, the parties could be given the responsibility of agreeing on the amount of the new award and filing a stipulation with the court setting forth the new amount.

The COLA system seems clearly better than the current system of fixed awards. Pursuant to the COLA system, the amount of the child support order is sporadically adjusted to maintain a relatively level real value. The COLA system requires no information from either parent. It is relatively simple and requires little court time. Furthermore, localized COLA indexes are relatively accurate in measuring the local inflation rate because they track changing prices in the local area; courts can use these indexes to ensure that COLA provisions effectively maintain the value of the child support order. Some administrative expense will be incurred to staff the child support office. In contrast to percentage-expressed orders, child support orders with COLA provisions retain the collection options available when the order is expressed in a fixed dollar amount. For example, the order may easily be enforced by a contempt order.

One disadvantage of the COLA mechanism is that it freezes the real value of the child support at the amount set forth in the initial decree. It does not automatically adjust because of any changes in the parties' circumstances; to obtain such an adjustment, one parent must initiate a legal modification action, unless some type of automatic review and adjustment system is created.

B. Adjusting for Changes in the Obligor's Income

Courts have been generally unreceptive to the automatic adjustment of the amount of child support based on postdecree changes in the obligor's income.[10] Courts especially disapprove of percentage-expressed orders, which set child support awards as specified percentages of the obligors' salaries.[11] Although some of this disapproval stems from statutory authority[12] and traditional attachment to the American rule,[13] many courts have articulated significant policy concerns with orders that automatically adjust to changes in the obligor's income. The following discussion evaluates the benefits of percentage-expressed orders and the major concerns with them.

1. The Benefits of Percentage-of-Income-Expressed Orders

The obvious benefit of the percentage-expressed order is that it requires no action to adjust to the obligor's current circumstances. This method is desirable for its very low transaction costs. Wisconsin now permits courts to express child support orders as a percentage of income, and this system apparently has worked fairly well for some types of obligors. Indeed, Wisconsin courts now use percentage-of-income orders about as frequently as fixed-sum orders (Bartfeld and Garfinkel 1994:7).

A few other states have accepted percentage-expressed awards.[14] Although Texas courts do not permit percentage-expressed awards by judicial decree, if the parties agree to such a provision, it is enforced.[15] An Indiana court affirmed a trial court order that required parents to exchange financial information and update the order annually; the updated amount would be computed based on the state guidelines.[16]

2. A Percentage-Expressed Order Neglects Relevant Factors

One criticism is that the obligor's income is not the only factor that should be considered when deciding the appropriate amount of child support.[17] For example, courts frequently note that percentage-expressed orders improperly ignore children's needs.[18] In particular, a substantial increase in the obligor's income may cause the payments to exceed the needs of the child.[19] This objection largely stems from a belief that a needs-based system is the appropriate model for calculating the amount of child support. According to this view, child support should be calculated based on evidence of the costs of the child rather than based on parents' incomes. The parties' relative incomes are relevant only in the allocation of the child support obligation between the parents.

Recognizing that a child's needs are to a large extent determined by parental resources, all states have moved away from a needs-based model toward guidelines based on the income of one or both parents. Drafters of guidelines have generally been persuaded that all divorced parents have the duty, postdivorce, to allocate to a child the same portion of their income that would have been allocated while the family was intact (Williams 1987:292). Under current guidelines, the needs of the child are not considered, except as a ground for deviation from the presumptive amount. Thus, current guidelines largely reject the needs-based approach.

Percentage-expressed orders also ignore the earnings of the custodial parent.[20] This criticism is more substantial than the previous one: only about one-third of all state guidelines now accept that the obligor's income should be the sole factor that determines the amount of child support. According to a 1990 report by the National Center for State Courts, about one-third of all states base child support solely on the obligor's income. About two-thirds reject this approach as too limited and follow the income-shares guideline or Melson formula, both of which consider the income of both spouses when calculating the presumptive child support award. The percentage-expressed model for child support adjustment therefore apparently could be applied only in those jurisdictions whose guidelines are based solely on the income of the noncustodial parent. A state following either Melson or income shares could accept a percentage-expressed order only under the assumption that the parents' incomes change in roughly the same relative amounts.

3. A Percentage-Expressed Order May Encourage Underemployment

Courts have also been concerned that percentage-expressed orders could encourage underemployment more than traditional fixed-sum orders.[21]

Given custodial parents' transaction costs of seeking modification, obligors with fixed obligations now may assume that they will retain all post-decree wage increases. Obligors with percentage-expressed obligations, conversely, would understand that they would have to share wage increases with custodial parents. To avoid the underemployment incentive and still permit children to share in later career advancement, the child support obligation could be based on a "normal" career path for someone with the obligor's experience and training rather than on what actually happens (Lazear and Michael 1988:175–77). The difficulty and expense of predicting the "normal" career path, however, make this alternative unworkable. These proposals are also probably unnecessary, since studies of underemployment disincentives under percentage-expressed orders have concluded that the obligor's work effort does not vary significantly from the work effort under a fixed-sum order (Klawitter 1994).

4. A Percentage-Expressed Order May Create Enforcement Problems

Percentage-expressed orders may also be difficult to enforce.[22] First, determining the obligor's "income" for purposes of the support calculation can sometimes be quite difficult.[23] The difficulty is often exacerbated by the obligor's incentive and ability to manipulate his apparent income. To avoid these problems, Wisconsin courts, lawyers, and child support workers are reluctant to use percentage-expressed orders for self-employed obligors. In addition, Wisconsin administrators find it difficult to determine whether an order expressed as a percentage of income is in arrears.[24]

Enforcement problems should be minimal where most of the obligor's income comes from a stable job. Employers can compute the amount of child support without great difficulty even where expressed as a percentage of the obligor's income, making garnishment a viable option despite changes in income. Basing guidelines on gross income, as Wisconsin does, further simplifies the employer's task. The guidelines should also clarify which employee benefits are considered income and which deductions from income are permitted. Percentage-expressed orders could also be useful if obligor's income oscillates and the obligor could afford different levels of child support at different times. Of course, this situation might cause the custodial household some uncertainty.

5. Possible Improvements to a Percentage-Expressed Child Support Order

Although the percentage-expressed order has generally been disfavored, courts have been more receptive to a percentage-of-increase method.[25] The percentage-of-increase method expresses the child support award as a fixed amount, computed from the guidelines based on the information that exists at the time of the decree, plus a specified percentage of any future increase in the obligor's salary. While the percentage-expressed order automatically adjusts downward when an obligor is laid off, the percentage-of-increase method automatically adjusts only upward; to lower the amount owed, the obligor must initiate an action for a modification. From the perspective of the recipient, the percentage-of-increase order is better than the percentage-expressed order because the former guarantees the custodial parent a specified minimum amount and lack of compliance is easier to detect. Of course, the percentage-of-increase order is less desirable for the obligor because the order does not automatically adjust downward.

Other variations could make automatic adjustments acceptable to more courts. For example, courts have approved orders that set a maximum amount the obligation can increase, regardless of how much the obligor's income increases.[26] This limitation would ensure that pursuant to automatic adjustment the obligor's payment would not substantially exceed the child's needs and would reflect in part the finding that families' spending on children as a percentage of income decreases with increases in income.[27] Similarly, a percentage-expressed order could be adjusted to accommodate the concerns of low-income obligors. A self-support reserve could be specified so that low-income obligors would not have to pay support until the minimum income level had been reached, which occurs under the Melson child support formula as well as under some systems in countries such as Australia and England.

C. Allowing Automatic Adjustment of Child Support

The current rejection of automatic adjustment mechanisms places the custodial parent at a substantial disadvantage. The custodial parent's inadequate information, the cost of legal action, and the vague standard for modification all discourage modification actions. If the award is not modified, inflation and the higher cost of children as they age force the custodial parent to bear an increasing portion of child-related expenses. Causing the custodial parent to bear an increasing portion of such expenses seems unfair as a social policy and unjustifiable unless the problems of automatic adjustment are substantial.

Current American child support practice bestows great hardship on the custodial parent. Policymakers should consider some means of automatic adjustment to child support orders to avoid the necessity of subsequent judicial proceedings. Periodic COLA review, at a minimum, is needed. Expressing a child support order as a percentage of the obligor's income rather than as a fixed amount could be a useful adjustment system when the obligor has a relatively stable job. Because the percentage-expressed order focuses only on the obligor's income, it seems unlikely that it will be accepted in states applying the income-shares approach or the Melson approach. Also, another automatic adjustment mechanism will be needed even in percentage-of-income states where the obligor is not an employee with a relatively stable job. In these instances, a COLA system would be more desirable.

The percentage-expressed order is best suited for those states that base child support only on the obligor's income. Certain variations to the percentage-expressed order, such as the percentage-of-increase method, as well as other possible changes to percentage-expressed orders discussed earlier, could remedy concerns about the obligor's ability to pay, hardship on low-income obligors, the custodial parent's need for stable payments, and the ability of the order to reflect the decreasing percentage of income that families dedicate to child support as income rises. Percentage-expressed orders apparently do not, as some courts have feared, cause more underemployment than do fixed payment orders. Finally, percentage-expressed orders create some enforcement problems but seem to work fairly well for obligors whose income comes mainly from a stable job.

D. Modification Actions Will Remain Necessary Even with Automatic Adjustment

Although automatic adjustment mechanisms will to some extent reduce the need for postdecree modification, such changes will remain necessary even if automatic adjustment is accepted. No automatic adjustment system addresses a substantial increase in the needs of the child. Also, no automatic adjustment mechanism considers what should occur if a parent establishes a new permanent relationship. If the guideline permits a court to consider the income of a new partner or an obligation to support a new partner (or additional children or stepchildren), new relationships could be grounds for modification of the child support award.[28] Some states allow modification for an obligor who assumes additional support obligations.[29] Substantial changes in the visitation arrangements may also justify modification (Melli and Brown 1994). Further, a COLA provision will not always keep up with postdecree increases in the obligor's income.

A recent pilot program was conducted to study, among other things, the extent to which old fixed-amount orders required modification. This study found that of the orders studied, relatively few that were more than three years old required adjustment. Of those that did, however, almost all were too low. The new orders were based on the child support guidelines then in effect and on each parent's current income. Of those orders that increased, the amount of the increase was significantly higher than what would have resulted with a COLA increase from the time of initial order (Caliber Associates 1992:172–85).

Depending on the automatic adjustment mechanism chosen, other situations would necessitate a modification. For example, even a COLA system requires modification if obligors are laid off or if their income substantially changes. Such would not be the case if child support was expressed as a percentage of the obligor's income but would be if the order were a percentage-of-increase order. If no automatic adjustment system is accepted, the need for modification would be even more pressing.

Federal Rules Regarding Child Support Modification

Recognizing that awards' failure to change over time has been a major cause of inadequate child support amounts, Congress has responded to the need for better ways to modify child support awards in the Family Support Act of 1988 and more recently in the Personal Responsibility and Work Opportunity Act of 1996 (the welfare-reform act).

The welfare-reform act[30] clearly establishes that the traditional American "substantial change in circumstances" rule is largely superseded, at least for those parents whose claims are being enforced by a child support enforcement agency. The law requires the states to review and adjust all child support orders for parents being served by a IV-D (child support enforcement) agency at least once every three years on request of the parent or, if the child is receiving welfare, on request of the state. If a parent seeks modification pursuant to this three-year review, the parent need not show a substantial change in circumstances. However, a showing of substantial change of circumstances is still required for any modification apart from the three-year cycle.

The welfare-reform act gives the states three possible ways to perform the three-year reviews: (1) applying the state child support guidelines to determine if the amount of the award differs from what it would currently be under the guidelines and, if appropriate, to adjust the order; (2) applying a COLA to the order under a formula developed by the state; or (3) using automated methods, including automated comparisons with wage or state income tax data, to identify orders eligible for review and make adjustments under standards established by the state. If the state chooses either the cost-of-living or automated review, it must permit either party to contest the adjustment and request that the support order be adjusted in accordance with the state's child support guidelines.

In addition to modifications resulting from the three-year cycle of review, the welfare-reform act provides for support-order modification on a showing of a change of circumstances—the traditional basis for modifying an award. However, once a showing of a change of circumstances has been made, the modification must be made in accordance with the state child support guidelines. Therefore, the child support guidelines remain the benchmark in these cases.

The welfare-reform rules on updating child support orders have been criticized because they do not require that child support awards be updated periodically. This issue is discussed later in this chapter.

New Ideas Regarding Child Support Modification

In most states, child support orders are expressed as fixed amounts, subject to modification only on a showing of a substantial and unforeseen change of circumstances (Clark 1988:727) (except for actions filed by a child support enforcement agency in connection with a three-year review). As stated earlier, custodial parents must assess their chances in modification actions without information about the obligors' financial situations or guidance in understanding what comprises a substantial change in circumstances. Although allowing automatic adjustment of child support will reduce the importance of modification for some parents, modification will still be needed in many instances. The continuing need to allow child support modification requires new ideas to better remedy the problems facing custodial parents. A number of relatively simple changes would improve the system governing modification of child support.

A. Information Exchange

Few states today make any effort to provide a parent with information about postdecree changes in the financial condition of the other parent.[31] Even if a parent is willing to devote the resources needed to pursue a modification proceeding, a parent still generally has little information to determine whether it would be wise to initiate a modification proceeding. It is likely that this lack of information more often than not works to the disadvantage of the custodial parent. If the custodial parent does not learn of any significant raises received by the other parent, the custodial parent may well defer or never initiate an action to increase child support, even though the action would have been successful. Of course, the lack of information could have the opposite effect if the custodial parent's income has significantly increased and the other parent is unaware of this change.

Some means should be found to provide an accurate periodic exchange of information between parents. One simple way of doing this would be to require parents to exchange copies of their tax returns by 1 May of each year. Such a procedure would be less than perfect. Some parents never file tax returns. Even if they do, there is no guarantee that the tax return is truthful. Also, if the parent has remarried and filed a joint return, the information would not be as useful, because the income of a new spouse, which would be included in the tax return, is not generally included in the guideline calculation. Still, such a procedure in many instances could give parents at least a rough idea of each other's financial condition. Also, tax returns include information other than wages that could be relevant to a child support determination, such as interest, rents, investment income, royalties, and capital gains.[32] This proposed disclosure procedure would require no direct governmental involvement. Also, it would not require the parties to draft an additional disclosure document; they merely would have to copy a document already created for another purpose. To verify the accuracy of the information exchanged, parents could be asked also to forward copies of their most recent W-2s as well as their most recent pay stubs (if the parents are salaried employees).

B. New Uses for and Changes in Child Support Guidelines

1. Various Possible Standards for Modification Actions

To integrate guidelines into the modification process, a number of different options are possible regarding the current system of modifying child support orders expressed as fixed amounts. For example, a state could abandon the substantial-change-of-circumstances concept and permit parents to file modification actions whenever they choose. The child support would be recomputed based on the guidelines and the parties' financial situation at that time. A few states have accepted this approach.[33] One fairly obvious benefit of the substantial-change-of-circumstances rule is that it attempts to balance the costs of the modification proceeding against the resulting benefit. In view of the legal and emotional costs of a modification action as well as the concomitant burden on courts, it seems wise to place some reasonable limits on a parent's right to initiate a modification action.

2. Establishing an Objective Standard for Modification Actions

A number of possible limits to modification actions are available. One alternative would be to limit the frequency of modification actions. For example, a parent could be barred from initiating a modification action for two years after any support action; some exception would be necessary for extreme hardship.[34] However, time-based modification rules focus on the wrong factor.

Another alternative would be to use the guidelines as an objective standard of substantial change of circumstances. Guidelines can provide an objective standard for child support modification actions by equating substantial change of circumstances with a deviation beyond a specified percentage between the original child support award (or the most recent revision) and the amount that would currently be awarded under the guidelines. The exact percentage chosen would depend on judgments about the appropriate balance between updating awards and judicial economy. Some precedent exists for choosing 10 percent, 15 percent, 20 percent, or 25 percent.[35] If the presumptive award would deviate from the current order by at least the prescribed percentage, the modification action generally should be permitted.[36] Of course, under such a system the moving party could also establish a substantial change in circumstances by other means, such as by showing a substantial change in the child's needs.

The objective standard for what constitutes a substantial change in circumstances should only create a rebuttable presumption that such a change has occurred. Therefore, if circumstances initially justified a deviation from the guidelines at the time of the entry of the order, and those circumstances remain unchanged, the presumption would be rebutted despite the deviation between the current award and the presumptive amount based on the guideline. Similarly, circumstances that now justify a deviation from the guidelines will rebut the presumption even if the initial order was based on the guidelines.

This proposed objective standard for what constitutes a substantial change in circumstances might permit more modification actions than the current standard, thereby potentially increasing court caseloads. Of course, because the proposed standard clearly establishes what needs to be shown to presumptively obtain a modification of the order, such an objective standard might actually reduce judicial caseload by both reducing unsuccessful filings and encouraging settlement where modification is indicated. Even if this proposed standard for modification would increase judicial caseloads, such a result should not cause this alternative regime to be rejected. First, a number of methods exist for easing burdens imposed on courts as a result of child support modification actions. One example is New Jersey's system of hiring hearing officers to handle almost all modification actions under judges' supervision. The result proposed by the hearing officer is then forwarded to the judge for final approval.[37] Also, even if this standard would increase judicial caseloads, this cost should not outweigh the societal benefits of updating child support orders to reflect parents' current circumstances.

3. Address Other Foreseeable Changes of Circumstances in the Guidelines

Guidelines will be less useful in modification actions if they do not address what should occur if either parent remarries or assumes responsibility for other children (Oldham 1990). An increasing number of guidelines do address such problems. For example, of the twenty-three states whose guidelines discuss what should occur if a parent establishes a new significant relationship, about half allow courts to consider the income of the new partner, while the other half forbid it (Judicial Council of California 1993:74–76; National Center for State Courts 1990:711). Some guidelines that specify how courts should calculate child support awards where the obligor has subsequent children do not allow downward modification, while others permit it, with some specifying how to make the calculation and others giving the court discretion regarding the amount of the appropriate reduction (National Center for State Courts 1990:121, 759). To the extent that guidelines do not clearly specify how to treat these common postdecree changes in parties' lives, the parties will not be able to predict the outcome of any contemplated modification action, thereby reducing the utility of guidelines in these situations.[38]

C. Provide Only Limited Automatic Periodic Review and Adjustment

As stated earlier, in response to recommendations that orders should be reviewed automatically and periodically, Congress has mandated that custodial parents being serviced by a IV-D agency be informed every three years of their right to attempt to modify the applicable child support order.

In an attempt to learn more about the costs and benefits of an automatic periodic review program, in 1992 Congress funded pilot programs in four states—Florida, Illinois, Delaware, and Colorado (Caliber Associates 1992). In these programs, custodial parents whose orders were at least three years old were randomly selected. If the parents were receiving AFDC benefits, the orders were automatically reviewed; other parents were contacted and informed that they could have their orders reviewed for possible modification.

This pilot project led to two surprising findings. First, a significant number of custodial parents did not want their orders reviewed. When contacted, parents gave a number of reasons for declining review. Some explanations were to be expected. For example, some parents were not receiving any child support and believed a review of the order would not be useful. Others were reluctant to go to court or thought that the obligors were paying all they could afford. Other explanations were not as obvious. A surprising number of parents did not consent to reviews because they did not want to undermine what they felt were good relationships with obligors. If the relationships were undermined, custodial parents were concerned that obligors would be less reliable regarding the payment of child support. Other custodial parents were concerned that their child support orders would be decreased rather than increased (Caliber Associates 1992:128–44, 229–36.)

Another finding is related to the first. Of the cases selected where the parents were not receiving AFDC, a surprisingly small percentage (6 percent) of the orders were modified. Although this finding may result in part from the low rate of consent to the review process, even among those consenting to review a full review of financial information was often unnecessary because the youngest child had become emancipated, the obligor was dead, no enforceable order existed, the agency could not locate the noncustodial parent, or the need for modification was otherwise obviously foreclosed.

Although only about 10 percent of all cases selected resulted in modification (15 percent of AFDC cases, 6 percent of non-AFDC cases), the modification was significant when it occurred: 85 percent of the AFDC cases receiving a full review were increased, 5 percent were reduced, and the rest remained unchanged. The result for parents not receiving AFDC benefits was lower: 77 percent of all such orders were increased, 8 percent were decreased, and 15 percent were unchanged. Of parents with AFDC benefits, orders, when modified, were increased an average of 115 percent. Of parents not receiving AFDC, the average increase amounted to 66 percent. These amounts were significantly higher than what would have occurred with COLA increases from the date of the order. There was a positive correlation between the age of the order and the percentage increase (Caliber Associates 1992:147–85).

The pilot project findings cast some doubt on the wisdom of automatic review of support orders at certain prescribed intervals. Substantial effort was expended to modify a relatively small percentage of the orders reviewed. If one of the automatic adjustment mechanisms suggested previously had been employed in the initial orders, an even smaller percentage of orders presumably would have been modified. It can be argued that, if an automatic adjustment mechanism for support is accepted, periodic review of all orders should not be automatic. Instead, either parent should be able to request a calculation of the presumptive child support amount that would result based on the parents' current financial information (see Reggio and Harhai 1993:8). If the state adopts an objective standard for a substantial change in circumstances and a program for exchange of financial information, as suggested earlier, parents should then be fairly certain whether modification would be possible and could act accordingly.

D. Establish a More User-Friendly Modification System

In most states, a party must initiate a judicial proceeding to modify a child support order. This process usually requires retaining a lawyer and therefore can be expensive. With the advent of guidelines and the growing tendency to define objectively what would presumptively establish a substantial change of circumstances, some states are now experimenting with various simplified procedures for modifying child support.

For example, a recent study proposed a system for pro se child support modification. Also, other states (and countries) are developing administrative procedures for child support modification. These developments could offer cheaper and more convenient procedures for parents who need to modify child support orders.

Alternate dispute resolution could also help. For example, if a petition to modify a child support order is filed in Delaware, mediation is mandatory, and mediators are provided. The parties are required to bring income verification (pay stubs and so forth) to the mediation.[39]

Conclusion

In almost all states, child support obligations are expressed as fixed amounts. Historically, this amount was not adjusted or modified unless parents could establish that the circumstances of one of the parents or the child had materially changed. This approach erodes the real value of child support unless the custodial parent initiates a new legal proceeding and is unfair to that parent. At a minimum, child support expressed as a fixed amount should periodically be adjusted automatically for increases in the cost of living. Alternatively, the child support obligation could be expressed as a percentage of the obligor's income, not as a fixed amount (or as a fixed amount plus a percentage of the obligor's income above a certain amount), with a minimum self-support reserve deducted and a specified cap for high-income obligors. Such a system could work well if the obligor has a stable job. This procedure would allow the award to adjust to changes in the obligor's financial situation without further court action. In most instances, either adjustment mechanism will result in higher awards for custodial families (Bartfeld and Garfinkel 1994:12).

Rules for modification of child support orders should be clarified. It would be unwise to let either parent obtain a modification whenever the application of the guideline would result in a minor change in the amount of child support owed. Some minimum threshold would be appropriate. Except in child support enforcement cases, orders currently may not be modified unless a parent proves the circumstances of one of the parties have substantially changed. No objective standard is provided in most states. The substantial-change-in-circumstances standard grants judges too much discretion and provides too little guidance to the parties, thereby potentially discouraging some valid claims and encouraging some spurious ones. If an objective standard for what presumptively constituted a substantial change in circumstances could be established, parents would have guidance regarding when modification would be successful, and consistent results would be facilitated. In addition, such an objective standard would encourage valid claims and discourage claims where the change in child support would not be significant.

Furthermore, spouses should be obligated to exchange financial information periodically, so each parent could judge (based on the promulgated objective standard) whether modification of child support would be possible. Given the complexity of many guidelines, state child support agencies should hire employees to calculate, on the request of either parent, the presumptive amount of child support owed based on the current circumstances of the parties. This information obviously would help parents determine whether modifications would be warranted.

NOTES

1. Child support orders would be 25 percent to 32 percent higher if adjusted for inflation, depending on the period and inflation rate being studied (Beller and Graham 1993:37–40). An order of $500 in 1976 would have declined in value to $261 by 1986 unless modified (Phelps and Miller 1988:210).

2. See generally, *In re Marriage of Stamp,* 300 N.W.2d 275 (Iowa 1980); *H.P.A. v. S.C.A.,* 704 P. 2d 205 (Alaska 1986); *Brevick v. Brevick,* 628 P.2d 599 (Ariz. Ct. App. 1981); *Branstad v. Branstad,* 400 N.E.2d 167 (Ind. Ct. App. 1980); *Hempton v. Hempton,* 329 N.W.2d 514 (Mich. Ct. App. 1982); *Bradley v. Earl,* 491 N.Y.S.2d 709 (App. Div. 1985); *Roya v. Roya,* 494 A.2d 132, 133–34 (Vt. 1985).

3. *In re Marriage of Phipps,* 379 N.W 2d 26, 29 (Iowa Ct. App. 1986); see also *Falls v. Falls,* 278 S.E.2d 546 (N.C. Ct. App. 1981).

4. *Edwards v. Edwards,* 665 P.2d 883 (Wash. 1983) (en banc). Another case that disapproves of court-ordered COLAs is *Morgan v. Ackerman,* 964 S.W. 2d 865 (Mo. App. 1998).

5. Minn. Stat. Ann. § 518.641 (West Supp. 1994).

6. See *In re Marriage of Garvis,* 411 N.W.2d 703 (Iowa Ct. App. 1987), *Roya v. Roya.*

7. See *McNeil v. McNeil,* 607 So.2d 1192, 1197 (Miss. 1992); *Wing v. Wing,* 549 So.2d 944, 948 (Miss. 1989); *Bradley v. Earl.*

8. Compare *In re Marriage of Pfeffer,* 443 N.W.2d 92, 95 (Iowa Ct. App. 1989) (deleting from the order an annual increase of 8 percent) with *Wallace v. Wallace,* 661 P.2d 455, 457 (Mont. 1983) (approving a provision calling for a 5 percent annual increase). See also *Morrison v. Kirkland,* 567 So.2d 363, 364 (Ala. Civ. App. 1990) (rejecting an order calling for a fifty-dollar-per-month increase every few years in the amount of child support due). Other courts have disapproved COLA provisions where the custodial parent earns a significant salary and receives a substantial amount of property at divorce. See *In re Marriage of Brown,* 462 N.W.2d 683, 685 (Iowa Ct. App. 1990).

9. Author's interview with Len Biernat, Hamline Law School; author's interview with Karen Smigielski, Office of Child Support Enforcement. For example, in 1995 34,369 cases were included within the Minnesota COLA process. The average increase in child support was $15.12 per month. The costs of the program were approximately $25,000, less than one dollar per case. Author's interview with Sherri Newes, Minnesota Department of Human Services.

10. See, e.g, *In re Marriage of Ferguson,* 566 N.E.2d 335 (Ill. App. Ct. 1990) (construing Ill. Rev. Stat. ch. 40, para. 505[a][5] [1989]); *In re Marriage of Mitchell,* 692 N.E.2d 281 (Ill. 1998) (child support must be determined by a fixed dollar amount and not ordered as a percentage of income). But see *Singletary v. Singletary,* 24 Fam. L. Rep. (BNA) 1048 (Ill. App. 1997) (where the Illinois court upheld a decree that ordered the obligor to pay $864 or 20 percent of his income, whichever was higher).

11. *Newsome v. Newsome,* 227 S.E.2d 347, 348–49 (Ga. 1976) (disapproving percentage-of-income method). Some state guidelines arrive at the amount of child support due by multiplying the obligor's income by a specified percentage. The child support obligation is expressed as a fixed amount, however.

12. See, e.g., *Marriage of Mitchell,* 1998 Ill. Lexis 351. Some courts have found that the percentage-of-income method is invalid under child support statutes allowing modification only under a substantial-change-in-circumstances standard because not every increase in income constitutes a substantial change in circumstances. See *Grover v. Grover,* 839 P.2d 871, 873 (Utah Ct. App. 1992).

13. Some courts, apparently uncomfortable with departures from the American rule, merely reiterate the idea that child support should be expressed in the form of a fixed dollar amount and that it should only be altered via a modification action after the court has heard all relevant information. See, e.g., *Breen v. Breen,* 471 N.Y.S.2d 617 (App. Div. 1984).

14. *Harris v. Harris,* 24 Fam. L. Rep. (BNA) 1352 (Vt. 1998).

15. See *Doss v. Doss,* 521 S.W.2d 709 (Tex. Civ. App. 1976). See also *Kittredge v. Kittredge,* 911 P.2d 903 (Okla. 1995); *Malone v. Malone,* 637 So. 2d 76 (Fla. Dist. Ct. App. 1994) (summarized in 20 Fam. L. Rep. [BNA] 1361 [1994]).

16. *Herron v. Herron,* 457 N.E. 2d 564 (Ind. App. 1983).

17. See, e.g., *Euston v. Euston,* 759 S.W.2d 788, 789 (Tex. Ct. App. 1988).

18. Id.; *Hunter v. Hunter,* 498 N.E.2d 1278, 1288 (Ind. Ct. App. 1986); see also *In re Marriage of Meeker,* 272 N.W.2d 455, 456 (Iowa 1978); *Stanaway v. Stanaway,* 245 N.W.2d 723, 725 (Mich. Ct. App. 1976); *Thrash v. Thrash,* 809 P.2d 665,

667 (Okla. 1991) (holding that court has no authority to order such an award but that parties may agree to it); *Picker v. Vollenhover,* 290 P.2d 789, 801 (Or. 1956); *Hood v. Hood,* 335 N.W.2d 349 (S.D. 1983); *Karim v. Karim,* 290 N.W.2d 479 (S.D. 1980); *Barlow v. Barlow,* 282 S.W.2d 429, 431 (Tex. Ct. App. 1995); *Grover v. Grover,* 873; *Jacobs v. Jacobs,* 254 S.E.2d 56 (Va. 1979); *Keyser v. Keyser,* 345 S.E.2d 12 (Va. Ct. App. 1986).

19. *Brevick v. Brevick,* 602 (rejecting a child support award expressed as 30 percent of the obligor's income); see also *Chasin v. Chasin,* 582 N.Y.S.2d 512, 514 (App. Div. 1992).

20. Id.; *Hunter v. Hunter,* 1288; see also *In re Marriage of Meeker,* 456; *Stanaway v. Stanaway,* 725; *Thrash v. Thrash,* 667 (holding that the court has no authority to order such an award but that parties may agree to it); *Picker v. Vollenhover,* 801; *Hood v. Hood; Karim v. Karim; Barlow v. Barlow,* 431; *Grover v. Grover,* 873; *Jacobs v. Jacobs; Keyser v. Keyser.*

21. See *Roszko v. Roszko,* 705 P.2d 951, 954 (Ariz. Ct. App. 1985). Under the American rule, voluntary reduction of postdecree income generally is not grounds for a modification of the child support award. See *In re Marriage of Powell,* 474 N.W.2d 531, 534 (Iowa 1991). A substantial body of case law, exemplified by these cases, discusses the possibility of underemployment. The question usually arises when the obligor petitions to reduce his child support obligation to reflect a postdecree salary decrease.

22. *Breiner v. Breiner,* 236 N.W.2d 846 (Neb. 1975); see also *Means v. Means,* 511 N.E.2d 323 (Ind. Ct. App. 1987); *Di Tolvo v. Di Tolvo,* 328 A.2d 625 (N.J. Super. Ct. App. Div. 1974), *rev'd sub nom. Petersen v. Petersen,* 428 A.2d 1301, 1303–4 (N.J. 1981); *Provenzano v. Provenzano,* 418 N.Y.S.2d 140 (App. Div. 1979).

23. See, e.g., *In re Marriage of Winne,* 606 N.E.2d 777, 783–84 (Ill. App. Ct. 1992) (considering whether amounts allocated by an employer to the parent's capital account were "income" for purposes of the child support guideline); *Mabee v. Mabee,* 617 A.2d 162, 164 (Vt. 1992) (discussing whether capital gains are income).

24. Letters from Gregg Herman, Bonnie Abramoff, Case, Drinka, and Diel, 17 June 1994 (on file with author); author's interview with Connie Chesnick, Wisconsin Department of Health and Social Services, 4 March 1994; letters from Bonnie Abramoff, Carlo Esqueda, Dane County (Wisconsin) Courts Division Manager, 7 June 1994 (on file with the author).

25. See, e.g, *Roszko v. Roszko,* 954 (upholding percentage-of-increase method); *Hayes v. Hayes,* 283 S.E.2d 875 (Ga. 1981); *Jensen v. Jensen,* 629 P.2d 765 (Mont. 1981); *Heinze v. Heinze,* 444 A.2d 559 (N.H. 1982); *Henderson v. Lekvold,* 621 P.2d 505 (N.M. 1980); *In re Marriage of Mahalingam,* 584 P.2d 971 (Wash. Ct. App. 1978); *Madison v. Madison,* 859 P.2d 1276 (Wyo. 1993). Kansas has approved this type of order in a maintenance award (*Marriage of Monslow,* 912 P.2d 735 [Kan. 1996]).

26. *Anneberg v. Anneberg,* 116 N.W.2d 794 (Mich. 1962); *Stanaway v. Stanaway,* 724–25 (order invalidated because no maximum amount was set forth); *Edwards v. Edwards.* But see *Hakken v. Hakken,* 298 N.W.2d 907 (Mich. Ct. App. 1980) (finding that ceilings are not required for escalator clauses).

27. Some guidelines provide that escalator clauses apply only up to a certain level of income. See, e.g., Tex. Fam. Code Ann. § 14.055(c) (West Supp. 1994); *Chasin v. Chasin; Nebraska Child Supp. Guidelines* Para. O (1 January 1990), National Center for State Courts 1990:582.

28. Not all guidelines expressly permit, and some forbid, courts' consideration of the income or needs of a new partner. See, e.g, Minn. Stat. § 518.551(5)(b)(1) (West Supp. 1994) (not providing for this consideration but allowing consideration of other factors); Tex. Fam. Code Ann. § 154.069 (West Supp. 1997) (not providing for this consideration but allowing consideration of other factors); Alaska R. Civ. P. 90.3 cmt. (6)(B)(6) (1994); Idaho R. Civ. P. 6(c)(6) (1994); id. 6(a)(4); *Ariz. Child Supp. Guidelines* part 5(f) (31 December 1989), in National Center for State Courts 1990:41; *Del. Child Supp. Formula* part III (January 1990), in National Center for State Courts 1990:121. In contrast, some guidelines direct courts to consider new partners. See, e.g, N.D. Guidelines for Absent Parent Child Supp. part IV, in National Center for State Courts 1990:710–12.

29. Some states do not permit a court to consider such obligations incurred after the entry of the initial decree. (See Judicial Council of California 1993:75–77). A number of other states permit courts to consider such children. See, e.g, Iowa Code Ann. § 598.21 (West 1981); Mo. Civ. P. Form no. 14 cmt. (Presumed Child Support Amount Calculation Worksheet). Under a third approach, some states do not permit an obligor to decrease child support due to subsequent children but permit the obligor to present evidence of subsequent children in response to a petition to increase child support. See, e.g., N.M. Stat. Ann. § 40-4-11.1(C)(2)(e) (Michie Supp. 1993); *Colo. Child Supp. Guideline* part III(B) (September 1986), in National Center for State Courts 1990:90; *Del. Child Supp. Formula* § III part X (25 January 1990), in National Center for State Courts 1990:124.

30. 42 U.S.C. § 666(a)(10) Review and Adjustment of Support Orders on Request.

31. Compare Colo. Rev. Stat. § 14-10-115(3)(b)(II) (West Supp. 1993) (providing that a court may, if it wishes, require an annual exchange of financial information). Guidelines proposed in 1996 for Canada would require an obligor to provide annual income information to the recipient. See Working Draft of (Canadian) Federal Child Support Guidelines 1996:§ 23.

32. Some guidelines include investments and royalties as income when computing the presumptive child support obligation. See, e.g., N.H. Rev. Stat. Ann. § 458-C:2(IV) (1992); Ohio Rev. Code Ann. § 3113.215(A)(2) (Supp. 1993); 231 Pa. Code § 1910.16-5 (Supp. 1994); Tex. Fam. Code Ann. § 154.062.

33. Washington apparently does permit a modification action without a showing of a substantial change in circumstances if the order has not been modified within two years. See Wash. Rev. Code § 26.09.170(8) (West Supp. 1994). North Dakota does not require a showing of a substantial change in circumstances if the order has not been modified for one year. N.D. Code § 14-09-08.4. Delaware permits a modification if the child support award would be changed by twenty-five dollars. *See* Del. Child Supp. Formula part X (January 1990), in National Center for State Courts 1990:124. In Massachusetts as of 1994, child support orders may be modified if the order is inconsistent with the guidelines (An Act to Improve the

Economic Security of Children of the Commonwealth, 1993 Mass. Acts ch. 460 [amending Mass. Gen. L. Ann. Ch. 119A, §§ 1, 13; id. Ch. 208, §§ 28, 28A (West 1994)]).

34. A few states have adopted similar approaches. See. e.g., Wash. Rev. Code § 26.09.170 (West Supp. 1994) (permitting a child support modification without requiring a change in circumstances if the order has not been modified within the previous twenty-four months but requiring such a showing if the decree has been modified within the past twenty-four months); Haw. Rev. Stat. Ann. Sec. 580–47(e) (permitting a modification without a showing of a change in circumstances if the order has not been modified for at least three years); American Law Institute, Principles of the Law of Family Dissolution, Tentative Draft no. 3, part II, (8 April 1998), § 3.22 (same). Also, federal legislation now permits modification every three years in IV-D actions without showing a change in circumstances.

35. See *In re Marriage of Pugliese,* 761 P.2d 277 (Colo. Ct. App. 1988); Vt. Stat. An. Tit. 15, § 660(b); Conn. Gen. Stat. § 46b-86; Fla. Stat. § 61.30; Ky. Rev. Stat. Ann. § 403.213(2) (Michie/Bobbs-Merrill Supp. 1992); Utah Code sec. 78-45-7.2; Ind. Code Ann. § 31-1-11.5-17 (Burns Supp. 1994); La. Rev. Stat. Ann. § 9:311.

36. Some states would not permit a modification unless the order has not been modified for a certain minimum period. For example, in Indiana and New Mexico the order must not have been modified for at least twelve months (Ind. Stat. Ann. § 31-15-7-3; N.M. Stat. Ann. § 40-4-11.4). In Utah, the order must not have been modified for at least three years (Utah Code § 78-45-7.2).

It is unclear how such a system would deal with a situation where the noncustodial parent was not initially ordered to pay any support and the modification action is to obtain some support. For an example of a court dealing with this issue under the traditional rule, see *S.A.B.S. v. H.B.,* 767 S.W.2d 860 (Tex. Ct. App. 1989).

37. Author's interview with Raymond Rainvill, New Jersey Administrative Office of Courts, 9 May 1994.

38. See, e.g., *In re Marriage of Ladely,* 469 N.W.2d 663, 665–66 (Iowa 1991) (providing little guidance to lower courts regarding how to respond when the obligor has additional children). See also *In re Marriage of Linberg,* 462 N.W.2d 698, 701 (Iowa Ct. App. 1990) (opining that trial courts could "consider" the income of a stepparent).

39. Letter from Barbara Corrozi, Delaware Family Court, 21 November 1995 (on file with author).

REFERENCES

Bartfeld, Judi, and Irwin Garfinkel. 1994. *Utilization and Effects of Payments on Percentage-Expressed Child Support Orders.* June. Madison, WI: Institute for Research on Poverty.

Beller, Andrea H., and John W. Graham. 1993. *Small Change: The Economics of Child Support.* New Haven: Yale University Press.

Caliber Associates. 1992. *Evaluation of Child Support Review and Modification*

Demonstration Projects in Four States: Cross-Site Final Report. Fairfax, VA: Caliber Associates.

Clark, Homer H. 1988. *The Law of Domestic Relations in the United States.* 2d ed. St. Paul, MN: West Publishing.

Eden, Philip. 1979. How Inflation Flaunts the Court's Orders. *Family Advocate* 1 (spring): 2–6.

Glendon, Mary Ann. 1989. *The Transformation of Family Law.* Chicago: University of Chicago Press.

Judicial Council of California. 1993. *Review of Statewide Uniform Child Support Guideline.* December. San Francisco: Judicial Council of California.

Klawitter, Marieka M. 1994. Child Support Awards and the Earnings of Divorced Noncustodial Fathers. *Social Science Review* 68:351–68.

Lazear, Edward P., and Robert T. Michael. 1988. *Allocation of Income within the Household.* Chicago: University of Chicago Press.

Lewin, Tamar. 1994. Private Firms Help Single Parents Get What's Due. *New York Times,* 21 May, A1.

Melli, Marygold S., and Patricia Brown. 1994. The Economics of Shared Custody. *Houston Law Review* 31:543–84.

National Center for State Courts. 1990. *Child Support Guidelines: A Compendium.* Arlington, VA: National Center for State Courts.

Oldham, J. Thomas. 1992. Putting Asunder in the 1990s. *California Law Review* 80:1091–132.

Phelps, Gale M., and Jerald M. Miller. 1988. The New Indiana Child Support Guidelines. *Indiana Law Review* 22:203–27.

Raggio, Kenneth C. and Stephen J. Harhai. 1993. Tools of the Trade: Make Excel a Family Law Power Tool. *Family Advocate* 15(winter):6–8, 12.

Robins, Philip K. 1992. Why Did Child Support Award Levels Decrease from 1978 to 1985? *Journal of Human Resources* 27:362–79.

Sidel, Ruth. 1986. *Women and Children Last.* New York: Viking.

Williams, Robert G. 1987. Guidelines for Setting Levels of Child Support Orders. *Family Law Quarterly* 21:281–324.

Part IV

Child Support: The Experience Elsewhere

Child Support as Distributive and Commutative Justice: The United Kingdom Experience

John Eekelaar

This chapter describes the experience of implementing reforms in the U.K. child support system. The chapter examines that experience from three perspectives: the goals of child support schemes, the conceptions of justice underlying the reform, and finally the choice of an administrative or judicial forum. The chapter explores two conceptions of justice underlying the purpose of child support—distributive and commutative justice—and illustrates how pursuit of one form of justice at the expense of the other in the U.K. reform resulted in a painful aftermath. This chapter examines the U.K. government's rationale in changing its child support scheme from a primarily judicial system to one that is primarily administrative and concludes that the system's structure may be immaterial to achieving child support goals.

Child Support Goals and Conceptions of Justice

Before describing the U.K. child support scheme and the dramatic public response to its implementation, it is useful to first examine the government's goals in initiating these changes. What might be the objectives of a good child support scheme? The primary aim must be to ensure that realistic levels of support are awarded so that every child who is living with only one parent has the benefit of sustained economic support from the absent parent at a meaningful level.[1] Another objective must be to achieve consistency in the awards made in comparable circumstances. Also, an overriding purpose of governments in initiating child support reforms has been to recoup from liable parents as much as possible of what the state is spending on their children through social security budgets. welfare budget reduction can be a goal in itself.

The U.K. government stated all three goals when in 1993 it moved from a judicial to an administrative model (Maclean and Eekelaar 1993;

Maclean 1994). The government added one further policy aim: to diminish legal costs by removing child support from the legal arena. All but this last goal are consistent with using either model and have been embraced by proponents of both. Therefore, the choice between the models does not seem to be dictated by the objectives pursued, unless reducing court-related costs has become an end in itself.

So realistic levels, award consistency, and welfare budget reduction are, in principle, achievable through either the court system or by administrative means. There exists, however, a deeper methodological divergence between the judicial and administrative models. It involves the well-known dichotomy between rule-based and discretion-based decisions, but that distinction does not completely explain the divergence. The rule-discretion dichotomy appears here as the contrast between formula-based decisions and guided discretionary decisions. Like the rule-discretion dichotomy, the contrast between these types of decisions is more one of degree than of kind; they represent opposite ends of a continuum (Schneider 1993).

The deeper issue, which is related to but not explained by this divergence, concerns two contrasting but complementary conceptions of justice underlying the purpose of ordering child support payments. One corresponds to distributive justice, which can crudely be seen as concerned with the distribution of common resources among groups of people (Finnis 1980; Morris 1995). Distributive justice is seen in the community standard setting a proportion of a parent's income (in the circumstances of separation from the child) for supporting that child, either by payment to the child's custodian or to the state on behalf of the custodian. The other conception, usually called commutative[2] justice, seeks to establish or reestablish some kind of equilibrium between the parents, taking into account a broader range of present and past circumstances and interactions.

The goals of distributive justice may be more easily met through formulaic decision making; those of commutative justice, through guided discretionary techniques. These conceptions of justice help to explain the difference between conceiving child support in terms of an obligation to discharge a basic and fundamental duty toward a child and seeing it as a broader device of balancing the income between two family groups (income sharing). In "A Comparative Approach to Child Support Systems: Legal Rules and Social Policies" (in this volume), Mavis Maclean and Andrea Warman characterize these two conceptions as a "predominantly legal approach" and a "predominantly social policy approach." That chapter should be read alongside this one.

Administrative and Judicial Models

Although the United Kingdom chose to implement a formula-based scheme using an administrative model, an examination of the way child support is handled in several countries illustrates that formula-based methods may be equally consistent with either judicial or administrative models.

In Denmark, where the state makes advance payments to mothers and underwrites fathers' obligations to support their children, an administrative mechanism sets the amount of child support according to well-established rules. In West Germany prior to unification, child support payments were set by regional courts in an essentially bureaucratic process. The common features of these schemes are more important than the difference between using administrative or judicial settings: first, both schemes operate according to standardized tables that relate payments to debtors' incomes and to the number and ages of children; second, both plans are not designed to achieve a balance of equity between two households but instead to ensure a basic level of child support from an absent parent, some of which will be met by the state if the debtor defaults. The average payments are therefore relatively low proportions of debtors' net incomes—for two children, around 10 percent. The schemes also run out when the debtor's earnings reach between 50 and 75 percent of average male earnings. In short, they operate in a relatively narrow range of income and determine relatively small but precise sums (Knudsen 1988; Willenbacher and Voegeli 1992; Willenbacher 1996; Dr. Linda Nielsen, personal communication).

In contrast, the American guidelines illustrate a judicial model that is more complex than these European examples. Rather than provide a quasi-subsistence level of support for children, the American system seeks to achieve a just sharing of income between the parents through one of two methods. The first method adds together the incomes of both parents and apportions the child support obligation between them. The second method, which is closer to the European examples, deducts a straight percentage from the debtor's income and is subject to discretionary adjustment when the recipient's income is large enough to become a factor. The objective of both methods is to achieve a conclusion that approximates what the absent parent would spend on the children if the separation had not occurred and his or her entire income was still available to the remnant family unit. Not surprisingly, this result is far more difficult to achieve than the simpler European objective, and by maintaining adjudication within the court system, it has been possible to take into account a wide range of equities between the parties, especially in complex family situations (Takas 1992, giving examples of practitioners persuading courts to make discretionary adjustments for complex families).

Australia and New Zealand employ derivatives of the American formula-based income-sharing schemes for establishing child support. New Zealand exemplifies how expanding the scope of factors to be considered complicates the use of percentage-of-income formulas and provides more opportunities for discretionary adjustment. There, an administrative agency situated in the Inland Revenue Department implemented a system that has among its objectives ensuring "that equity exists between custodial and noncustodial parents, in respect of the costs of supporting children." This system allowed formula-based awards to be adjusted by the courts through "departure" orders that take into account the parties' respective financial positions and any hardship the formula award might create (Child Support Act 1991:§§4[h] and 105). The courts have been sparing in their exercise of discretion, resulting in a sense of grievance and feeling of injustice among applicants for such orders (Atkin 1994; Bainham 1996).[3] In response to the large volume of applications and in an attempt to reduce costs, New Zealand directed an administrative officer to handle the departure requests. Australia also transferred the processing of departure orders from the courts to an administrative structure when the court system proved too costly and cumbersome.

Reforms in the United Kingdom: The Child Support Act of 1991

Elements of the Child Support Scheme

U.K. policymakers shared objectives common to those that motivated other child support schemes (Maclean and Eekelaar 1993).[4] The lowness and inconsistency of the discretionary-based court orders were criticized, and the government felt that much more could be recovered from the fathers of children whose mothers were receiving social security payments than was being achieved under existing social security law and practice. This concern overshadowed the others and is reflected in the way the formula for establishing liability is structured. The formula creates a target liability (the maintenance requirement) equivalent to the social security paid or payable to the debtor's child and its caretaker when eligible. The award is set at half of the debtor's assessable income (that is, net income less certain exemptions), irrespective of the number of children needing support. If, however, the resulting award would exceed the target, the debtor pays the target sum and an additional amount based on lower percentages of the remaining assessable income related to the number of children needing support. The caregiving parent's income is taken into account, although it usually has only a slight impact on the outcome.

Two elements of this technique sowed the seeds of considerable later difficulty. First, basing the target sum on social security paid or potentially payable to children and caregivers and publishing target savings for the social security budget created the perception that the purpose of the exercise was to save money rather than to help children. This perception was confirmed by (1) the requirement that a mother identify the father of a child on whose behalf she was receiving benefits or face reduction of benefits; (2) the fact that the Child Support Agency (CSA), established to administer the scheme, initially pursued as a priority debtors whose former families received social security; and (3) that the salary of the CSA's chief executive was related to social security budget "savings."

Second, the 50 percent levy on income was imposed in the belief that it was the highest extraction that could be made without destroying work incentives. Because agency-assessed awards supersede previous court orders, the effects of such a levy on debtors with medium and low incomes was significant, sometimes amounting to more than 30 percent of net income. But although the formulation made a small gesture toward income-sharing goals by factoring in caregivers' income (but not the income of their new partners) and reducing awards at certain levels, the plan ignored the effect on debtors' income of the formation of new families. The only costs that could be deducted in determining assessable income were those that debtors would have incurred in maintaining themselves and any of their own natural children at subsistence level, including reasonable housing costs. Costs incurred in maintaining and housing new partners or stepchildren were ignored. Furthermore, award calculations allowed no adjustments for other circumstances facing debtors, such as high costs in traveling to work or visiting children and debts incurred for the benefit of the former family. In other words, having used the European technique of fixing a subsistence sum that determined the obligation come what may, the U.K. plan set the figure so high that issues of equity between the parents could not be avoided. Yet the scheme resolutely resisted addressing those issues.

No provision was made for fine-tuning awards (apart from the rigid elements of the formula) in part because the government wanted to keep administration of the scheme outside the jurisdiction of the courts. All child support claims were to be processed by the CSA, a quasi-independent body (with its own chief executive and budget) operating under the supervision of the Department of Social Security. The courts lost jurisdiction to order support except in certain cases, such as if a wealthy debtor paying the maximum award had ample excess income; if the award was to cover school fees; if the child was disabled; or if the award was to support a stepchild. However, unless the caregiving parent was receiving social security benefits, courts retained jurisdiction for a transitional period if the court had already ordered child maintenance or if the court order simply reflected a written parental agreement (Child Support Act 1991 [Commencement no. 3 and Transitional Provisions] Order 1992; Child Support Act 1991:§8[5]). Appeals from a CSA assessment were confined to matters of fact or law (that is, evaluations of circumstances were excluded) and were confined within the administrative system (by being heard by child support officers and then by the Child Support Appeal Tribunal) (Child Support Act 1991:§§18–21).

Part of the reason for wishing to marginalize the courts so completely was the belief that the costs of legal representation were too high and too heavy a drain on legal aid funds. Nevertheless, these measures alone would do little to resolve that issue because in more costly cases, child support is likely to be only one of a number of matters in dispute. Indeed, removing child support matters to a separate agency could enhance overall costs where the dispute resolution requires involvement of both courts and the CSA. It might have been possible to build more discretion into the administrative system. For example, child support officers or the Child Support Appeal Tribunal could be allowed wider discretion to consider the kinds of issues that would be relevant to the exercise of judicial discretion. However, the government held firm because this modification raised the specter of endless delay as well as the fear that demands might be made for legal representation before the child support officers or tribunals.

The "Retrospectivity" Problem

The Australian child support scheme described in Maclean and Warman's essay in this volume set a specific date for its commencement. Formula-based assessment of child support applies only to separations occurring after the given date (Harrison 1993). In contrast, the U.K. scheme is retrospective. CSA assessment is compulsory for caregiving parents receiving social security. CSA assessment is available even where the separation occurred before commencement day unless the caregiving parent is not receiving social security and a court order or written agreement was in force between the parents at commencement day (in which case commencement was postponed until 1996). Thus, in cases covered by the act (all cases where the caregiving parent receives social security), assessment will be made without taking into account any special arrangements effected between the parents, such as payment of debts or (notably) transfer of lump sums or property. A father would not have the award against him reduced even if he had earlier transferred property to the mother in the expectation that doing so would count against child support liability.

The government offered a number of reasons for maintaining this position. Where a house was encumbered by a mortgage, it was often advantageous to the father to transfer it to the mother in return for reduction or extinction of his support liability. This situation depended on the circumstances, but the government's resistance to discretionary investigation precluded opening up the examination of individual cases. In any event, it was argued that the formula was designed to operate in the context of existing circumstances. The past was irrelevant to determining what was now a just distribution between the father and his child (or the state that was supporting the child), and factors relating to the father's present housing needs (though not those of his new family) were considered in the formula. In terms of the conceptions of justice mentioned earlier, distributive justice was pursued at the expense of commutative justice.

The Aftermath

Thus established, the system seemed bound to fail. How could it be expected that such drastic incursions into income and interpersonal conflict could be resolved by rules alone, untempered in any way by considerations of personal equity? During 1993 and 1994 protests against the scheme became increasingly vociferous. Cases in which men had apparently committed suicide on receipt of assessments received great publicity. Marches against the scheme were organized around the country, and the matter twice came before parliamentary select committees. People likened the scheme to the notorious poll tax, which was an important element in the downfall of Prime Minister Margaret Thatcher, and expressed fears that the plan significantly increased the government's unpopularity.

Within six months of its inception, the scheme came under the investigation of Parliament's Social Security Select Committee. However, the committee recommended only minor adjustments (*First Report* 1993; Eekelaar 1994), which alleviated its impact slightly on the poorest debtors. Opposition mounted amid reports of excessive delays,[5] endemic errors,[6] and poor training and intimidation by its staff. The CSA's chief executive was rumored to be driven in a bulletproof car and eventually resigned. After a further review by the Social Security Select Committee (*Fifth Report* 1994), in January 1995 the government announced significant modifications, which were enacted in the Child Support Act of 1995 (*Improving Child Support* 1995). These changes are instructive in evaluating the shortcomings of the techniques adopted and will be considered in detail.

Salvaging the System

Reducing "Excessive" Awards

The first step in the political program to save the system was a crude reduction of seemingly high awards through imposing a general ceiling of 30 percent of net income or 33 percent if arrears are owed. Furthermore, wealthier debtors will benefit from a decision to halve the maximum amount payable as the "additional element" (the amount payable by richer debtors who have assessable income left over after meeting the maintenance requirement). These decisions have little to do with securing greater equity between families (they reduce, for example, the scope for differentiation based on the number of children needing support) but reflect a political decision to ameliorate the redistributive effect of the original formula.

Attempts at Better Fine-Tuning

The reform package also introduced two elements that would allow more attention to be given to individual circumstances. The first added to the categories of exempt income; the second introduced an element of discretion.

(1) New Exemptions

Whether a debtor's assessment reaches 30 percent of his net income depends on the amount of his assessable income (net income minus exemptions). The original formula allowed exemptions only for a sum equivalent to what debtors would need to spend on themselves and any children of their own living with them, including reasonable housing costs. Exemption was not allowed for expenses in supporting or housing new partners or stepchildren, which debtors were expected to fund out of what was left of their assessable income after extraction of the 50 percent child support award. By increasing the possibility of further exemptions, the changes reduced the amount of net income to which the 50 percent applies.

Two new exemptions were introduced: one allows the costs of housing (but not supporting) a new partner or stepchildren to be added to the debtor's exempt income (*Child Support and Income Support* [*Amendment*] *Regulations* 1995); the other allows costs of travel to work to be added on a ten pence/mile basis if the "straight-line distance between an employee's home and place of work is in excess of 150 miles a week" (*Improving Child Support* 1995; *Child Support and Income Support* [*Amendment*] *Regulations* 1995).

The government also sought to address the retrospectivity problem through additions to income exemptions. When a property transfer took place before the scheme took effect in 1993, additions to exempt income are allowed corresponding to the value of the property transferred. As a result, child support awards will be reduced as the value of the property transfer grows, according to a banding system (*Child Support and Income Support* [*Amendment*] *Regulations* 1995).

(2) The Introduction of Discretion

The second element of saving the system was provision for departure from the formula-based assessment (*Child Support Act* 1995; *Child Support Departure Direction* [*Anticipatory Application*] *Regulations* 1996). Either the debtor or the caregiving parent may apply, but the grounds are specified. Debtors must show special circumstances falling into one or more of the specified categories and the possibility of hardship if they were held liable under the formula. The specified categories are: exceptionally high costs of travel to work; high costs of travel to maintain contact with the child; particular expenses connected with long-term illness or disability or that of a dependent; certain debts of the former relationship between the parents; commitments the debtor had entered into before the scheme was introduced from which it would be unreasonable or impossible to withdraw; and where the formula adjustment for prescheme transfers (mentioned previously) yields an inappropriate result (*Improving Child Support* 1995). Costs incurred in supporting stepchildren may be a ground for departure, where the absent parent incurred them before the scheme came into effect in April 1993. This limitation maintains the scheme's hostility toward allowing an absent parent's newly acquired social obligations toward stepchildren to affect liability toward natural children.[7] Either parent may seek a departure on a variety of general grounds, such as "the assessment is unrealistically low because, although the absent parent has been able to demonstrate a low income, he has substantial assets or an extravagant lifestyle inconsistent with income at that level," or where one of the parents has a wealthy partner who is meeting housing costs (*Improving Child Support* 1995; *Child Support Departure Direction* [*Anticipatory Application*] *Regulations* 1996).

The discretion will first be exercised by a CSA official, but either parent may appeal to the Child Support Appeal Tribunal. However, the government attempted to place tight controls on the way the discretion is exercised. The decision maker is to keep in mind the general principles of the scheme: parents are responsible for maintaining their children whenever they can, and this obligation is owed equally to all natural children. Furthermore, departure is allowed only if "just and equitable," which allows consideration of the financial circumstances of the parents and the welfare of the child but excludes consideration of matters such as whether the child's conception was planned; the responsibility for the breakdown of the parents' relationship; the fact that either parent has formed a new relationship; the arrangements for contact and whether it is being exercised; and failure to make payments under any order or agreement (*Child Support Act* 1995).

Reducing the Administrative Burden

It has become clear that the CSA was established without sufficient preparation. It was failing to meet modest targets in processing applications and was embarrassed by repeated criticism from the parliamentary commissioner for administration (the ombudsman), who detailed many cases of serious administrative failure (*Third Report* 1995). By October 1996 assessments had attained only 77 percent accuracy (Bennett 1997). The government responded by announcing that it would extend the transitional period that retained the jurisdiction of the courts in cases where the caregiving parent was not receiving social security benefits and there was a court order or written agreement for child support already in existence. It seems likely that this deferral of these cases from the scheme will be indefinite. These cases remain within the jurisdiction of the courts, to which the parties may turn should they desire any variation. More drastic, however, was the decision not to pursue "for the time being cases where we issued a maintenance application form over six months ago which has either not been returned or has been returned with insufficient information to progress it" (*Third Report* 1995). It looks as if the CSA has abandoned attempts to trace or follow up recalcitrant debtors, concentrating its energies on extracting as much as it can from more cooperative parents. This conclusion is confirmed by a large-scale study that concluded that although the amounts paid to recipients increased over the scheme's first eighteen months, the proportion of lone parents receiving payments had not changed (Marsh, Ford, and Finlayson 1997).

More seriously, there is evidence that the CSA is failing to enforce the assessments that it does make effectively. One reason why the courts were considered to have failed was that their enforcement mechanisms were weak, dependent as they were on the initiatives of the custodial parents. The CSA was intended to be proactive in enforcement, which does not seem to be the case in actuality, and in many cases the agency's officers negotiate a sum with the debtor short of the assessed amount (Davis, Wikely, and Young 1998).

Some Help from the Courts

Although the government was initially unmoved by the retrospectivity argument and refused to allow formula-assessed child support liability to be influenced by prior capital settlements, debtors could always request that the courts modify settlements in light of later increases in child support liability. In one case the court refused to make any modification, arguing that it had never been possible to exclude the possibility of later orders for child support (*Crozier v. Crozier* [1994], 1 FLR 126), but in another case the court made an adjustment allowing the father to claim an indemnity against the mother for any child support liability he might later incur (*Smith v. McInerney* [1994], 2 FLR 1077). This ability is, however, of limited practical value if the parent with the child is not in a financial position to satisfy the indemnity.

Conclusions

The problems that befell the CSA may in part be attributed to poor planning, undue haste, and overzealous pursuit of treasury objectives. It is still unknown whether the 1995 modifications will save the scheme or how they will work in practice. Although objections to the scheme persist, they have become much less vociferous since the 1995 changes. But it must also be asked whether there were design failures that throw some light on the theoretical bases underpinning child support schemes.

Balancing the Conceptions of Justice

It seems clear that the moral justification for the shape of the scheme in its original form was some idea of distributive justice. It was simply deemed that a particular proportion of absent parents' incomes should be removed from them and applied toward the costs of their children on no other ground than parentage. As in general taxation, the income liable to attack could be reduced by allowances (exemptions), reflecting, in this case, minimal expenses debtors would incur to house and support themselves and any new children. But other calls on debtors' income (including those made by a new family toward which he might have social or moral obligations), the circumstances of the family unit in which the children to which he was indebted were living, and the overall financial relationship between debtors and creditors were virtually eliminated from consideration.

Can child support be appropriately characterized in this way? The European experience suggests that it can, but only to a limited degree. It is of course true that the cost of raising a child goes well beyond the sums necessary to provide for the goods the child actually consumes. The child is dependent on the economic infrastructure that supports the home and the caregiving parent. But the more that the absent parent is required to contribute to that infrastructure, the harder it becomes to avoid considerations of commutative justice: of comparing all the circumstances between the child's family environment and those of the absent parent. There is no magic cutoff point below which it is possible to say that the debtor must make a contribution irrespective of the relative circumstances of the two households and above which those circumstances become relevant. If a line is to be drawn, it must (as in other cases of distributive justice) be a question of political judgment. It seems clear that the U.K. government initially drew that line in the wrong place.

Hence, part of the modification to the scheme involved redrawing the line. But the payments can still be at such a level that questions of commutative justice arise. There is clearly a case, on grounds of commutative justice, for an absent parent to contribute to the infrastructure of his child's new family unit, and the British scheme deals with this situation partly through even more detailed regulations and partly through an element of discretion (departures), which is nevertheless highly structured. The question that is then raised of how far this strongly rule based, formulaic method can successfully deal with issues of commutative justice. The wealth of detailed information that needs to be assembled, much of which is contestable and subject to frequent variation, risks defeating the objective of rapid assessment by a proactive bureaucracy with minimal scope for making value judgments. The extent of the details to be processed and kept up to date brought about near paralysis of the administration of the scheme, which in turn affected the CSA's capacity to enforce its assessments and led to an apparent willingness to compromise at the enforcement stage. The danger now is that the primary objectives of moving from the courts to an agency-based scheme—which include rapid processing of cases, regular reviews of assessments, and more efficient enforcement—may not be easily achieved, and the overall goal of reducing the state's costs will be frustrated. Wealthy parents, whose potential liability exceeds the maxima of the administrative scheme, still have access to the courts but will usually meet the costs of using them. Although the CSA charges a fee,[8] it is not clear whether the scheme will be cost-effective, especially if it becomes involved with many issues of commutative justice between poorer parents.

Commenting on the first two years of the CSA's work, its new chief executive wrote,

> It has been evident for some time that the task set for the Agency has proven to be more difficult in practice than had been anticipated when the scheme was devised. In particular, I do not think it was fully appreciated that the Agency's intervention into the most personal and sensitive areas of people's lives would make such a negative impact;

> nor was it realised how many people would actively resist or reject prioritising child maintenance above nearly all other financial commitments. (*Third Report* 1995)

What Did We Learn?

The lesson to be learned may be as follows: formulaic determinations of child support liability can provide a basis for reallocation of resources based on the principles of distributive justice but can have only a relatively limited effect. What is essentially a distributive tax on procreation may work, but it can bite into income only at a low level. Such determinations can be administered through either administrative agencies or courts; whichever is cheaper and more efficient depends on the nature of the court and administrative structure of a particular society. These matters often will be settled rapidly by lawyers without requiring any official determination.[9] When an attempt is made to impose child support liability above a certain level, the demands of commutative justice, which have traditionally been met through the court system, become overwhelming.

It is too early to say how well administrative procedures will deal with child support in the long run. The main lesson to be learned, perhaps, from the British experience is that any start should be gradual, and care must be taken not to overload the system by seeking to achieve too much too quickly. It may be that a firmer line should be drawn between distributive and commutative justice in the context of child support and that simple, mechanical, and rapid modes of assessment and enforcement should be concentrated on achieving the former, leaving scope for commutative justice to be pursued through other means in cases where it is appropriate.

NOTES

1. There might be policy subtexts to the goal of making parents (especially fathers) more responsible for their behavior and equalizing the burden of child care between men and women.

2. The term *commutative* "can cover the whole field in which, problems of allocation of common stock and the like apart, the problem is to determine what dealings are proper between persons (including groups)" (Finnis 1980:179).

3. The law and practice on departure orders constitutes by far the longest section of the account of the scheme in Butterworth's *Family Law Service* for New Zealand.

4. The scheme is neutral between mothers and fathers. However, for these purposes, the person looking after the child (the "caregiving parent") will be assumed to be the mother and the "absent parent" will be assumed to be the father.

5. During its first year, it arranged maintenance for only 31.5 percent of eligible applications it received; 41 percent took more than a hundred days to clear (*First Two Years* 1994).

6. The agency was accused of making errors or failing in its statutory requirements in 86 percent of its assessments (*Annual Report* 1994).

7. This attitude differs markedly from the attitude toward stepchildren in the New Zealand legislation: the debtor parent's obligations toward up to four children currently dependent on (him) (whether step or natural) may be taken into account (Child Support Act 1991 § 30; Family Law Service § 5.212).

8. Because of its poor service and the backlog of cases, the CSA is suspending charging its fee for two years (*Improving Child Support* 1995).

9. See the position in the Netherlands described by Griffiths (1986).

REFERENCES

Annual Report of the Chief Child Support Officer 1993–94: Report by the Comptroller and Auditor-General. 1994. HC 670-IX. London: Her Majesty's Stationery Office.

Atkin, W. R. 1994. Child Support in New Zealand Runs into Strife. *Houston Law Review* 31:631–45.

Bainham, Andrew, ed. 1996. *The International Survey of Family Law 1994.* The Hague: Martinus Nijhoff.

Bennett, F. 1997. *Child Support: Issues for the Future.* London: Child Poverty Action Group.

Child Support Act 1991. New Zealand.

Child Support Act, 1991, c. 22. United Kingdom.

Child Support Act 1995. New Zealand.

Child Support Act, 1995. United Kingdom.

Child Support Departure Direction (Anticipatory Application) Regulations 1996. 1996. S.I., no. 635.

Child Support and Income Support (Amendment) Regulations 1995. 1995. S.I., no. 1045.

Davis, Gwynn, Nick Wikely, and Richard Young. 1998. *Child Support in Action.* Oxford: Hart Publishing.

Eekelaar, John. 1994. Third Thoughts on Child Support. *Family Law* 24:99–102.

Family Law Service. Wellington, NZ: Butterworths.

Finnis, John. 1980. *Natural Law and Natural Rights.* Oxford: Clarendon Press.

Fifth Report of the Social Security Committee, the Operation of the Child Support Act: Proposals for Change. 1994. Session 1993–94, HC 470. October. London: Her Majesty's Stationery Office.

First Report of the Social Security Committee: The Operation of the Child Support Act. 1993. Session 1993–94, HC 69. 1 December. London: Her Majesty's Stationery Office.

The First Two Years. 1994. Child Support Agency. London: Her Majesty's Stationery Office.

Griffiths, John. 1986. What Dutch Lawyers Actually Do in Divorce Cases. *Law and Society Review* 20:135–61.

Harrison, Margaret. 1993. The Australian Child Support Scheme. In *Parenthood in Modern Society: Legal and Social Issues for the Twenty-First Century,* ed. John Eekelaar and Petar Sarcevic. Dordrecht and Boston: Martinus Nijhoff.

Improving Child Support. 1995. CM 2745. January. London: Her Majesty's Stationery Office. Summarized in *Family Law* 25 (1995): 98.

Knudsen, Rita. 1988. Denmark. In *Child Support: From Debt Collection to Social Policy,* ed. Alfred J. Kahn and Sheila B. Kamerman. Newbury Park, CA: Sage Publications.

Maclean, Mavis. 1994. Child Support in the U.K.: Making the Move from Court to Agency. *Houston Law Review* 31:515–36.

Maclean, Mavis, and John Eekelaar. 1993. Child Support: The British Solution. *International Journal of Law and the Family* 7:205–29.

Marsh, A., R. Ford, and L. Finlayson. 1997. *Lone Parents, Work, and Benefits.* Research Report 61, Department of Social Security Research. London: Her Majesty's Stationery Office.

Morris, Andrew. 1995. On the Normative Foundations of Indirect Discrimination Law: Understanding the Competing Models of Discrimination Laws as Aristotelian Forms of Justice. *Oxford Journal of Legal Studies* 15:199–228.

Schneider, Carl E. 1993. Discretion, Rules, and Law: Child-Custody Decisions and the Best Interests Standard. In *The Uses of Discretion,* ed. K. Hawkins. New York: Oxford University Press.

Takas, Marianne. 1992. Improving Child Support Guidelines: Can Simple Formulas Address Complex Families? *Family Law Quarterly* 26 (3): 171–94.

Third Report of the Parliamentary Commissioner for Administration, Session 1994-4; Investigation of Complaints against the Child Support Agency. 1995. HC 135. January. London: Her Majesty's Stationery Office.

Willenbacher, Barbara. 1996. The Changing Role of Professionals in Divorce in Germany. *International Journal of Law, Policy, and the Family* 10:159–76.

Willenbacher, Barbara, and Wolfgang Voegeli. 1992. Child Maintenance in the Federal Republic of Germany. In *Economic Consequences of Divorce: An International Perspective,* ed. Lenore J. Weitzman and Mavis Maclean. New York: Oxford University Press.

A Comparative Approach to Child Support Systems: Legal Rules and Social Policies

Mavis Maclean and Andrea Warman

Introduction

Comparative reviews across national frontiers run the risk of presenting no more than a descriptive guide to the idiosyncracies of other countries' ways of arranging such difficult matters as the need to provide financial support for children living apart from a parent. This chapter will not offer a comprehensive description of worldwide practice. Instead, this chapter avoids the descriptive approach by examining two aspects of the nature and purpose of several child support systems—the location of the support system within the machinery of government and the support system's focus.

A clear difference exists between countries where child support is identified as primarily a legal issue for the judicial system and those in which child support is seen as primarily a matter for social policy. Under the predominantly legal approach, the aim of the system is to identify and enforce the rights of children and perhaps their resident parent to a share in the income and wealth of the other parent. In a predominantly social-policy setting, the system may seek to reduce child poverty, to reduce social security expenditure, or to enforce parental responsibility. Under a social-policy approach there will be more discussion of the distribution of resources within social groups rather than of individual rights. Whereas the legal approach can only allocate the existing resources of the parents, under a social-policy approach additional resources can be allocated from general revenue or by fiscal adjustment.

The second dimension to this comparative analysis, that of the focus of the support system, reflects a change discussed by June Carbone in "Child Support Comes of Age: An Introduction to the Law of Child Support" (in this volume). The support system is moving away from concern with the legal relationship between parents toward an increasing interest in the continuing relationship between parents and children. Given the changing attitudes toward the economic relationship between parents after divorce and the growing realization that economic difficulties accompany the task of child rearing, resources formerly discussed and allocated as spousal support are now more likely to be discussed and allocated under the heading of child support. But whether talking of child support, spousal support, or family support, the concern is how societies can raise children who are not receiving adequate resources from their parents. Whether this activity is framed as making American fathers pay their debts to their children (Lieberman 1986) or as developing social mechanisms for dealing with serial monogamy (Maclean 1991, 1995), the same issues arise of conflicting demands on both public and private resources.

This chapter first presents examples from the codified law and welfarist traditions of Eastern and Western Europe. Other chapters in this volume deal in detail with the new British system (John Eekelaar, "Child Support as Distributive and Commutative Justice: The United Kingdom Experience") and the developments in the United States (Marsha Garrison, "The Goals and Limits of Child Support Policy"). This chapter examines in greater detail the new Australian child support system, which brings together a strong social-policy interest with a common-law tradition. This comparative analysis seeks to discuss the context and focus of child support systems that differ in both their approach and their outcomes.

European Systems: Legal Codes in Welfare States

European child support systems are excellent illustrations of both dimensions of this comparative analysis—the legal/social policy aspect of the system and the changing focus from the legal relationship between parents to that between parents and children.

Evidence from a recent study, which examined spousal and child maintenance in Western European countries as part of an attempt to define "family obligations" (Millar and Warman 1996), supports the suggestion that the responsibilities of parenthood are becoming far more important than those of ex-partners to each other. Although some of these countries still have systems that award ongoing spousal maintenance, the legal duty to maintain a former partner is increasingly subject to debate, and in practice awards tend to be low. In contrast, child maintenance, whether addressed through the legal system or not, is always defined as an ongoing obligation, and although in some cases parents are able to set levels of support themselves, the state is far more likely to be involved in this process—sometimes even guaranteeing payments—which never happens for spouses.

Sweden provides a clear example of this different approach to spousal and child maintenance. Following divorce, both spouses are obliged to support themselves. There are only two exceptions to this general rule. Long-term subsistence may be claimed if a former spouse can prove that he or she had a long-standing relationship that involved complete financial dependence on the former partner. More commonly, a transitional award may be made to a former spouse to enable him or her to study, acquire new skills, and in the long term become financially independent.

This contrasts with the Swedish approach to child maintenance: it must always be paid by the noncustodial parent, whether or not the parents are married. Parents may make their own arrangements, but the courts will become involved in disputed cases. In these cases, the child's needs and the financial situation of both parents are taken into account. Importantly, though, the Swedish state sets a certain minimum level of support to which every child is entitled. When the noncustodial parent cannot pay this amount, the state assumes responsibility for the payment. In other words, every child has the right to a basic level of support—a right not shared by a former spouse. Indeed, the advanced maintenance scheme that pays child support directly to lone mothers (payments which are then reclaimed from the child's father, if possible, through the Public Social Insurance Office) is further evidence that the state is far more willing to intervene in the relationship between parents and children than in relationships between former partners.

Child maintenance is guaranteed not only in Sweden and the other Scandinavian countries. Advance payments are made in eight of the sixteen Western European countries examined for the study, including Austria and France (Millar and Warman 1996). Conversely, such payments are never made to former spouses. It is interesting to speculate on the impact of child support guarantees (which, in effect, turn the family obligations of absent parents into debts to the state) on the attitudes of separated fathers to their parental responsibilities. For although advance payments are possible in countries where the legal system deals with child maintenance (as in Austria, for example), there is perhaps more room for this type of intervention in a social-policy setting.

In Denmark, the state, through local authorities, takes a far more active role in setting rates of child support and ensuring that payments are made. The Ministry of Justice produces a set of rules for calculating normal *bidrog* (maintenance), modifiable for children with special needs. The local authorities make these payments in advance and take on responsibility for recouping the money and for enforcing this parental obligation when necessary. In practice, legal powers rarely need to be used, and there is a collection rate of better than 90 percent (Koch-Nielsen 1996).

In Denmark, then, as in Sweden, child support is clearly a concern for social policy, with resources provided by the community as well as the parents. The link between private and public child support systems is clear and well understood, though contentious (see Agell 1992). Furthermore, the Scandinavian countries also appear to share the more general feature of official attention to and regulation of the parent-child relationship, while there is far less regulation of relationships between adults.

In Norway, active state involvement is part of the broader policy aim of promoting parental responsibility. Parents may make their own child support arrangements, but more usually the local social-insurance office becomes involved, setting a rate based on a formula established at the national government level. Once again, advance payments are made and then recovered by the local social-insurance office, which has the authority to make deductions from the salaries of persistent debtors. Indeed, a central register of child support debtors is kept, partly to keep track of individuals who move away from their children but also perhaps to promote a sense of shame among those who do not take their parental obligations seriously (Leira 1996). This degree of intervention into private family life is obviously contentious, but it communicates a clear message that responsibilities toward children do not end when the relationship between their parents does and, perhaps even more importantly, that all children should have access to a basic minimum income as a right.

In Germany (the former Federal Republic of Germany), the Civil Code establishes the right to maintenance as the right of the child itself. As such, maintenance is intended to meet the individual needs of the child and is not seen as part of the household income of the custodial parent. Parents must share their income with their children even if this results in poverty for the parent. There is no distinction in law between parents living with the child and parents living elsewhere, and the code contains no amounts for maintenance. To avoid the expense and conflict of litigation, the levels of support are now based almost universally on the Dusseldorf table of amounts, which was taken from the state procedure to enforce a support obligation for nonmarital children. The assessment procedure is carried out by a junior court official and is more administrative than judicial in character. The state regularly updates the minimum levels of support for nonmarital children, and since 1976 the simplified procedure has been available for children of divorcing parents.

Similarly, enforcement has been simplified, with the power to issue an order for the attachment of earnings vested in a junior court official. Of course, there are problems of lack of compliance, and order amounts are not high (about 10 percent of the father's income), particularly when seen in the context of women's absence from the labor market while there are young children and of the absence of wife support. There is an interesting and effective balance between courts and welfare involvement in the problem in that the child support system remains in the hands of the court, but procedures for assessment and enforcement are administrative in character, and the levels set are based on the social-policy requirements for children born outside marriage (see Willenbacher 1996).

The weaknesses of systems that rely too heavily on the courts alone are evident in a country such as Spain. Under the Spanish Civil Code, parents have legal obligations to support their children whether or not the parents are married. It is important that "support" in this legislation includes not only food and shelter but also medical care and education and must be sufficient to maintain the standard of living to which the child is accustomed. However, although the Spanish courts do have the power to enforce these obligations, in practice "the best guarantee of alimony or child support being paid is the willingness of the payer to pay. Guarantees established by law might help in certain cases, but in general their usefulness is very limited" (De Delas 1992). Legally, failure to pay child support is an offense that can result in a fine or even imprisonment. Yet estimates of the numbers of parents who do not pay child maintenance range from 20 percent to as high as 80 percent (Valiente 1996), and the state never guarantees or makes advance payments.

Spain illustrates some of the weaknesses of a system that relies on the courts without the balance of administrative assessment and enforcement evident in the German system. In Spain, although legal obligations to support exist, they are rarely enforced, not least because court proceedings are slow and expensive and many single mothers simply cannot afford to hire lawyers. Levels of maintenance are set at the discretion of judges and are variable and unrealistic. No one appears to take this obligation seriously, and there appears to be less sense of the authorities sharing or enforcing parental responsibilities than in the countries described earlier.

France and Italy share the same approach, relying heavily on the courts with the additional shared feature of discretionary powers for judges to set child support levels largely at will. In both cases it seems that awards are usually low, and, in Italy at least, unreliable and small payments may be one reason that separated and divorced women are far more likely to work outside the home than those who are married (Triffiletti 1996).

In Eastern Europe until the changes of the 1990s, society expected all women to work, inexpensive child care was widely available, and though divorce rates were increasing, the economic aspects of divorce were not of immediate concern (Fuszara 1997). As employment for women becomes less surely available and as welfare provision in cash and kind diminishes with the economic difficulties of transition to the market economy, these issues may well come to the fore. But there is strong legal protection for children in divorce. For example, in Hungary a minor child has a right to remain in the family home, and in Poland the court has the power, though it is rarely used, to refuse to grant a divorce if it is considered to be against the interests of the children of the marriage (Szlezak 1995).

In this part of Europe it is customary for parents to remain economically responsible for their children until their mid- or late twenties, giving financial help even after marriage. This tradition of strong respect for the family unit is overlain with the former communist emphasis on the need to subordinate individual needs to those of the wider social group, including first the family and then society as a whole. Support for the next generation is a part of the socialist natalist philosophy: the socialist state needs many workers to build the new world (Kurczewski 1994).

Australian Developments: The Social Policy Drive Toward Delegalization

The recent development of the new Australian system for child support provides a clear example of social-policy goals driving the matter away from the domination of courts and lawyers. The combination of a serious review of social policy—in particular social security entitlements and expenditures—with a wish to relieve pressure on an overloaded and ineffective part of the family court system led to the establishment of an administrative system.

If the aim of social policy is to alleviate the poverty and economic uncertainty experienced by female-headed households after divorce, then any policy strategy must seek to achieve income for these families that is both adequate and reliable—that is, a guaranteed-maintenance system. To achieve the maximum advantage, these payments must supplement rather than replace the mother's earned income. It is not possible, even in a socialist republic, for the majority of women who are heads of households to earn adequate family income—partly as a result of loss of human capital due to family formation and partly because of the low level of wages paid for the work women do combined with the constraints and costs of child care. Transfer payments from the other parent, whether or not he is a former legal partner, and the state (or the community or public purse, whichever term is preferred), are required to provide an adequate standard of living to offer the affected children any kind of parity with the children of two contributing parents. Irwin Garfinkel describes such a scheme in

"The Limits of Private Child Support and the Role of an Assured Benefit" (in this volume). This chapter will report only on the impact of his proposals in Australia.

Background

In the mid-1980s, New Zealand introduced an administratively based child support scheme for welfare recipients. This innovation was of interest in Australia but was thought to have some major problems, in particular the inability of the Department of Social Security to locate absent parents or to collect from those it did locate (Edwards 1989). Collection of money was simply not a departmental skill. Developments underway in Australia were strengthened by the convergence of interest from the legal and social security perspectives. Brian Howe, then minister of social security in the Australian government, mounted a major investigation into the workings of the social security system. At the same time Justice Fogarty, who chaired the Family Law Council, was concerned about the amount of court time consumed by maintenance claims and their enforcement and was eager to explore alternative approaches. At this propitious moment, Garfinkel was invited to Australia to explain his ideas to policymakers.

A ministerial committee was set up with the following objectives: (1) noncustodial parents should share the cost of children according to their capacity to pay, an argument based on equity between the parents; (2) all children living apart from a parent should receive adequate support, an antipoverty argument; (3) the state should minimize expenditures on the collection process, a public policy argument; (4) work disincentives should be minimized, also a public policy goal; and (5) any procedures should not invade individual privacy, a human-rights argument. This complex mix of motives and constraints neatly crosses the divide between legal and social policy objectives and shows how well integrated the combined approach was becoming even at early stages of developmental planning.

After considering these aims, the committee secretariat identified the following key questions that needed to be answered before policy could be taken further:

1. Where should payments be collected, and by whom? Ministers on advice decided that collection must be undertaken by the tax office, as only the Inland Revenue Service had experience in locating individuals, good relationships with employers, and expertise in the task of revenue collection. This decision was particularly important for the problematic group of self-employed agricultural workers.

2. Should the scheme apply only to welfare clients, as in New Zealand? The Ministry of Social Security argued convincingly for all new cases to come under the new scheme, as policymakers were anxious to avoid creating any disincentive to coming off welfare. The welfare population is not static, and movement into and out of benefit must be maintained and not distorted by inappropriate incentives.
3. Should the scheme continue to use court-based judicial assessments of levels of child support payments or look to an administrative procedure for assessment, as in New Zealand and some European jurisdictions? Ministers decided in favor of administrative assessment because the courts were overburdened with these kinds of cases and subject to serious delays.
4. Should a formula for assessment be used, and if so, should it be based on income sharing or income pooling? What protections should be offered to the payer and his current household, and what account should be taken of the resources of the custodial parent and any new members of her household? These questions were concerned with detail rather than principle, and decisions were held over for the period of consultation that followed the publication of the child support discussion paper. Modifications were considered, particularly the inclusion of the custodial parent's income if it exceeded a certain level (1.5 times the national average earnings).

Implementation

Although the ministerial committee had considered far-reaching issues and sought broad-based consultation, opposition to the proposals developed quickly and vociferously in 1986–87 from a number of sources. Noncustodial parents, who had not previously formed an alliance, came together seeking publicity for their cause, buying time on commercial television to state their case. The legal profession through the Law Council of Australia opposed both administrative level setting and the loss of judicial discretion. Welfare-rights groups argued that the entire scheme was designed to save public expenditure on welfare to one-parent families, without concern for reducing poverty among them. Perhaps surprisingly, women's groups also objected that the scheme included a rather stringent proposal to require women to identify the fathers of their children.

The child support scheme was clearly a radical innovation, and in view of the anxieties expressed during the consultation period, the government decided to implement the proposals in two stages.

Stage 1: Collection

In June 1988 the Child Support Agency was set up under the auspices of the tax office, with responsibility for anyone with an existing court order or court-registered agreement. Automatic withholding was to be implemented wherever possible, particularly for new entrants to the scheme. Research in the United States had shown consistently that compliance with orders was more likely when a pattern of regular payment was established at an early stage (see, for example, Pearson, Thoennes, and Anhalt 1992). The Department of Social Security would distribute funds collected by the agency. The Family Law Act (1975) was amended to give child support payments priority over other calls on the parties' resources. In addition, the Department of Social Security established a maintenance-income test for welfare eligibility that would disregard the first fifteen dollars of maintenance plus five dollars for each child and then 50 percent of any further maintenance paid. This test was quite separate from any test carried out with respect to earned income. The court orders, the social security system of exemptions, and the collection and disbursement systems were closely integrated.

Problems arose with the parents who lacked orders and who needed to obtain them to participate in the scheme. The subsequent delays reduced the revenue collected, but levels paid increased rapidly from an average of twenty-five dollars to forty-five dollars received by those on benefit.

Stage 2: Assessment

In October 1989, the second stage set up the machinery to implement assessment by formula. The formula offered exemption from assessment for the personal expenses of the noncustodial parent, equal to the rate of benefit for a single person without children, and then withheld a fixed percentage of his assessable income according to the number of children. If he had remarried and had more children (excluding stepchildren), then the exemption was set at the level of benefit for a married man with children.

In special circumstances, however, the court may make orders that depart from the formula—for example, if a man has high access costs or a disabled child by another partner. The noncustodial parent may also ask the court to substitute a generous property settlement for a part of the child support obligation—perhaps giving his former wife the couple's house—on the understanding that this represents his major contribution to the welfare of his child. Such a substitution may not exceed 75 percent of the total cash-transfer liability and may not be permitted where the sole parent is on welfare. The required percentages of current taxable income after exemptions are 18 percent for one child, 27 percent for two, 32 percent for three, 34 percent for four, and 36 percent for five or more children. The total amount available for deduction is limited to 2.5 times the average annual earnings. These percentages are based on studies of actual expenditure on children (Lovering 1984). In this respect, the percentages differ from the recently adopted British formula described by Eekelaar, which is based on the welfare entitlement of the single-parent family as a household.

The approach taken in Australia makes it more difficult to take into account the hidden costs of child rearing (that is, the impact on the care-giving parent's ability to earn, her child-care costs, the extra costs of housing for a larger household, and so on). However, Australia's approach also does not consider any of the custodial parent's new partner's income, though Australia does give some consideration to the income of the mother herself when her income exceeds 1.5 times the average annual earnings, an unusual circumstance for a sole parent.

Compared with the former court procedure, the procedure in the new Australian scheme is simplified: the single parent simply completes a form at the local social security or tax office. The assessment is related to capacity to pay and is updated annually by the tax office as tax is paid on the previous year's income. Private child support arrangements are still possible, but the Department of Social Security may intervene in benefit cases if the levels are too low.

Court Involvement

Overall, the new system offers better integration of the social security and legal systems, while retaining, unlike the British system (as of 1995), the right to go to court. The main functions of the Australian court, however, have changed. The court was once the main arena for every assessment and review in every case of child support and the sole arena for enforcement actions. Now it is the locus for urgent cases and for determining if a case warrants departing from the formula or permitting a level of substitution of property for cash transfer or arrears.

The Child Support Agency expected that less than 20 percent of cases would have contact with the court. Academic lawyers predicted a higher level, as the changes were so extensive and introduced so quickly that they would result in a large number of appeals, requests for departure, and substitution orders. Others predicted a rise in the number of custody disputes, as it was argued that men who were being asked to pay for the first time would respond by demanding contact with their children. An additional sum was set aside to provide for the expected increase in calls on the legal aid fund.

However, in practice, calls for substitution orders have been few. Departure orders cover only very rare circumstances. Custody battles have not materialized. The main reason for seeking a court appearance is to deal with the problem of child support arrears, which accumulate from the date of entitlement, long before fathers are found and asked to pay, and may be considerable sums.

Evaluation

The new Australian child support system was established following extensive research and consultation at home and abroad. It was part of an integrated attempt by the Departments of Social Security, Tax, and Employment (which retrained sole parents for return to the labor market) and the legal system to address the increasing problem of serial monogamy combined with continuing parenting. The economic problems of sole parents were attacked by bringing together in the most effective combination the resources of the absent parent, maximizing the earning capacity of the custodial parent, and adding these resources together with additional support when necessary from the community, state, or taxpayer through the benefit system. The key feature was that instead of expecting one possible form of support to substitute for another, the plan brought together all possible forms of support through a maintenance disregard, an earnings disregard, and an effective system of assessment and enforcement of the private support obligation.

How is the system working? The Australian Department of Social Security and Treasury are disappointed. The predicted $200 million savings in the social security budget has not materialized. From national data, it was thought that only 15 percent of absent parents would not be eligible to pay. The Australian government (like the British government) was hopelessly optimistic about the level of resources available to noncustodial fathers and about the cost of collecting small amounts of money from large numbers of very reluctant payers. The Australian Inland Revenue Service achieved a 99 percent contact rate and a 70 percent collection rate, with an average payment of eighty-four dollars per week in the first year. Nevertheless, the low level of the amounts recovered and the high costs of collection considerably reduced the direct savings expected by government. For the 1993–94 financial year, the estimated reduction in social security spending as a result of the scheme was $55.2 million, with 41 percent of single parents on benefit reporting maintenance income, compared with 25 percent before the scheme came into operation (Rhoades 1995). The back-to-work program for sole parents was less successful than had been hoped, largely because Australia began to be affected by the worldwide recession.

The child support scheme itself received harsh criticism in the press, but the detailed evaluation carried out by Harrison, Snider, and Merlo (1996) reveals a rather different picture. Men are angry about having to pay more, but women, not surprisingly, are pleased about receiving more, in part because, unlike the new British system, which carries a penalty for failing to participate, the Australian approach has an incentive to cooperate in the maintenance-assessment process. There has been no widespread resort to the courts. Again, the British system differs in that legal aid is less easily available for such matters in Australia than in the United Kingdom. Concerns that the child support scheme would affect men's willingness to leave the home for the family have not proved well founded. Conventional wisdom in Australia now describes the house as the bargaining chip for the wife to use when giving up her claim to a share of the husband's occupational pension.

But above all, there has been an unprecedented upsurge of interest and public concern about the plight of children who are without the financial support of both their parents and a serious shift in public attitudes toward child support. It is no longer a matter of dispute but an entitlement. Australia has moved, in Martin Rein's terminology (1976), from claims to rights. Procedures are simple. Enforcement is much improved. The costs, both direct and indirect, of child rearing are acknowledged and understood in a way that would have been inconceivable ten years ago, when in Australia as in other common law jurisdictions, support for children was almost an adjunct of spousal support. As increasing numbers of children are born outside marriage, it is even more important that their right to support should be recognized as their own, not related to or dependent on the legal nature of the relationship between their parents and that this support should come from both parents and from the community as a whole (Weitzman and Maclean 1992).

Conclusion

In the comparative analysis in this chapter, European and Australian child support systems were examined from the perspective of whether child support is seen as a matter of social policy or as a legal problem in the arena of courts and lawyers.

The social-policy approach to the problem as a whole may lead to the availability of greater resources and, if integrated with access to the courts in unusual or complex cases, may yield a larger measure of social justice, even if there is a price to be paid in terms of justice for some individuals. Furthermore, systems that rely less on the courts may well be more effective over time in changing attitudes toward parental responsibilities than those that rely heavily on legal obligations.

Evidence from Spain illustrates that the existence of formal legislation and a legal right to support from parents is no guarantee that obligations to children are accepted at the level of everyday life. In contrast, the social-policy approach taken in Scandinavia, with its emphasis on the responsibilities of all parents, has opened up debate about the more general role of fathers in family life (Bjornberg and Eydal 1996). Indeed, it is even suggested that this emphasis has influenced the formation of the identity of fathers, who are more willing to take on financial obligations but at the same time may not want to take a more active part in other aspects of parenthood. This development raises important questions about the impact of child support guarantees, which are then recouped from separated fathers. Does this process turn a family obligation into a debt to the state, and what effect might doing so have on the identity of separated fathers and their future involvement with their children?

In the countries examined a clear and desirable trend has appeared. A majority continue responsibility for children beyond marriage, divorce, and remarriage. The central concept is the personal link between parents and children, regardless of other new dependencies and resources. Increasingly, child support systems offer clarity, predictability, and increasing access to good and speedy enforcement.

If current moves away from court-based decision making toward private ordering and alternative dispute resolution for the other aspects of divorce-related matters continue, then whatever the outcome, at least the financial needs of the children will have a firm basis as rights and must be removed from the bargaining process. Redefining child support as an obligation beyond dispute has much to recommend it.

REFERENCES

Agell, A. 1992. Grounds and Procedures Reviewed. In *Economic Consequences of Divorce,* ed. L. Weitzman and M. Maclean. Oxford: Clarendon Press; New York: Oxford University Press.

Bjornberg, U., and G. Bjork Eydal. 1996. Family Obligations in Sweden. In *Defining Family Obligations in Europe,* ed. J. Millar and A. Warman. Bath, Eng.: Centre for Social Policy Analysis, University of Bath.

Chambers, D. 1979. *Making Fathers Pay.* Chicago: University of Chicago Press.

De Delas, M. 1992. *Divorcio, Separacion, y Nulidad: Problemas y Soluciones.* Barcelona: Plantena.

Edwards, M. 1989. Unpublished paper on file with the Family Policy Studies Centre, London.

Fuszara, M. 1997. Divorce in the Opinion of Those Divorcing. In *Family Law and Family Policy in the New Europe,* ed. J. Kurczewski and M. Maclean. Brookfield, VT: Dartmouth Publishing.

Harrison, M., G. Snider, and M. Merlo. 1996. *Who Pays for the Children?* Melbourne: Australian Institute of Family Studies.

Koch-Nielsen, I. 1996. Family Obligations in Denmark. In *Defining Family Obligations in Europe,* ed. J. Millar and A. Warman. Bath, Eng.: Centre for Social Policy Analysis, University of Bath.

Kurczewski, J. 1994. Introduction to *Families, Politics, and the Law,* ed. M. Maclean and J. Kurczewski. Oxford: Clarendon Press; New York: Oxford University Press.

Leira, A. 1996. Family Obligations in Norway. In *Defining Family Obligations in Europe,* ed. J. Millar and A. Warman. Bath, Eng.: Centre for Social Policy Analysis, University of Bath.

Lieberman, J. 1986. *Child Support in America.* New Haven: Yale University Press.

Lovering, K. 1984. *Cost of Children in Australia.* Working Paper no. 8. Melbourne: Australian Institute for Family Studies.

Maclean, M. 1991. *Surviving Divorce: Women's Resources after Separation.* New York: New York University Press.

———. 1995. Economic Ties. In *Women, Men, and Marriage: Talks from the Tavistock Marital Studies Institute,* ed. Christopher Clulow. London: Sheldon.

Millar, J., and A. Warman. 1996. *Family Obligations in Europe: The Family, the State, and Social Policy.* London: Family Policy Studies Centre.

Pearson, J., N. Thoennes, and J. Anhalt. 1992. Child Support in the United States: The Experience in Colorado. *International Journal of Law, Policy, and the Family* 6:321–37.

Rein, M. 1976. *Social Science and Public Policy.* Harmondsworth, Eng., and New York: Penguin.

Rhoades, H. 1995. Australia's Child Support System: Is It Working? *Tolley's Journal of Child Law* 7 (1): 26–37.

Szlezak, A. 1995. Allocating Resources. In *Family Law and Family Policy in the New Europe,*ed. J. Kurczewski and M. Maclean. Brookfield, VT: Dartmouth Publishing.

Triffiletti, R. 1996. Family Obligations in Italy. In *Defining Family Obligations in Europe,* ed. J. Millar and A. Warman. Bath, Eng.: Centre for Social Policy Analysis, University of Bath.

Valiente, C. 1996. Family Obligations in Spain. In *Defining Family Obligations in Europe,* ed. J. Millar and A. Warman. Bath, Eng.: Centre for Social Policy Analysis, University of Bath.

Weitzman, L., and M. Maclean. 1992. The Way Ahead: A Policy Agenda. In *Economic Consequences of Divorce,* ed L. Weitzman and M. Maclean. Oxford: Clarendon Press; New York: Oxford University Press.

Willenbacher, B. 1996. The Changing Role of Professionals in Divorce in Germany. *International Journal of Law Policy, and the Family* 10:159–76.

Part V

Replacing the Current System

The Limits of Private Child Support and the Role of an Assured Benefit

Irwin Garfinkel

Introduction

The past quarter century has seen revolutionary changes that have transformed and strengthened the private child support system in the United States. Improving the private child support system is good public policy. It increases the economic security of children eligible for child support, it reduces dependence on welfare, and it reinforces the widely shared value of parental responsibility. While the nation can and should further strengthen enforcement of private child support obligations, there are limits to what enforcement can accomplish. In "The Goals and Limits of Child Support Policy" (in this volume), Marsha Garrison notes how little child support reform has accomplished in reducing child poverty, and as the title of her essay in this volume suggests, Martha Albertson Fineman concludes that "Child Support Is Not the Answer." Therefore, makers of public policy need to explore the possibilities of other approaches to remedying the poor performance of the United States on child poverty.[1]

This article examines the promise of an assured child support benefit as a partial solution to child poverty among single-parent families. Consideration of an assured child support benefit is particularly critical at this time because it fits closely with the current approach to welfare benefits and work in the welfare-reform legislation. The assured benefit assumes that mothers will work to support their families, relying on the benefits to supplement their income.

The Concept of a Child Support Assurance System

The child support assurance system (CSAS) (Garfinkel and Melli 1982) was one of the proposals for reform stimulated by Congress's interest in the 1970s in creating a new child support enforcement program. The

CSAS has served as the model for most recent legislation to improve child support collection. The CSAS replaces the local judicial discretion of the traditional private system with the bureaucratic regularity of the federal social security system and, like survivors' insurance, simultaneously prevents poverty and reduces dependence on welfare by providing aid to beneficiaries in all income classes.

Child support assurance is based on a partnership of responsibility between parents and government. Parents are responsible for sharing income with their children. Government is responsible for enforcing private support and for insuring a steady flow of income to all children with absent parents.

The CSAS has three components: (1) child support awards are set by a legislated formula based on a percentage of the nonresident parent's income; (2) payments are deducted from the absent parent's earnings, just like Social Security deductions; and (3) the government guarantees a minimum level of child support to all children legally entitled to private child support—an assured benefit. In those cases where child support payments by nonresident parents fall below a certain minimum, the child is entitled to an assured benefit. The assured benefit is financed from a very small addition to the Social Security payroll tax.

Like survivors' insurance, child support assurance aids children of all income classes who suffer income loss due to parental absence. Survivors' insurance compensates for the loss of income arising from widowhood. Child support assurance compensates for the loss arising from divorce, separation, or nonmarriage. Withholding a flat percentage of the nonresident parent's income makes the bulk of the financing of child support assurance similar to a proportional payroll tax, which is used to finance all U.S. social-insurance programs. In the child support assurance case, however, the "tax" applies only to those who are legally liable for child support. The assured-benefit component of child support assurance makes the benefit structure of the system like all other social-insurance programs in that it provides greater benefits to low-income families than are justified on the basis of the family's contributions or taxes.

The 1984 Child Support Act and the 1988 Family Support Act took giant strides on the collection side toward this new system of child support assurance by requiring states to adopt numerical child support guidelines for determining child support awards and universal wage withholding of child support obligations. States were also required to strengthen paternity establishment. Congress also took very small strides on the benefit side in 1984 and 1988 by directing the secretary of Department of Health and Social Services to grant Wisconsin and New York waivers to use federal money that would otherwise have been devoted to Aid to Families with Dependent Children (AFDC) to fund a version of an assured child support benefit.

Despite this legislation, the nation has only begun the transition from the traditional to the new child support assurance system. Although the federal government has offered to pay 90 percent of the costs to states for automating their child support record-keeping systems for more than a decade, most states have yet to automate. Most states lack the administrative capacity to receive, monitor, and disburse all child support payments and were therefore unable to implement universal income withholding by 1994. While child support guidelines have been enacted in all states, the degree to which they are being utilized, especially in nonwelfare cases, is unclear. Indeed, there is debate in many states about whether Congress really meant the guidelines and withholding provisions to apply to all cases (Williams 1994). Demonstrations of periodic updating suggest that until there is a way to routinize updating—by, for example, establishing child support orders as a percentage of income—in practice, the vast majority of cases will not be updated (Bartfeld and Garfinkel 1996). All states are a long way from universal establishment of paternity, and crossing state lines still remains a very effective way to avoid child support obligations.

Moreover, neither the federal government nor any state has adopted an assured child support benefit.

The Limits of Private Support and the Case for an Assured Benefit

Strengthening public enforcement of private child support continues to have bipartisan support and is good public policy because it will increase the economic security of children potentially eligible for child support, reduce dependence on welfare, and reinforce the widely shared value of parental responsibility. But there are limits to what private child support enforcement can accomplish. Perfection in enforcement would reduce the poverty gap for children potentially eligible for child support by 24 percent (Garfinkel 1992:54); 76 percent of the poverty gap would remain. Moreover, perfection is unlikely to ever be achieved. More realistically, if child support award rates and collection rates improved halfway between current performance and perfection and award levels were established and updated, the poverty gap would be reduced by 12 percent (Garfinkel 1992:54).

Private enforcement is limited by the ability of nonresident fathers to pay support. A large proportion of the fathers of children receiving welfare have low and irregular earnings. As long as such is the case, their child support will also be low and irregular (Michalopoulos and Garfinkel 1989). To expect otherwise is wishful thinking.

The limits of private child support enforcement create a case for an assured child support benefit, the third component of a new system of child support assurance. Thus, the remainder of this discussion focuses on the benefits and costs of an assured benefit.

An assured benefit promotes economic security, setting a secure floor under payments. Because child support assurance is available to all families legally entitled to support irrespective of income, it prevents poverty and dependence on welfare. Families need not become impoverished to qualify. While an intermediate improvement in enforcement of private child support by itself reduces the poverty gap by 12 percent, with the addition of an assured benefit of $3,000 for the first child, the poverty gap is reduced by 24 percent (Garfinkel 1992:54).

An assured benefit also increases the incentive to establish paternity. To qualify for an assured benefit, the child must be legally entitled to receive private support, which, in the case of an out-of-wedlock birth presupposes paternity establishment. Paternity establishment is a critical weak link in private child support enforcement.

Of course, an assured benefit also has costs. I have estimated that even with the inadequacies of the current child support enforcement system, the cost of an assured benefit of $3,000 for the first child, $1,000 each for the second and third child, and $500 each for the fourth and fifth child would be equal to $4.7 billion (Garfinkel 1992:54).[2] If, however, child support enforcement were to improve to a more respectable level, the cost of this child support assurance system as a whole (the collection as well as the benefit side) would be only $2.1 billion because improvements in collections save $2.6 billion (Garfinkel 1992:54).[3]

How can a government program not limited to poor families be so cheap? First, the collection-side aspects of child support assurance save money. Second, despite the fact that it insures children of all income classes, the assured benefit per se is not very costly. Men and women tend to mate with people from the same sort of backgrounds. This assortative mating guarantees that in the overwhelming majority of cases with a wealthy custodial parent, the nonresident parent will be equally wealthy and there will be no public subsidy. In rare cases, of course, there will be a poor nonresident parent of a child residing with a wealthy parent. Counting the public portion of the assured benefit for income tax purposes substantially reduces this already small leakage.

An assured benefit has other costs. It creates adverse incentives with respect to paying support and marriage. Nonresident parents who would pay less than the assured benefit and are motivated to pay out of concern for their children lose this motive because their children are guaranteed the support whether or not the parents pay. Improved enforcement may counter any adverse incentive to pay. Furthermore, it is possible to design an assured benefit that rewards private payments of support, just as the earned income tax credit rewards work.

Because the assured benefit is available only to families with nonresident parents, it may subsidize marital dissolution. However, evidence from studies of the effects of welfare on marriage suggest that the adverse effects on marriage will be small (Moffit 1992). The potential adverse effects provide a rationale for limiting the generosity of the assured benefit. They also provide a rationale, as does practical experience in administration, for beginning implementation with state demonstrations. To date, however, the only American jurisdiction to conduct a major trial of a version of an assured child support benefit is New York state. The New York Child Assistance Program (CAP) limits the assured benefit to families that qualify for welfare, provides intensive social services along with the assured benefit, and includes no attempts to strengthen child support enforcement. Experimental findings include increases in family income, work, and private child support awards, decreases in welfare dependence and costs, and no improvements in support payments. The cost savings are growing over time (Hamilton et al. 1996). On the one hand, some—indeed, possibly all—of the benefits may be attributable to the social services rather than to the assured benefit. On the other hand, limiting the assured benefit to the poor undermines the principle of universality that is critical to preventing poverty and dependence on welfare. This aspect strengthens the case for testing a purer version of an assured benefit that is neither entwined with social services nor income-tested.

A non–income tested assured benefit will cost more in benefits than New York's CAP. But the pure version of an assured benefit will also cost much less to administer than the CAP version. Indeed, the administrative costs of a universal assured benefit will be quite small. Once income withholding is fully implemented and states or the federal government receive and disburse all child support payments, the additional costs of administering an assured benefit will consist primarily of modifying computerized record-keeping systems.

Since 1990, two bipartisan commissions—the National Commission on Children (1991) and the U.S. Commission on Interstate Child Support (1992)—have recommended federally financed state demonstrations of an assured benefit. The case for an assured child support benefit is strong enough to warrant at least a trial.

NOTES

1. The United States ranks near the bottom among industrialized nations in an examination of eighteen nations by the Luxembourg Income Study, a nonprofit group based in Walderdange, Luxembourg (*New York Times,* 14 August 1995, A7).

2. The assured benefit would be treated as unearned income for the purpose of determining AFDC benefits and also would be taxable under the federal income tax.

3. The medium-run improvement entails an increase in award rates (the proportion of cases with child-support awards) and collection rates (the proportion owed that is collected) halfway between the current level and perfection and in an increase in awards to the level of the Wisconsin child-support guidelines—17 percent of gross income for one child, 25 percent, 29 percent, 31 percent, and 34 percent for two, three, four, and five or more children, respectively. The assured benefit for the first child would be $3,000 and would increase for the second and third child by $1,000 per child and for the fourth, fifth, and sixth child by $500 per child. The assured benefit would be treated as unearned income for the purpose of determining AFDC benefits and also would be taxable under the federal income tax. For more details, see Garfinkel 1992.

REFERENCES

Bartfeld, Judi, and Irwin Garfinkel. 1996. The Impact of Percentage-Expressed Child Support Orders on Payments over Time. *Journal of Human Resources* 31:794–815

Garfinkel, Irwin. 1992. *Assuring Child Support: An Extension of the Social Security System.* New York: Russell Sage Foundation.

Garfinkel, Irwin, and Sara S. McLanahan. 1986. *Single Mothers and Their Children: A New American Dilemma.* Washington, DC: Urban Institute Press.

Garfinkel, Irwin, and Marygold S. Melli, eds. 1982. *Child Support: Weakness of the Old and Features of a Proposed New System.* Special Reports nos. 32A, 32B, 32C. Madison, WI: Institute for Research on Poverty.

Hamilton, William, Nancy Burstein, August Baker, John Blomquist, and Stephanie Gluckman. 1996. *The New York State Child Assistance Program: Five Year Impacts, Costs, and Benefits.* Cambridge, MA: Abt Associates.

Michalopoulos, Charles, and Irwin Garfinkel. 1989. *Reducing the Welfare Dependence and Poverty of Single Mothers by Means of Earnings and Child Support: Wishful Thinking and Realistic Possibility.* Discussion Paper 882-89. Madison, WI: Institute for Research on Poverty.

Moffitt, Robert. 1992. Incentive Effects of the U.S. Welfare System: A Review. *Journal of Economic Literature* 30:1–61.

National Commission on Children. 1991. *Beyond Rhetoric: A New American Agenda for Children and Families.* Washington, DC: National Commission on Children.

U.S. Commission on Interstate Child Support. 1992. *Supporting Our Children: A Blueprint for Reform.* U.S. Commission on Interstate Child Support's Report to Congress. Washington, DC: U.S. Government Printing Office.

Williams, R. 1994. Implementation of the Child Support Provisions of the Family Support Act: Child Support Guidelines, Updating Awards, and Routine Income Withholding. In *Child Support and Child Well-Being,* ed. Irwin Garfinkel, Sara S. McLanahan, and Philip K. Robins. Washington DC: Urban Institute Press.

Why Child Support Assurance Won't Work

Allen M. Parkman

Introduction

This chapter provides an economic analysis of the child support assurance system (CSAS) described and advocated by Irwin Garfinkel in "The Limits of Private Child Support and the Role of an Assured Benefit" (in this volume). As Garfinkel explains, the three essential components of that system are: (1) child support guidelines, which establish a child support award as a percentage of the nonresident parent's income; (2) routine income withholding, which deducts child support owed from wages and other sources of income, just like income and payroll taxes; and (3) an assured child support benefit, which provides a government guarantee of a minimum level of child support to the resident parent of a child legally entitled to private support (Garfinkel, McLanahan, and Robins 1992:3–25). Because the philosophical premise underlying the CSAS is that parents are responsible for sharing income with their children and that government is responsible for ensuring that children who live apart from a parent receive the share to which they are entitled (Corbett 1992:32), an implicit component of CSAS must be the identification of children's parents, especially their fathers, since increasing numbers of parents are not married. The proponents of CSAS do not present it as a welfare program but instead pattern it after the survivor benefits available under the old age, survivors', and disability insurance (Social Security) program.

The analysis presented in this chapter questions the desirability of government-assured child support because it creates perverse incentives that reduce the effectiveness of the program's other essential and desirable components. It is fundamental for children's welfare that their parents are identified and forced to assume responsibility for their support. A concern for children's welfare that is primarily addressed by increasing the money and services available to custodial parents—often from public sources—

shifts the public policy focus away from the primary problem facing children today: unprepared and irresponsible parents. Being a successful parent requires much more than just the desire for or acceptance of a child. Assured child support will in some cases encourage the wrong people to become parents.

Incentives for Parents

Child support assurance would encourage some unprepared and irresponsible people to become parents. These parents are often unwilling to accept the costs of parenthood associated with a long-term commitment to each other and the sacrifices necessary to prepare their children for life. Government-assured child support would have many of the problems that have been associated with welfare programs such as Aid to Families with Dependent Children (AFDC) (Murray 1984).[1] Paramount among these problems are the incentives for ill-prepared parents to have children and the disincentives for the parents to establish two-parent households. There is general agreement that living in a two-parent household is preferable for a child than a single-parent household (McLanahan and Sandefur 1994).

By only addressing the financial predicament of some children, the proponents of CSAS have tended to ignore the traditional role of parents (Garfinkel and McLanahan 1986:3).[2] Parenting goes far beyond just putting food on the table: it consists of nurturing as well as creating children. Parents have played an important role throughout history preparing their children for life by educating them and providing them with important social values. While the educational role has been assumed to some extent by the government, parents still have an important role in education and the central function in establishing critical social values (Walker and Sylwester 1991).[3] The decline in the family has been associated with a decrease in the recognition of these values by the current generation.

The Costs and Benefits of Parenthood

While the creation and nurturing roles of parents are instinctive, the choices made in conjunction with those roles are influenced by their costs and benefits (Parkman 1995:21–52). Being a successful parent can be costly, requiring substantial investments of time, energy, and money, as well as potentially the most beneficial and rewarding life experience. Social welfare is increased by activities whose benefits exceed their costs, as is true with parenting. When parents make substantial investments of time and money in their children, it is highly likely that these children will turn into productive members of society. Society and the families are better off.

Alternatively, when people produce children who are disruptive in their youth and antisocial as adults, the costs may exceed the benefits.

For much of history, parents had incentives to avoid producing the latter type of child as the best interests of the parents coincided with those of society. Most costs and benefits of children were internalized in the family because parents could anticipate a lifelong relationship with their children, especially in agrarian societies in which geographic mobility was limited. Because parents lived in close proximity to their children, even as adults, poor parenting could impose a substantial cost on parents, so they were encouraged to devote substantial time, money, and effort to that activity. In addition, the children were the cornerstone of their parents' support in their old age, and poor parenting could have a devastating effect at that time. As a result of these incentives for responsible parenting, the families were better off, and so was society.

An additional impetus for adults to be responsible parents was based on parenthood traditionally being a privilege rather than a right, as the barriers to parenthood were substantial. The first constraint was usually marriage, which normally required a couple to wait until they had accumulated enough resources to establish their own household. Marriage was especially important because premarital sex could create substantial problems for society, and, therefore, strong sanctions were imposed to discourage it. Faced with limited opportunities to dissolve a marriage by divorce, adults had incentives to invest substantial time and effort in choosing mates. In summary, the requirement of minimum resources before marriage and the stability provided by the expectation of a long marriage generally worked to the advantage of children.

That pattern has changed dramatically, as some parents now expect a much weaker attachment to their children, in part because of much greater geographic mobility but also because society shoulder's responsibilities and costs once assumed by parents. With fewer responsibilities, it is easier for parents to limit their involvement in their children's lives. Before there was government aid for dependent children, parents, especially fathers, were expected to support their children. If the fathers were unable or unwilling to assume that role, the burden fell on mothers or their families. They often did not assume this role happily, thereby making it difficult for fathers to avoid their responsibilities. Not only has society assumed responsibility for the financial obligations of some fathers, it has also assumed a custodial responsibility for children. When parents have done a poor job of raising a child, the child is now more commonly sent to a publicly funded institution. Between 1950 and 1990, the number of children in juvenile institutions rose from 37,000 to 104,000 (U.S. Bureau of the Census 1976:419; U.S. Bureau of the Census 1994:69). The dramatic increase in the homeless population is another reflection of weaker links between parents and their children (Jencks 1994:80).[4]

Because of the decline in the parents' presence in their children's lives, the costs and benefits of children increasingly have fallen on others. These costs range from taxes for education to antisocial behavior such as crime, while the benefits can consist of social interactions as well as increased productivity. Some parents associate fewer costs with poor parenting and fewer benefits from expending substantial efforts to be good parents. The most obvious of these parents are those who do not participate in the rearing of their children, which increasingly has been fathers. Between 1950 and 1994, the percentage of American children living in mother-only families has climbed from 6 to 27 percent (U.S. Bureau of the Census 1994:61 table 71). According to the U.S. Bureau of the Census data (1994:65 table 78), 16 million children were living in families with no father present in 1994. The fatherless families often live in neighborhoods where more than half of all families with children are headed by a woman with no husband present (Casey Foundation 1995:5). In some cases, the fathers have no contact with their children at all. Thirty percent of all children born in 1992 were born to unmarried women (U.S. Bureau of the Census 1994:73 table 88). While in some cases, the children were born to cohabitating parents, such often was not the case. In 1992, there were 354,000 births to unmarried women aged fifteen to nineteen, up from 190,000 in 1970 (U.S. Bureau of the Census 1994:77 table 94). If half of today's children are expected to spend some of their childhoods in single-parent homes, the ties between the parents and their children later in life would also be expected to be weaker than in the past. In many cases, therefore, parents will assume less of a burden for poor parenting than they did previously.

Because some people are shifting the cost of their children to society, the basic components of CSAS are highly laudable and necessary for increasing social welfare. Some parents, especially fathers, currently escape or limit their parental costs. Yet social welfare would be enhanced if parents were confronted with a substantial share of parental costs to encourage them to have children only when that choice will benefit the children, their parents, and society. Some people, when confronted with these parental costs, might decide that they would prefer not to be parents. They can only be confronted with these costs when they know that paternity will be diligently pursued followed by predictable and enforceable child support obligations. Meanwhile, child support provided by the government can reduce the costs of parenthood, which in some cases is encouraging the wrong people to become parents.

Long-Term Commitment

The problems facing children are particularly acute when their parents have not made a long-term commitment to each other, resulting in single-parent households. While this problem is particularly acute if the parents never lived together, it is also a problem when cohabitating or married couples separate. As Sara McLanahan and Gary Sandefur note,

> Children who grow up in a household with only one biological parent are worse off, on average, than children who grow up in a household with both of their biological parents, regardless of the parents' race or educational background, regardless of whether the parents are married when the child is born, and regardless of whether the resident parent remarries. (McLanahan and Sandefur 1994:1)

Living in a single-parent household has a detrimental effect on performance in school, decreasing the likelihood of completing high school by about 5 percent for white children and 13 percent for blacks (McLanahan 1985:883).

A large proportion of single mothers were teenagers when they bore their first children, with the result that the mean age at first birth for women receiving AFDC in 1993 was 20.3 years (U.S. Bureau of the Census 1995:4). Having children at an early age is associated with lower educational attainment and higher fertility for the mother and the children, both of which limit their opportunities to develop skills and relevant experience, thereby reducing their earning capacities (Moore and Burt 1982). Not only do single parents often have low earning capacities, but they are less able to instill important social values in their children. Almost two-thirds of rapists, three-quarters of adolescent murderers, and the same percentage of long-term prison inmates are young males who grew up without fathers in the house (Kristol 1994:A13). Children living in single-parent families headed by never-married young women have far greater delinquency rates than do children from two-parent families (Wilson and Petersilia 1995).

Parents below the Poverty Level

Children benefit from parents who have made a long-term commitment to each other and are able and willing to incur the substantial parental costs, of which financial expenses are only one component. Still, it would seem reasonable that being financially capable of supporting a child should be a fundamental requirement for parenthood. Many low-income people have children that impose a substantial burden on the parents, but the children's welfare is important to the parents, and the sacrifice is made willingly. However, some people create children that they are unable or unwilling to support, which often must be viewed as an irresponsible act reflecting a fundamental lack of concern for the children's welfare. People have children without being able or willing to support them because of public financing. Child support assurance would either replace or augment current welfare programs for many poor parents. People who are unwilling or unable to fulfill the financial obligations associated with parenthood often are less likely to fulfill the other parental obligations, such as educating and socializing their children (Haveman and Wolfe 1995).[5]

The arguments that have been made against unlimited welfare can also be made against the assured child support component of CSAS. Welfare programs have reduced the cost of children for some parents, thereby increasing the quantity demanded. Since mothers without mates have more readily qualified for aid, the growth of these programs in recent years has contributed heavily to the sharp growth in the ratio of illegitimate to legitimate birth rates (Becker 1991:139). For example, the number of recipients in the AFDC program rose from 9.7 million in 1970 to 14 million in 1992 (U.S. Bureau of the Census 1994:377 table 589).

While the value of AFDC payments adjusted for inflation has declined since 1970, the academic literature has concluded that AFDC and the other welfare programs have created incentives for unmarried women to have children (Tanner, Moore, and Hartman 1995:240).[6] While early research on welfare programs, especially AFDC, produced mixed results, more recent research associates those programs with the increase in illegitimacy rates and the poverty of unmarried mothers and their children (Winegarden 1988; Plotnik 1990; Fossett and Kiecolt 1993).[7] Others have argued that even though AFDC payments adjusted for inflation fell after 1970, the large increases in those payments during the 1960s encouraged unmarried women to have children, and then many social restraints on illegitimacy eroded as out-of-wedlock births became more common (Murray 1994). Even when the early research did not establish a statistically significant relationship between AFDC payments and the number of unmarried mothers, it is difficult to escape that without the substantial increase in welfare programs, eligibility, and payments that have occurred since the 1960s, unmarried mothers generally could not have established independent households.

Not only does welfare permit women with poor employment opportunities to establish independent households, usually under poverty conditions, but it also acts as an inducement for women with employable skills to become mothers and often to forsake employment and thereby join the ranks of the poor (Kimenyi and Mbaku 1995). These women's fall below the poverty level is based on the relative attraction of low-paying jobs and motherhood. Low-paying jobs are also often unattractive jobs. The turnover rate at McDonald's is legendary. Alternatively, tending one's own children is often viewed as an enjoyable experience. So while the income from welfare may not be as high as working in a low-wage job, it can make motherhood more attractive than employment in a low-paying, monotonous job. The result is a household that would not otherwise be classified as poor joining that group.[8]

To the extent that welfare discourages paternal presence by providing an alternate source of maternal support, welfare encourages fathers to limit their parental responsibilities. In one study, about 24 percent of the children living with a divorced mother and about 33 percent of the children living with a never-married or remarried mother had no contact with their fathers during the past year (McLanahan and Sandefur 1994:96). Given society's expectations, it is difficult for a man to participate in a family for which he is not the primary source of support. Being a good provider is still regarded as one of the central roles that men are expected to perform. A 1990 poll found that 77 percent of young women felt a good-paying job was an essential requirement for a husband (*Time* 1990:14).

Parenthood has shifted from being a privilege to a right, with the government assuming the financial role that traditionally had been assumed by the father. With AFDC, the government required and then encouraged female-headed households and the absence of the father, often to children's detriment. While much of the thrust of social policy and practice has been to write off absent fathers, there is a growing body of research emphasizing the important role paternal involvement can play in children's positive cognitive, emotional, and social development (Davidson 1990; Popenoe 1996). Research shows that children born to single, teenage mothers are more likely to drop out of school, to give birth out of wedlock, to divorce or separate, and to be dependent on welfare (Garfinkel and McLanahan 1986:1–2). A recent report indicates that most young men in the juvenile justice system spent at least part of their childhood in single-parent households (Casey Foundation 1995:13). The process has its own momentum, as the high dropout rate of one generation leads to poor employment opportunities and absent fathers in the next generation (Garfinkel and McLanahan 1986:12).[9]

In summary, among the poor, CSAS would expand the incentives for parenthood that welfare programs create for some people who had not met the most fundamental financial requirements for parenthood. If, after government financial support, all children had equally qualified and motivated parents, government support would be a success. But such does not appear to be the case; thus, government support encourages some less-qualified and less-motivated people to become parents.

Parents above the Poverty Level

Even among parents above the poverty level, child support assurance has a perverse effect because assured child support—although generally not as large as that provided by state guidelines—would be available to all children. Women's search for reliable spouses is often masked by romantic notions of marriage (Becker 1991:108–34). Marriage can be a precarious institution, since marrying irresponsible men can impose substantial costs on women during marriage and at divorce, especially if there are children. These costs are often financial, but they can also bring a reduction in the quality of life. Solo parenting can be much more difficult, and custody of any children can be a major impediment to an active social life.

Knowing the costs of a poor choice encourages women to critically assess potential mates and to maintain marketable skills during marriage (Parkman 1992b). As marriage has become a more vulnerable institution, in part because of the enacting of no-fault divorce by all states between 1969 and 1985, adults have been delaying marriage. The fault divorce grounds of adultery, cruelty, and desertion provided some protection for spouses who worked at home. That protection was dramatically reduced by the introduction of no-fault divorce, which permitted unilateral divorce subject to only limited compensation (Weitzman 1985; Parkman 1992a). While most women are not familiar with the change in the divorce grounds, they are familiar with the deleterious impact of divorce on middle-aged mothers who limited their careers. As women have approached marriage with more caution, the average age at first marriage for women has increased from 20.8 in 1970 to 23.7 in 1988 (U.S. Bureau of the Census 1994:103 table 145).

While potentially costly, children are also a source of great joy. Women would normally be expected to be reluctant to bear children with clearly irresponsible men. However, the availability of government financial assistance for mothers encourages women to screen potential mates less severely and to work less diligently to make relationships work. This process is called moral hazard—people with insurance are encouraged to increase the activities for which the insurance is provided (for example, auto insurance encourages people to dump their cars into rivers and then file stolen-car claims) (Kerr 1992:A3). Although the proponents of CSAS have described child support assurance as similar to the survivors' benefits contained in Social Security, the impact would be very different. While moral hazard can be a problem with any type of insurance, the opportunities for abuse under child support assurance are more numerous than under the survivor benefits in Social Security. The survivors' insurance program requires the death of the insured worker as a precursor to government support, an alternative that is clearly not attractive, even with the insurance.

In summary, child support assurance would provide an incentive for women to scrutinize potential mates less closely and work less diligently to make marriages work, resulting in more single-parent households. The problems associated with a child growing up in a single-parent household are not unique to poverty-level households.

Incentives for Government Officials

If government officials had the capacity and motivation to force parents to assume financial responsibility for their children, the incentives for irresponsible parental behavior caused by child support assurance and the funds necessary to finance it would be limited. However, it is unlikely that the actions of government officials will be effective. While the CSAS would place a much larger administrative burden on governments, especially the federal government, the child support enforcement programs enacted to date have produced poor results. A cornerstone of CSAS must be the identification of nonresident parents followed by the requirement that they contribute to their children's support, with a limited role for government-assured child support. A review of past performance and future incentives suggests that CSAS proponents have been overly optimistic about the effectiveness of government officials in this process. As a result, the children qualifying for support and, therefore, the incentives discussed earlier will probably increase dramatically.

Although the federal government has been involved in child support enforcement since 1975, as Marsha Garrison points out in "The Goals and Limits of Child Support Policy" (in this volume), the government's record is not impressive. Using 1983 data, Garfinkel and Sara S. McLanahan estimated that only about 40 percent of absent white fathers and 19 percent of absent black fathers pay child support; among those who do receive money, the average amount was $3,129 for white mothers and $1,698 for black mothers. Placing these figures in perspective, these payments accounted for about 10 percent of the income of single white mothers and for about 3.5 percent of the income of black mothers (Garfinkel and McLanahan 1986:24).

Despite a decade and a half of child support reform, by 1990 some indicators suggested that there had been little additional progress

(Garfinkel, McLanahan, and Robins 1994:6). Of the 11.5 million custodial parents in 1991, only 54 percent had obtained child support awards. Custodial mothers received an annual average of $3,011 in child support payments, but 25 percent of mothers with awards did not receive any payments, and another 24 percent received only partial payments (U.S. Bureau of the Census 1994:391 table 616). (Daniel R. Meyer provides more data in "Fathers and the Child Support System," in this volume.)

There are vast differences across the states in the extent to which the reforms are being implemented. For example, the paternity-establishment rate for children born outside marriage ranges from a low of 5.5 percent in Arizona to a high of 67 percent in Georgia (McLanahan and Sandefur 1994:148). An analysis of the paternity-adjudication process in three counties in Wisconsin in 1990 demonstrated a range of results within a state, with substantially higher adjudication rates in smaller counties. In the largest county, Milwaukee County, only 42 percent of cases were adjudicated, and sanctions were rare, in part because a staff of 104 was responsible for 77,776 cases (McLanahan, Brown, and Monson 1992:137). Even though the federal government has been willing to pay 90 percent of the states' costs to automate their child support record keeping, most states have yet to automate. During the 1980s, the likelihood of a custodial mother's obtaining an award and receiving full payment did not change (U.S. General Accounting Office 1993:2). A recent Urban Institute study showed that potential child support collections amount to as much as $46 billion in 1995 dollars (Garfinkel and Oellerich 1992:73). Yet only $15 billion in awards are currently in place, and only $10 billion is paid, leaving a collections gap of approximately $36 billion. Overall, average awards and payments declined by 25 percent in real terms between 1978 and 1985, although some of the change can be explained by a change in the composition of the parents (Garfinkel, McLanahan, and Robins 1994:6).

As late as December 1994, the General Accounting Office (GAO) pointed out that management weaknesses were hindering the efforts of the Office of Child Support Enforcement (OCSE) to lead the program effectively, to judge how well the program is working, and to set effective policies (U.S. General Accounting Office 1994:3). Despite twenty years of required performance reporting, OCSE has not developed universally understood data definitions, and states collect data in ways that make aggregation and comparison impractical. Therefore, OCSE was in no position to know how the national program was actually performing. By the early 1990s, OCSE's monitoring role had come into greater prominence, with more than half of the OCSE staff devoted to compliance audits. State program staffs reported to the GAO that the audits helped them gain state legislative support, but the audits were too detailed and untimely to be useful management tools, with audit reports sometimes issued two years after the period audited.

Who Is at Fault?

When programs fail, the usual conclusion is that it is not the fault of the personnel but of the underlying legislation. The solution is often new legislation. Frequently ignored are the incentives for government officials who generally find it difficult to make onerous decisions such as forcing parents to face up to their financial responsibilities (Messmer 1994; Earls 1994; Greco 1992).[10] Separated parents usually are supporting two households, so it is no surprise that their finances are strained. Many noncustodial fathers have a legitimate claim to hardship. It is easier for officials to ignore delinquent fathers and substitute an available social program rather than to force parents to live up to their obligations. If public programs become more generous relative to paternal resources, officials will have even more incentive to provide public funding. This outcome is also influenced by the high cost of collecting from delinquent parents. In 1994, the federal government spent $1.2 billion to collect $7.3 billion in child support (U.S. General Accounting Office 1995:9–10). The child support collected was probably the easiest to collect, so the return on additional efforts would be expected to be even less.

The problems associated with government officials identifying and collecting from nonresident parents is compounded by the potential lack of cooperation from custodial parents who want to avoid imposing costs on noncustodial parents. Demands for child support tend to strain any possible relationship (McLanahan et al. 1994:239). Alternatively, the custodial parent may not want to have an ongoing relationship with the noncustodial parent or fear retaliation if child support is imposed. Therefore, even if support can be conditioned on cooperation by the custodial parent, that cooperation may be limited in many cases. Only if the custodial parent wants to impose a cost on the noncustodial parent—or there is no other source of funds—will the custodial parent have an incentive to cooperate with the process. Noting custodial parents' reluctance, bureaucrats will be even more inclined to take the easy way out by reporting that a diligent effort has been made to identify and collect from noncustodial parents, thereby qualifying the family for the government-assured support.

The Financial Cost of a Child Support Assurance Program

Another consideration is the financial cost of the program. Proponents of CSAS have generally had a more optimistic view of the program's financial impact than others have had. Having stated the underlying premise—that parents are responsible for sharing income with their children and that the government is responsible only for ensuring that children who live apart from their parents receive the share to which they are entitled—the proponents of CSAS initially calculated the cost by implementing the program only with a limited group of children in families with current awards. A program for these families with medium improvements in awards and collections and assured benefits of $2,000 or less would reduce government expenditures (Meyer et al. 1992:174). In more recent research, the proponents of CSAS have expanded its coverage and recognized that it can be an expensive program with a net cost of between $3 billion and $9 billion in 1988 dollars, depending on the benefit level and whether an award or merely cooperation was required to participate in the program (Meyer and Kim 1994:12). Other researchers have expressed concerns about the potential cost of the program, along with its limited impact on poverty because most children eligible for an assured benefit are not poor (Sorensen and Clark 1994). None of these studies adequately consider the dynamic effects resulting from the incentives for less-responsible people to become parents that have been discussed earlier in this chapter, and those costs can be substantial.

Conclusion

This chapter has argued that while identifying both parents and enforcing their obligation to support their children is laudable, necessary, and to be encouraged, providing assured child support by the federal government will work to the detriment of those programs and encourage less-reliable parents to have children and less-responsible adults to marry. While well intentioned, the assured child support component of the CSAS is fundamentally flawed. Children ideally will have parents who are capable of preparing them for life and committed to that responsibility. Unfortunately, child support assurance has perverse incentives for parents and government officials that reduce the likelihood that children will grow up in that type of environment.

The CSAS has a fundamental appeal by directing money to deserving people. It is an easy response, especially if the perverse incentives created are ignored. As with welfare programs that encourage unmarried mothers to have children, when the perverse incentives created by the program are recognized, it is questionable whether the benefits of a government-assured child support program exceed the costs.

A harder and certainly less appealing program may ultimately be better for society. People who have not made long-term commitments to each other and have not demonstrated the capacity to make a financial commitment to their children are becoming parents. Current policies condone and to some extent encourage this behavior. Viewing parenthood as a privilege rather than a right and recognizing society's obligation to protect children would encourage a different program. The cornerstone of any program must be identification of parents coupled with the enforcement of their financial obligations to their children. An earned-income credit that is less dependent on the number of children might also be desirable. Still, children should not be subjected to unreliable and irresponsible parents. Rather than funding irresponsible parents, society should consider placing these children—for their own benefit—in foster homes or orphanages with the understanding that when at least one parent has demonstrated the ability to be responsible, they can resume custody. For the sake of the children, the period in a foster home or orphanage could be limited, permitting adoption by people who are willing and able to provide acceptable environments.

Some people argue that adequately funded orphanages are more expensive than current programs. However, this contention overlooks the true cost of current programs in terms of lower education and employment attainment by children, poorer adjustment by them, and, in some cases, extreme antisocial behavior. Orphanages, adoption, and foster homes are clearly a second-best solution to a child growing up in a loving, competent household. Although government-assured child support hopes to provide those households, this chapter has argued that such programs are more likely to be destructive to that environment.

NOTES

1. While AFDC payments are often identified as the only source of support for unmarried, poor mothers, the package of benefits can be much larger and can include food stamps, Medicaid, public housing, nutrition assistance, and utility assistance. The incentives created by these programs are discussed in Murray 1984.

2. While proponents of CSAS acknowledge that economic theory suggests that increasing the income of families headed by single women will enlarge the number of women and children living in such families, CSAS advocates also contend that "increasing the incomes of families headed by single women will reduce some if not all of their present problems [and] it might also reduce the negative consequences associated with growing up in such a family" (Garfinkel and McLanahan 1986:3).

3. According to an Oregon longitudinal study, the single best predictor of adolescent criminal behavior is a long-established pattern of early antisocial behavior

in school associated with a dysfunctional family situation (Walker and Sylwester 1991).

4. Two-parent households give children access not only to their parents but also to a network of aunts, uncles, and grandparents. This network is usually smaller and weaker when the child grows up in a single-parent household (Jencks 1994:80).

5. Haveman and Wolfe (1995) present a summary of the research on the factors that influence children's attainments later in life. The authors note that growing up in a poor family appears to have a particularly negative effect on later work and earnings.

6. The welfare programs available to unmarried, poor mothers can include AFDC, food stamps, Medicaid, public housing, nutrition assistance, and utility assistance. If someone qualified for all of these programs, their value would be equivalent to pretax earnings of between $27,760 in Hawaii and $13,059 in Mississippi. If someone qualified only for AFDC, food stamps, and Medicaid, the benefits would be equivalent to pretax earnings of between $21,300 in Alaska and $6,100 in Mississippi (Tanner, Moore, and Hartman 1995:18).

7. Nearly all of the earlier investigations used cross-sectional state or SMSA data. It is difficult to establish causation with contemporaneous cross-sectional data and conventional regression techniques. To avoid these problems, more recent studies have used time-series data (Winegarden 1988; Plotnik 1990). Other researchers have established a substantial and consistent relationship between the size of public assistance payments and illegitimacy by using a more closely focused sample of young women in metropolitan areas (Fossett and Kiecolt 1993).

8. Since CSAS might not be means-tested, it would provide stronger incentives than AFDC for mothers to work.

9. Even after income is taken into account, children who grow up in mother-only households are still far more likely to become single parents themselves than are children who grow up in two-parent households (Garfinkel and McLanahan 1986:12).

10. While the record of states collecting child support is poor, some states are using innovative techniques. States such as Nebraska and Iowa have begun building electronic funds-transfer networks to collect payments (Messmer 1994). In Massachusetts, child support collection was shifted from the welfare agency to the Department of Revenue (DOR). In two years the state boosted its child support and alimony compliance rate from 59 percent to 78 percent. The DOR has a better database, and its employees are probably much less sympathetic to delinquent fathers (Earls 1994). In contrast to the lack of incentives for government officials, private businesses with a profit motive have a strong incentive to collect from "deadbeat" fathers. For example, companies such as Child Support Services charge an application fee of thirty-five dollars and a 25 percent contingency fee based on what they collect. Using the classic techniques of the bill-collection trade, Child Support Services locates about 85 percent of its targets. These companies are particularly effective because the 1977 Fair Debt Collection Practice Act restrictions do not apply to court-ordered child support obligations (Greco 1992).

REFERENCES

Becker, Gary S. 1991. *A Treatise on the Family.* Enlarged ed. Cambridge, MA: Harvard University Press.

Casey, Annie E., Foundation. 1995. *Kids Count Data Book.* Baltimore: Annie E. Casey Foundation.

Corbett, Thomas, 1992. The Wisconsin Child Support Assurance System: From Plausible Proposals to Improbable Prospects. In *Child Support Assurance: Design Issues, Expected Impacts, and Political Barriers as Seen from Wisconsin,* ed. Irwin Garfinkel, Sara S. McLanahan, and Philip K. Robins. Washington, DC: Urban Institute Press.

Davidson, Nicholas. 1990. Life without Father: America's Greatest Social Catastrophe. *Policy Review* 51:40–44.

Earls, Alan R. 1994. Dialing for Deadbeats. *Computerworld,* 27 June, 129.

Fossett, Mark A., and K. Jill Kiecolt. 1993. Mate Availability and Family Structure among African Americans in U.S. Metropolitan Areas. *Journal of Marriage and the Family* 55 (2): 288–302.

Garfinkel, Irwin, and Sara S. McLanahan. 1986. *Single Mothers and Their Children.* Washington, DC: Urban Institute Press.

Garfinkel, Irwin, Sara S. McLanahan, and Philip K. Robins. 1992. Findings of the Wisconsin Child Support Reform Project: Introduction and Summary. In *Child Support Assurance: Design Issues, Expected Impacts, and Political Barriers as Seen from Wisconsin,* ed. Irwin Garfinkel, Sara S. McLanahan, and Philip K. Robins. Washington, DC: Urban Institute Press.

———. 1994. Child Support and Child Well-Being: What Have We Learned? In *Child Support and Child Well-Being,* ed. Irwin Garfinkel, Sara S. McLanahan, and Philip K. Robins. Washington, DC: Urban Institute Press.

Garfinkel, Irwin, and Donald T. Oellerich. 1992. Noncustodial Fathers' Ability to Pay Child Support. In *Child Support Assurance: Design Issues, Expected Impacts, and Political Barriers as Seen from Wisconsin,* ed. Irwin Garfinkel, Sara S. McLanahan, and Philip K. Robins. Washington, DC: Urban Institute Press.

Greco, Susan. 1992. The Collectors. *Inc,* December, 148–57.

Haveman, Robert, and Barbara Wolfe. 1995. The Determinants of Children's Attainments: A Review of Methods and Findings. *Journal of Economic Literature* 33:1829–78.

Jencks, Christopher. 1994. *The Homeless.* Cambridge, MA: Harvard University Press.

Kerr, Peter. 1992. Blatant Fraud Pushes up the Cost of Car Insurance. *New York Times,* 13 October, A3.

Kimenyi, Mwangi S., and John Mukum Mbaku. 1995. Female Headship, Feminization of Poverty, and Welfare. *Southern Economic Journal* 62 (1): 44–52.

Kristol, Irving. 1994. Life without Father. *Wall Street Journal,* 3 November, A13.

McLanahan, Sara S. 1985. Family Structure and the Reproduction of Poverty. *American Journal of Sociology* 90:873–901.

McLanahan, Sara S., Patricia R. Brown, and Renee A. Monson. 1992. Paternity Establishment in AFDC Cases: Three Wisconsin Counties. In *Child Support Assurance: Design Issues, Expected Impacts, and Political Barriers as Seen from Wisconsin,* ed. Irwin Garfinkel, Sara S. McLanahan, and Philip K. Robins. Washington, DC: Urban Institute Press.

McLanahan, Sara S., and Gary Sandefur. 1994. *Growing Up with a Single Parent: What Hurts, What Helps.*. Cambridge, MA: Harvard University Press.

McLanahan, Sara S., Judith A. Seltzer, Thomas L. Hanson, and Elizabeth Thomson. 1994. Child Support Enforcement and Child Well-Being: Greater Security or Greater Conflict? In *Child Support and Child Well-Being,* ed. Irwin Garfinkel, Sara S. McLanahan, and Philip K. Robins. Washington, DC: Urban Institute Press.

Messmer, Ellen. 1994. Child Support Law Prompts States to Build EFT Networks. *Network World,* 21 February, 14.

Meyer, Daniel R., Irwin Garfinkel, Donald T. Oellerich, and Philip K. Robins. 1992. Who Should Be Eligible for an Assured Child Support Benefit? In *Child Support Assurance: Design Issues, Expected Impacts, and Political Barriers as Seen from Wisconsin,* ed. Irwin Garfinkel, Sara S. McLanahan, and Philip K. Robins. Washington, DC: Urban Institute Press.

Meyer, Daniel R., and Rebecca Y. Kim. 1994. *Incorporating Labor Supply Responses into the Estimated Effects of an Assured Child Support Benefit.* Discussion Paper no. 1033-94. Madison, WI: Institute for Research on Poverty.

Moore, Kristin A., and Martha R. Burt. 1982. *Private Crisis, Public Costs: Policy Perspectives on Teenage Childbearing.* Washington, DC: Urban Institute Press.

Murray, Charles. 1984. *Losing Ground: American Social Policy 1950–1980.* New York: Basic Books.

———. 1994. Does Welfare Bring More Babies? *Public Interest* 115 (spring): 17–30.

Parkman, Allen M. 1992a. *No-Fault Divorce: What Went Wrong?* Boulder, CO: Westview Press.

———. 1992b. Unilateral Divorce and the Labor-Force Participation Rates of Married Women, Revisited. *American Economic Review* 82 (3): 671–78.

———. 1995. The Deterioration in the Family: A Law and Economics Perspective. In *The Individual, the Family and Social Good: Personal Fulfillment in Times of Change,* ed. Gary Melton. Lincoln: University of Nebraska Press.

Plotnik, Robert D. 1990. Welfare and out-of-Wedlock Childbearing: Evidence from the 1980s. *Journal of Marriage and the Family* 52 (August): 735–46.

Popenoe, David. 1996. *Life without Father.* New York: Martin Kessler Books.

Sorensen, Elaine, and Sandra Clark. 1994. A Child Support Assurance Program: How Much Will It Reduce Child Poverty, and at What Cost? *American Economic Review* 84 (2):114–19.

Tanner, Michael, Stephen Moore, and David Hartman. 1995. The Work versus Welfare Tradeoff. *Policy Analysis* 240:1–53.

Time. 1990. The Road to Equality in *Women. The Road Ahead.* Special issue. *Time.* 136(19):10–15.

U.S. Bureau of the Census. 1976. *Historical Statistics of the United States: Colonial Times to 1970.* Washington, DC: U.S. Government Printing Office.

———. 1994. *Statistical Abstract of the United States, 1994.* Washington, DC: U.S. Government Printing Office.

———. 1995. *Mothers Who Receive AFDC Payments.* SB/95-2. Washington, DC: U.S. Government Printing Office.

U.S. General Accounting Office. 1993. *Child Support Assurance: Effect of Applying State Guidelines to Determine Fathers Payments.* GAO/HRD-93-26. Washington, DC: U.S. Government Printing Office.

———. 1994. *Child Support Enforcement: Families Could Benefit from Stronger Enforcement Program.* GAO/HEHS-95-24. Washington, DC: U.S. Government Printing Office.

———. 1995. *Child Support Enforcement: Opportunities to Reduce Federal and State Costs.* GAO/T-HEHS-95-181. Washington, DC: U.S. Government Printing Office.

Walker, Hill M., and Robert Sylwester. 1991. Where Is School along the Path to Prison? *Educational Leadership* 49:14–16.

Weitzman, Lenore. 1985. *The Divorce Revolution.* New York: Free Press.

Wilson, James Q., and Joan Petersilia. 1995. *Crime.* San Francisco: ICS Press.

Winegarden, Calmon R. 1988. AFDC and Illegitimacy Ratios: A Vector-Autoregressive Model. *Applied Economics* 20 (December): 1589–1601.

Why Child Support Assurance Won't Work: A Rejoinder

Irwin Garfinkel

Allen Parkman has written a splendid brief against an assured child support benefit. By ignoring the virtues of assured child support—such as reducing the economic insecurity of millions of single mothers and their children—Parkman need only show that an assured benefit has some vices.[1]

An assured child support benefit would be bad public policy, he argues, because it will "encourage some unprepared and irresponsible people to become parents." Indeed, Parkman asserts, "People have children without being able or willing to support them because of public financing." Thus, rather than funding irresponsible parents through any form of public assistance, Parkman favors "placing these children—for their own benefit—in foster homes."

Parkman also argues that marriage is a good institution for children and parents and that public enforcement of private child support obligations is desirable. I agree with both propositions. Given the weakness of his case, Parkman's lengthy discussion of these topics is a clever diversionary tactic.

To return to the main issue, however, men and women have been having children they are unable or unwilling to support since long before the advent of public financing. Before public provision, the mothers and children were helped by other members of their family, by churches, and by other institutions, such as feudal lords. People have children without being able or willing to support them because of human nature. What to do about the children and parents is a matter of public policy.

Throughout its history, capitalism has been accompanied by public financing of aid to the poor. Public aid for the poor has always been opposed by the most extreme libertarians. On occasion, people sharing Parkman's views have gained ascendance. Indeed, one century ago, poor single mothers, then overwhelmingly widows, were denied outright cash relief in a large number of American cities. Instead, the children were taken away from the mothers, sent to orphanages, and called half-orphans.

As the younger generation says, "Been there. Done that." Americans have already tried Parkman's prescription. With the support of President Theodore Roosevelt, one state after another—forty between 1910 and 1920—rejected the policy of taking children away from poor mothers and placing them in orphanages and instead enacted state mothers'-pension programs to help poor single mothers take care of their children. In 1935, the federal government made the program national as part of the landmark Social Security Act.

After dismissing Parkman's view that children should be taken away from their parents, the question becomes what is the best way to aid poor parents, including poor single mothers, to raise their own children. No way is perfect. All have vices as well as virtues. My chapter attempts to weigh the costs versus the benefits.

Finally, Parkman says that advocates underestimate the costs of an assured child support benefit. As evidence, he notes that if child support awards are not required for eligibility for an assured child support benefit, the costs will be many times higher than if awards are required. This contention is true. Costs will be much higher if a loosely designed program is enacted, which is one reason why I have always favored limiting eligibility for an assured child support benefit to parents legally entitled to receive private child support. I leave it to the reader to determine whether this proposal constitutes underestimation or sensible judgment.

NOTE

1. Parkman does acknowledge that an assured benefit promotes work for women who might otherwise be dependent on welfare.

Child Support Is Not the Answer: The Nature of Dependencies and Welfare Reform

Martha Albertson Fineman

Child support is merely one component of a complex series of issues surrounding the question of who should bear the economic and social costs of caring for dependent members of society. The United States is in crisis, with more than 20 percent of children living in poverty. Divorce and never-married motherhood are blamed for that shameful situation, and policymakers seek to re-create, through paternity proceedings and child support collection mechanisms, a world in which the "head of the household" assumes economic responsibility for his dependents, removing the need for collective response.

In the current atmosphere of reform, welfare is cast as evil, and child support is cast as the moral solution embodying the ideal of self-sufficiency whereby families assume responsibility for their own economic well-being. This construction, however, serves only to obscure the real issue: the need to take responsibility for children beyond the private family. Child support is based on an outmoded and inadequate belief that the private family can and should provide for those such as children who are unable to provide for themselves. This chapter discusses these issues in the context of the universal problem of dependency and the need for caretaking and concludes that child support is not the answer.

Dependencies and Subsidies

The fact of subsidy is not remarkable—the question is why some subsidies but not others are stigmatized. Relevant to the answer is the role of the mythical, idealized family in American society. The family serves on an ideological level as the alternative to collective responsibility for dependents. This family (which is hierarchical and patriarchal) is an abstraction that is central to the creation and maintenance of an unequal and unjust system of allocating societal resources. The family is the unit to which the collective responsibility for caretaking has been delegated

I use the term *unjust* in the context of the lack of societal support for family units that deviate from the traditional nuclear family norm. So, while all families need and receive resources to care for children and other dependents, only some families receive unstigmatized assistance.

Therefore, the place to begin a discussion about welfare, child poverty, and reform is with the observation that everyone is dependent on public subsidy in the United States, whether the subsidies come in the form of direct assistance, such as welfare, or indirect assistance, such as exemptions, child-care deductions, and other tax breaks for wage-earning families. Politicians have manipulated public sentiment with rhetoric that distorts and misleads about basic statistics when recent figures show that little of the federal expenditures actually go to welfare—1 percent of the federal budget, or 3 percent if food-stamp expenditures are included (Andrejco 1995:A18; Rosen 1994:B7). This amount should be contrasted with the amounts involved in subsidies to the middle class, such as student loans, Veterans Authority and Federal Housing Authority mortgage programs, deductions for mortgage interest, and the vast public subsidies for highway construction, savings and loan bailouts, and farming—examples of funded programs that give unstigmatized benefits to certain members of society. As recipients of such widespread federal assistance, everyone is a welfare recipient.

Other incentives or private subsidies have implications for the public purse: provisions for untaxed employer contributions to pension funds and health-insurance programs and spending accounts for medical and child-care expenses mean that workers gain compensation but do not pay taxes on a percentage of it. Lost revenues must be supplemented by taxation on other endeavors and sources of income. Whether the money is collected and distributed or never collected at all, the resulting loss of public revenue to family "preservation" is the same.

In revealing these subsidies to certain families to show that there is unfulfilled collective responsibility for all children and other dependents, I challenge the dominant way of understanding the allocation of responsibility for dependency in American society. Families must be understood as functional social institutions with defined responsibilities. It is important to realize that within families there is an entrenched system of injustice, found in the important but invisible type of subsidy of uncompensated family labor. This labor needs to be made an explicit part of the public discussion about dependency. This subsidy of time and energy occurs when others sacrifice market participation to facilitate the success of those for whom they care. Caretaking work is taken for granted. Labor supplied overwhelmingly by women working as mothers, wives, and daughters is not considered in calculating the gross national product. The recipients of this subsidy are not taxed on the value they receive and do not consider themselves dependent as a result of the donation of another's time and effort. This labor substitutes for and relieves the necessity of collective responsibility for dependent citizens. Given this important social role of the family as the primary caretaking institution, it seems logical that the core family connection should not be the sexual or reproductive affiliation exemplified by marriage but rather the nurturing, caretaking relationship between a mother and a child—used here as a metaphor for the caretaker-dependent relationship, including all dependency relationships found within the family context, whether the young, ill, frail, elderly, or disabled are in need of care.

The most important governmental question should be how to devise policies that assist the family in its caretaking role. Governmental assistance is justified by the family's assumption of responsibility for dependents. There is a fundamental obligation in a just society for the collective to provide for its weaker members. The relevant policy question should be what policies are consistent with the fulfillment of collective responsibility and what actions interfere with or evade that goal.

It is necessary to begin with the recognition that dependency is both inevitable and universal in that it is associated with infancy and often accompanies old age, illness, and disabilities. Dependency is, therefore, a biologically based, natural part of all human experience. This construction does not include psychological or economic dependencies that may accompany biological and developmental dependency but are not viewed as inevitable and universal (Fineman 1995:161–63).

Biological dependency is not considered pathological in American society. The most appealing example of biological dependents are children—symbolic innocents who are perceived as having a legitimate claim to the resources of others. Much of the criticism regarding recent attempts at welfare reform highlights the harm of such proposals to "innocent children." Critics produced images of children but often dropped the family context. Marian Wright Edelman emphasized that welfare reform measures would "hurt and impoverish millions of children"; a Roman Catholic bishops spokesman said that hungry children were unfairly targeted; Hugh Price of the National Urban League spoke of "the end [of] the war on poverty and the begin[ning] of the war on poor children" (Gray 1996:A23). Republican rhetoric runs along the same lines: Presidential candidate Bob Dole, while denouncing President Bill Clinton's record on work-welfare reform and pronouncing on the need to "confront dependency" and "encourage the return of men to their responsibilities," also spoke of creating "a safe harbor of childhood" (*New York Times* 1996a:D21). There is a near consensus in America that inevitable dependents are viewed as the "deserving poor" and are not to be punished—at least not directly.

If inevitable dependents are deserving and have legitimate claims on resources, to whom may or must they turn? This question raises theoretically problematic consequences of inevitable dependency. Caretakers of inevitable or biological dependents are themselves often dependent on the resources of others to be able to provide that care—a type of "derivative dependency" (Fineman 1995:162–63). There is no societal consensus that derivative dependents have legitimate claims to social resources. In fact, in the context of the welfare debate and the attention directed to the increased rate of single motherhood, American society has rejected the idea that caretaking supplies a justification for societal resources.

Yet it seems a simple, irrefutable observation that caretakers need resources to perform their functions and are often dependent on others as a result. This derivative dependency is socially produced, defined, and assigned. Caretakers are referred to the private family for resources, but in continuing to allocate dependency automatically to the private sphere, society forgoes the opportunity to develop a theory of collective responsibility for children and other dependents. The ideology of independence and autonomy has funneled the needs and claims of derivative dependency away from the state to the nuclear family. Derivative dependency has historically been privatized and kept hidden as a widespread social phenomenon worthy of public attention and resources.

In U.S. society, derivative dependency, while not universal or inevitable, is gendered. Caretakers, within as well as without the family, are typically women (Estin 1992–93). Women are socially assigned their caretaking roles as wives, mothers, and daughters within families—an assignment of dependency that is even more pronounced (and less challenged) when it comes to care for the elderly or ill. Elderly parents look to daughters (or daughters-in-law) for expected accommodations (Nelson and Nelson 1992:747). Women are also overwhelmingly found in caretaking positions as the "hired help" receiving low wages and typically no social security or other benefits (Niemi 1994:13). Women are the societal caretakers within the uncompensated sphere of the private family. "[C]aregiving remains invisible . . . because the law construes family care as a matter of love and obligation, not . . . personal choice or arm's-length bargaining" (Estin 1992–93:776). "Today . . . it is women who perform the work of the family, women who seek to escape the work, and women who eke out a living performing the work—for other women" (Siegel 1994:1214; see also Davis n.d.:16–17). To continue to consider dependency a private matter and fail to compensate caretakers is an injustice that has serious implications for all women and children.

Inconsistent and Incompatible Political Responses

In what sense is it just to assign the burdens of dependencies to women who are uncompensated or undercompensated? At a minimum, if dependency is inevitable and there is a larger societal obligation to care for dependents, then caretakers must be valued and caretaking rewarded. Provisions for justly sharing the collective responsibility for the dependent and weak should have been the basis of our politicians' "Contract with America" rather than the mean-spirited measures assembled and signed by the president under the umbrella Welfare Reform Act.[1]

Fulfilling societal obligations in a just manner will have redistributive (or market-correcting) consequences. As those who care for inevitable dependents are finally compensated, economic resources will be reallocated. Most of the movement will be from those who occupy stereotypical male (or market) positions to those who perform stereotypical female (or caretaking) roles, but there will also be significant implications for the existing economic disparity between white and black communities.

Instead of looking at dependency as natural and inevitable and considering pragmatic responses framed in terms of justice given empirical realities, U.S. policymakers resort to the rhetoric of failed social institutions, such as traditional marriage. They also unrealistically rely on the market to provide opportunities for maternal work.

The solution most often offered for inevitable and derivative dependency in the welfare debate is marriage or, in its absence, the establishment of male economic responsibility through paternity proceedings and child support. Women who do not conform—either by refusing to marry or to participate in paternity proceedings—are faced with threats that their children will be placed in orphanages or that restrictive measures and conditions will be attached to their societal subsidies. Maternal work serves as a fail-safe measure.

Resort to both of these "solutions" illustrates the way myth has overtaken reality in contemporary policy debates. Self-induced ideological blindness blocks more pragmatic responses to poverty—responses that would articulate the collective responsibility and justify continuing and broadening the subsidy rather than its elimination or curtailment.

The proffered solutions of marriage and maternal market work seem incompatible. In the traditional model of marriage, the male role is as the head of household and the female is the subservient helpmate. Husbands fulfill their role by meeting economic obligations and providing discipline and control over wives and children. Wives provide services, including child care and homemaking.

The problem with this ideal arises because of the new egalitarian expectations for marriage wherein both partners are considered equals, entitled to pursue market rewards and expected to share domestic tasks. Dependency and perceived resulting inferiority within the family has become unacceptable to many women. In the past decade, as a result of feminist agitation and evolution in equal-protection jurisprudence, female market participation has become the new norm (Siegel 1994:1214) applicable to all women, even mothers. This alteration of the traditional expectations for mothers is evident in the divorce context and the current welfare-workfare debate (Fineman 1983:851–52).

The norm of maternal work is incompatible with the traditional model of marriage, implicating independence and a range of choices for women that would confound the old hierarchical order. Even if women wanted to stay at home and act in a more traditional manner, the head-of-household/homemaker model is no longer economically feasible. The family of today needs a wage and a half to maintain the middle-class standard of living achievable by a sole wage earner a few generations ago (Miller 1995:D1).

The more significant difficulty with maternal work, however, is that it is imposed within the ideological confines of the old order. Today, women may be expected to work even if they are mothers, but this expectation occurs in the context of unchanged, largely unchallenged, institutions that operate as though workers are free of domestic responsibilities. Studies indicate that across cultures, employed mothers still perform the vast majority of child care and housework despite the existence in some countries of shared responsibility laws (International Labor Organization 1992). Worldwide, women work more for less pay than men (Briscoe 1992; Quindlen 1992:A21; Xinhua News Agency 1992). Employed women still spend twice as much time with child care and housework as do their husbands, and fathers participate in child care only slightly more than they did in 1967 (Drakich 1989:83–87). There may be new expectations about mothers and market work, but there is no accommodation in the market for the demands of mothering on workers. Child care, paid parental leave, and flexible schedules to facilitate caretaking are not the workplace reality for most mothers.

Even if such external family-related difficulties were accommodated, resort to the solution of maternal work will not eradicate poverty. Market discrimination remains a problem, particularly for some segments of the female workforce. Jobs traditionally held by women are often comparatively underpaid (Niemi 1994). Unemployment and downsizing frequently affect newer workers, who are often female. Perhaps most relevant for the welfare debate, there are no guarantees that jobs will be available even for mothers who are willing and able to work.

Confronting the Empirical Realities

The traditional family model cannot be the solution in a world where families need two working adults, and many women refuse to adopt a dependent posture and choose to develop market careers. There are additional, empirically-based questions raised about the continued viability and desirability of the traditional family. Empirical questions also surround the maternal work solution offered to reduce welfare dependency. It is illuminating to compare myths with reality in both contexts.

Traditional Marriage

Aside from the changed role expectations associated with egalitarian marriage, current empirical information refutes the general applicability of the traditional ideal of a male who, as head of the household, provides financially for his wife and children. Legal attachment of men to women and children is the popular panacea for many social ills (certainly for child poverty), and marriage is seriously offered as *the* appropriate social policy. Mothers who deviate from this family norm are subjected to criticism and punished through the deprivation of social support. Punitive disincentives for unmarried women to reproduce are increasingly accepted as appropriate. Women who do not cooperate in forming attachments to men (either by marrying or participating in paternity proceedings) are threatened with orphanages for their children and restrictions on already meager economic subsidies.

The resort to marriage and the traditional family as a reformist ploy is grounded in the myths of autonomy, independence, and self-sufficiency that represent ideals for families as well as individuals. A properly functioning family does not call on societal resources. It is self-sufficient, finding internally the resources needed to perform its function.

Given the characteristics of the prevailing market, a self-sufficient family seems to be one where roles are well defined. If the needs are for private or family subsidized caretaking, then the complementary roles of breadwinner and caretaker seem natural and inevitable. As a result, society gravitates toward the family populated in traditional form: husband/father, wife/mother, and dependent/minor children. This biological/reproductive unit is considered natural as a social organization and is not questioned.

As a functional matter, the natural family is ideally a private family—the social institution that will raise the children, care for the ill, the needy, the dependent. It is a self-contained and self-sufficient unit in accomplishing those tasks—located within the larger society, complementing the state that protects it but not explicitly demanding public resources to fulfill its role. The ideal of the private family is the way responsibility for inevitable dependency moves from the public (state) to the private family. Overt responsibility for dependency is ideologically directed to the private entity.

Subsidies are invisible, particularly the subsidy of women's labor in the family. In this regard the concept of the natural and private family has important political currency. Its existence as an ideological construct masks and hides dependency and allows official and public rhetoric to spin out in terms of ideals of capitalistic individualism, independence, self-sufficiency, and autonomy.

Whatever the rhetorical attachment to the institution of marriage, empirical indications are that it is a failure when measured against the traditional ideal. The most-often-cited statistic indicating the decline of the traditional family is the divorce rate. The U.S. Bureau of the Census estimates that half of all marriages entered into since 1970 could end in divorce (Lugaila 1992:8). Recent census figures show an increase in white never-married mothers, suggesting that single-motherhood is becoming a viable option for women of all races and social classes.[2] Other indications of disaffection with marriage include the increase in the median age at marriage and the number of childless couples. Households comprised of married couples living with their children declined from 44.2 percent in 1960 to 26.3 percent in 1990; at the same time, other families with children almost doubled in number, to 8.3 percent (Schultz 1994). The percentage of married couples without children remained at around 30 percent (Lugaila 1992:15).

In addition, over the past few decades much has been revealed about the potentially violent implications of traditional marriage. Domestic abuse is increasingly recognized as a widespread problem transcending race and class lines.[3] The nature and extent of private violence calls into question the wisdom of policies designed to coerce women to stay with male partners to avoid poverty and governmental censure.

Even if the institution of marriage was not plagued with violence, there are other problems—in addition to changed expectations of equality—that make the traditional model inappropriate in today's world. Many women have rejected the traditional model of the homemaker confining her time and energy to the demands of the family. That role is no longer considered sufficient by women who are unwilling to sacrifice career advancement for full-time, uncompensated caretaking. A new ideal of the egalitarian family has been fashioned on these changing premises.

As an economic institution, marriage also seems to have failed when measured against the expectations implicit in the model envisioned by traditionalists. Given a variety of market realities, the breadwinner/housewife model is not an institution that can adequately take care of dependency. This situation holds true for the middle class and particularly for the working poor. In the United States, many people work but are nonetheless poor. The working poor's dire economic position seems destined to be compounded as Congress dismantles programs aimed to help them, such as the earned-income credit (Rimer 1995:A1).

Reliance on men and marriage as social policy ignores the reality of both unemployed and poor men who can barely provide for themselves, let alone assume responsibility for women and children. Even among the middle class, there has been a real loss in wages and opportunities in the past few years. Men who experience downsizing are effectively denied the ability to provide for their families as they find themselves on a downwardly mobile career path. Middle-class males who are victims of the global market and economic readjustment increasingly cannot be counted on to provide sufficient amounts of child support to lift children out of poverty, whether married to the children's mothers or not.

Statistics indicate that there are additional problems with the reliance on men to support children. Aside from the fact that many men find themselves in dire economic straits, there are problems caused by the independence of women that are reflected in the divorce rate and the increase in never-married mothers. Men increasingly do not live within the family unit. The emerging social reality is a family composed of a single mother, whether divorced or never married, and her children. The response to this changing demographic has been to label it a problem and to define the solution for this dilemma as tying the absent male to the family unit in legal and economic terms. The preferred resolution for child poverty is based on the traditional model of male as economic provider. The institution of child support is deemed adequate to fulfill male economic responsibility after the dissolution of the marriage. Establishment of the paternal tie and, hence, the duty to support outside of the marriage context is done through paternity proceedings, a process that has policy problems for some and is far from universally successful in establishing a legal bond between fathers and their children (Fineman 1995:212).

Furthermore, as Marsha Garrison and Irwin Garfinkel note in this volume, difficulties abound with the idea of child support as the solution to poverty.

Maternal Work

Perhaps statistical and empirical information like that cited in the previous section has caused policymakers increasingly to turn to maternal work as the solution to child poverty.

In view of the current political rhetoric, it is necessary to make the basic point that mothering is work. If motherhood in general entails work, poor motherhood entails even more work and, while receiving welfare, is one of the most burdensome types of mothering imaginable. Poor women dependent on public assistance and/or charity must deal with impersonal, formalized bureaucrats and bureaucracies (Simon 1983). To meet day-to-day needs, poor women and their children endure the hardships and confront the obstacles that the process and its personnel place in their way. Also relevant are the horrendous conditions in which many are forced to raise their children. Single-mother families are disproportionately found in poor neighborhoods essentially abandoned by police and increasingly deprived of social-welfare programs. Motherhood in these neighborhoods means daily encounters with potential violence. It is no wonder that some poor mothers "fail" at raising their children to become productive, tax-paying citizens—the real wonder is that so many succeed in mothering under such adverse conditions. It is essential to remember when considering the solution of maternal work for poverty that the demands of mothering do not disappear when women enter the work market.

The second fundamental point that needs to be considered in the context of the maternal work debate is the assumption that jobs are waiting for welfare recipients. This assumption is essential to the logic underlying the Welfare Reform Act and is central to much of the criticism of welfare recipients.

The logic of workfare rests on the premise that the problems of the poor are the product of their own choices and individual weakness and failures. However, studies indicate that welfare recipients do not lack the will to work. Instead, the problems faced include finding a permanent job that pays enough to provide for a family and dealing with child-care responsibilities that remain even after a job is found (Handler 1995). Makers of public policy currently are in a state of euphoria over rapidly decreasing welfare rolls and job opportunities for welfare mothers, helped by the low unemployment rate. But states and the federal government have tried work programs in the past, and most of them have failed through no fault of the welfare participants but because of low wages and other problems.

For example, in one study, California officials acknowledged that graduates of a training program needed to earn a minimum of eleven dollars per hour to stay off welfare, yet their wages averaged only $6.50 per hour (Abramovitz 1988:221, 246). A 1986 study of work programs revealed that low wages forced 43 percent of Massachusetts training graduates back onto welfare (Walsh 1988:32). Many mothers on welfare who get jobs have difficulty keeping them because of low pay, lack of training, harsh working conditions, and other problems, including lack of social skills, lack of child care, lack of health insurance, and resentful boyfriends. Consequently, at Project Match in Chicago, almost half of these women lost their jobs within six months and nearly three-quarters did so within a year (DeParle 1994b:A1, 14; DeParle 1994a:3; Wilkerson 1995:A1, A18).

Real Reform

What would real welfare reform look like? First, the misperceptions and myths that obscure the problem should be eliminated in favor of recognition of and addressing the fact that motherhood is work. As important work, it should be compensated. Most industrial democracies do so through a universal governmental transfer in the form of a child allowance or through a basic income guarantee (Rainwater and Smeeding 1995; see also Garfinkel, "The Limits of Private Child Support and the Role of an Assured Benefit," in this volume).

It is also important that caretaking benefits be universal. Bearing the burden of dependency in a society should be considered work deserving of public compensation, regardless of other sources of caretaker wealth. The universal nature of such programs underscores the inappropriateness of partitioning certain children and other dependents and their caretakers into stigmatized, need-based programs where they become easy targets (Fineman 1995:115–16). Any problem generated by an unwarranted accumulation of resources by the wealthy caretaker could be addressed through a progressive tax system.

Also, social policies must be based on the realization that the needs of inevitable dependents do not disappear if the caretaker is engaged in market work. There are still caretaking tasks to be done, and market work is often incompatible with these tasks. Significant structural changes must be contemplated in market institutions to allow the reconciliation of motherhood with market work. In furtherance of this objective, it would be helpful to reframe the current workfare discussion so that issues associated with work did not focus exclusively on poor welfare mothers, thereby isolating them from other women. All women have problems if they try to combine market work and motherhood.

Once a more inclusive perspective is gained, it is clear that the real issue is not whether there is an obligation for women to work but whether there is a right to work that is to be protected and supported by social policies. This stance presents the family and work issue from the woman's perspective. Reform should not be driven by the anonymous, unembodied taxpayer of the welfare debates but by the mother who is seeking to combine work and caretaking in a way that will not sacrifice the demands of either. Such an emphasis would mean not only a serious attempt to create jobs and training programs for poor unemployed women and men but also regulation of the wage structure and standardization of health, pension, and other benefits.

Taking the position that there is a right to work also means making necessary changes in the workplace for day-care services and provisions for paid family leave. Employers will be required to pay family wages to working mothers. On an ideological level, such structural reforms refute the assumption underlying today's workplace that the American worker is an unencumbered person, free to participate in an inflexible nine-to-five schedule without concern for ill children, school vacations, or other caretaking glitches, because some woman is taking care of all of those things at home for free.

Conclusion

Reorientation of the workplace to accommodate caretaking would mean that women could realistically be both economic actors and mothers. As women perform in both spheres the question of men's role arises. But a true reevaluation of fatherhood and of masculinity that is neither hierarchical nor patriarchal has yet to occur. Perhaps such a reevaluation is too painful or even threatening, since the dominant roles men have historically occupied in the traditional family are challenged by the revisioning of gender equality. Thus, it is easier to resort to myth than to engage in substantive change. It is no longer possible to refuse to confront the fact that substantial injustice is perpetuated when family policy in this country is fashioned and formulated on myths and symbols that are no longer valid as an empirical matter or desirable to many citizens on an ideological level. Policies that rely on the traditional nuclear family as the means to escape poverty and provide for inevitable and derivative dependents foster the assumption that the maintenance of intimacy—everything from contraception to responsibility for the day-to-day care of children—is primarily a private task. The norm of marriage and the dominant ideology surrounding that institution obscure the nature and extent of dependency in American society. The idea and idealization of the family masks dependency and hides the costs of caretaking.

Furthermore, it seems apparent that more than mere money or concern with poverty is at issue in this debate, which is why everyone must care about this issue. It seems that the real concern for many politicians is the imposition of their own morality, which entails the prevention of unmarried women having children and the curtailment of divorce. The attacks on welfare motherhood are attacks on women who are unsupervised by men in their intimate, reproductive family lives. Divorced women are also targets of marriage rhetoric, as are middle-class and older women who are not mothers. Women who choose abortion or birth control over bearing children operate outside of the conventional morality.

One burning desire that emerges in the family-values debate is the need to "discipline" those women who do not conform to roles associated with the traditional family but rather live outside the hierarchical, patriarchal family. The message is that responsible reproduction (indeed, responsible sexuality) occurs only within the context of the traditional family. In 1949, Justice Panken of the New York Family Court stated,

> Man enters a marital relationship to perpetuate the species. The family is the result of marital relationship. It is the institution which determines in a large measure the environmental influences, cultural backgrounds, and even economic status of its members. It is the foundation upon which society rests and is the basis for the family and all of its benefits.[4]

There has historically been an "insistence on the traditional family as the sole permissible locus of childrearing" (Carbone 1994:398). As a result, in constructing the problems presented by as well as the solutions for the never-married mother and the divorced mother, the physical absence of a male is considered central. Male presence, in the form of economic support accompanied by "rights" over children, introduces discipline and control and make the family "complete" in some mystical way. "He" is social policy: the universal answer, the means offered for resolving the problems of poverty and despair.

It should be clear that the current form of the debate about single mothers, welfare, and work is not about real reforms; it is not even about real problems. Expressed through potent symbols, the debates are really about gender, race, and disciplining women who fail to confine themselves to the patriarchal family. Like the war on drugs, the war on poverty—now recast as the war on welfare—has the underlying passion of a moral crusade. Anger and accusation proclaim the existence and extent of evil evidenced by the deviation from traditional family norms. The noose tightens as women and children are misperceived as appropriate targets of fury rather than as the victims of misguided social policies and the scapegoats of the blind failings of politicians.

NOTES

1. The welfare reform bill, signed by President Clinton in August 1996, ends the federal guarantee of cash benefits to poor children. The bill, substantially similar to two others that he previously vetoed, is the culmination of two years of debate in the Republican-dominated Congress. Congress's "sense . . . that prevention of out-of-wedlock pregnancy and the reduction of out-of-wedlock births are important Government interests" (Welfare Reform Act, title IV, subsection A) informs the structure of the new regimen. To this end, AFDC is abolished (§ 4103) in favor of block grants to the states. The states will administer a single temporary assistance (TEA) program designed to assist "needy families either already with or expecting a child . . . in becoming self-sufficient" (Id.). Priority is to be given to engaging adults in two-parent families and in single-parent families with "older pre-school or school-age children" in job-related and education programs. Refusal to participate by adult members of families "without small children needing child care" will result in benefits reduction; such is also the case for those who do not cooperate in paternity establishment procedures. In any case, all cash benefits financed from federal sources will usually cease after a five-year lifetime maximum. No additional cash is to be provided for any new children born to families already receiving TEA; instead, vouchers, good only for certain government-designated child-care-related needs, will be made available. State-specific TEA plan requirements include a ten-year plan with numeric goals for reducing illegitimacy; states will be rewarded with additional grants for attaining these goals and for "high performance" in TEA objectives. In some states, bounties will be paid for population increases, presumably where they are accomplished with a concurrent drop in out-of-wedlock births. In addition, benefits will be denied to young women under eighteen years of age who are unmarried and not living under adult supervision. These mothers must also stay in school to qualify for TEA. Elsewhere in the bill, nutrition programs, including food stamps, the Women, Infants, and Children Program, and school lunch/breakfast programs, are reduced or cut (Id., title III, subsections C, D), effecting estimated savings of some $18 million over the next four years by ending the entitlement status of these programs.

2. A survey of unmarried women aged eighteen to forty-four showed an increase in the rate of never-married motherhood from 15 percent in 1982 to 24 percent in 1992. The rate of births by unmarried women with at least one year of college education increased from 5.5 percent to 11.3 percent (Murray 1992:A14). For women in professional or managerial positions, the rate rose from 3.1 percent to 8.3 percent (Bachu 1993:xix). The media have paid a great deal of attention to the increase in out-of-wedlock births (Beck 1993; Cohen 1993; DeParle 1993; Lawson and Lamott 1993; Pollitt 1993; Whitmire 1993). Before too readily embracing the view that marriage is the best antidote to poverty, educational failure, and psychological distress, it might be instructive to study two-parent families devastated by layoffs in the steel, defense, timber, and auto industries—families whose children now exhibit most of the emotional and cognitive problems generally blamed on divorce (Coontz 1993).

3. "[I]n the United States a 1984 National Crime Survey found that women were victims of family violence at a rate three times that of men, and that of all spousal violence crimes, ninety-one percent were victimizations of women by their husbands or ex-husbands" (Thomas and Beasley 1994–95:1128). In response, Congress passed the Violence against Women Act (42 U.S.C.A. §§3796gg-3796gg-5 [West 1994]). The act provides funds for prevention and education, for battered women's shelters, and for the support of police and prosecutors.

4. *Lester v. Lester,* 87 N.Y.S.2d 517, 520 (New York Family Court 1949).

REFERENCES

Abramovitz, Mimi. 1988. Social Disservices: Why Welfare Reform Is a Sham. *Nation,* 26 September, 221, 238–41.

Abramovitz, Mimi, and Fred Newdom. 1995. Women on Welfare—Myths and Realities. *Resource: Women, Work and Welfare* (January):8. Pamphlet.

Alpert, Bruce. 1996. Strange Allies Snag Welfare Reform, Breaux Says. *New Orleans Times-Picayune,* 28 June, A14.

Andrejco, Marlene. 1995. A New Contract Is Needed That Will Favor the Poor and Combat Poverty. *Pittsburgh Post-Gazette,* 11 May, A18.

Bachu, Amara. 1993. *Fertility of American Women.* Bureau of the Census Current Population Report. June. Washington, DC: U.S. Government Printing Office.

Beck, Joan. 1993. Nation Must Stem the Tide of Births out of Wedlock. *New Orleans Times-Picayune,* 6 March, B7.

Briscoe, David. 1992. "All Work and No Pay" World. *Times* (London), 8 September, 7.

Carbone, June. 1994. Income Sharing: Redefining the Family in Terms of Community. *Houston Law Review* 31:359–415.

Cohen, Richard. 1993. Judging Single Mothers. *Washington Post,* 16 July, A19.

Coontz, Stephanie. 1993. Dan Quayle Is Still Wrong: Why the "Two Parent Paradigm" Is No Guarantor of Happiness. *Washington Post,* 9 May, C5.

Davis, Joyce. N.d. Enhanced Earning Capacity/Human Capital: The Reluctance to Call It Property. Manuscript in possession of the author.

DeParle, Jason. 1993. Big Rise in Births outside Wedlock. *New York Times,* 14 July, A1.

———. 1994a. Gauging Workfare's Employability. *New York Times,* 6 March, section 4, p. 3.

———. 1994b. Welfare Mothers Find Jobs Are Easier to Get Than Hold. *New York Times,* 24 October, A1, A14.

Drakich, Janice. 1989. In Search of the Better Parent: The Social Construction of Ideologies of Fatherhood. *Canadian Journal of Women and Law* 3:69–87.

Estin, Ann Laquer. 1992–93. Maintenance, Alimony, and the Rehabilitation of Family Care. *North Carolina Law Review* 71:721–803.

Fineman, Martha Albertson. 1995. *The Neutered Mother, the Sexual Family, and Other Twentieth Century Tragedies.* New York and London: Routledge.

Fineman, Martha L. 1983. Implementing Equality: Ideology, Contradiction, and Social Change: A Study of Rhetoric and Results in the Regulation of the Consequences of Divorce. *Wisconsin Law Review* 1983 (2): 789–886.

Fisher, Ian. 1995. Moynihan Stands Alone in Welfare Debate. *New York Times,* 27 September, B1.

Gray, Jerry. 1996. Amid Praise, a Peppering of Criticism and Dismay. *New York Times,* 1 August, A23.

Greenberg, Mark. 1994. *Contract with Disaster: The Impact on States of the Personal Responsibility Act.* Washington, DC: Center for Law and Social Policy.

Handler, Joel. 1995. *The Poverty of Welfare Reform.* New Haven: Yale University Press.

Holmes, Steven J. 1996. Study Rethinks Relationship between Welfare and Work. *New York Times,* 4 June, D21.

International Labor Organization. 1992. *Report of the International Labor Organization.* 6 September.

Jencks, Christopher, and Kathryn Edin. 1990. The Real Welfare Problem. *American Prospect* 1:31–50.

Kasindorf, Martin. 1996."It Is Welfare Repeal": Moynihan Lashes out at Bill to Change System. *Newsday,* 2 August, A7.

Lawson, Carol, and Anne Lamott. 1993. Single but Mothers by Choice. *New York Times,* 5 August, C1.

Lugaila, Terry. 1992. *Households, Families, and Children: A Thirty-Year Perspective.* Washington, DC: U.S. Government Printing Office.

Miller, Ursula. 1995. Two Incomes More the Norm: Higher Living Costs Make It Harder for One Paycheck to Provide Any Extras. *Cincinnati Enquirer,* 13 February, D1.

Murray, Charles. 1992. The Coming White Underclass. *Wall Street Journal,* 29 October, A14.

Nelson, Hilde Lindemann, and James Lindemann Nelson. 1992. Frail Parents, Robust Duties. *Utah Law Review* 1992 (3):747–63.

New York Times. 1996a. In Their Own Words: Bob Dole. 17 July, D21.

New York Times. 1996b. Text of President Clinton's Announcement on Welfare Legislation. 1 August, A24.

Niemi, Albert W., Jr. 1994. Education: Women's Ticket to Pay Equality. *Georgia Trend,* May, 13.

Pear, Robert. 1996a. A Computer Gap Is Likely to Slow Welfare Changes. *New York Times,* 2 September, 1, 12.

Pear, Robert. 1996b. A Popular Child-Support Bill Is Being Stalled by Politics. *New York Times,* 13 May, A13.

Pollitt, Katha. 1993. Bothered and Bewildered. *New York Times,* 22 July, A23.

Quindlen, Anna. 1992. Abhors a Vacuum. *New York Times,* 9 September, A21.

Rainwater, Lee, and Timothy M. Smeeding. 1995. *Doing Poorly: The Real Income of American Children in a Comparative Perspective.* Luxembourg Income Study Working Paper 127. Maxwell School of Citizenship and Public Affairs, Syracuse University.

Rimer, Sara. 1995. Cutting Tax Credit Means Much to Those with Little. *New York Times,* 16 October, A1.

Rosen, Ruth. 1994. Which of Us Isn't Taking "Welfare": Poor Children Rank Low in Government Largesse; Why Is the Comfortable Class So Mean? *Los Angeles Times,* 27 December, B7.

San Diego Union-Tribune. 1987. Moynihan Supports Welfare Reforms Forcing Fathers to Pay Child Support. 24 July, A18.

Schultz, T. Paul. 1994. Marital Status and Fertility in the United States: Welfare and Labor Market Effects. *Journal of Human Resources* 29:637–69.

Siegel, Reva B. 1994. Home as Work: The First Woman's Rights Claims Concerning Wives' Household Labor, 1850–1880. *Yale Law Journal* 103:1073–217.

Simon, William H. 1983. Legality, Bureaucracy, and Class in the Welfare System. *Yale Law Journal* 92:1198–269.

Thomas, Dorothy Q., and Michele E. Beasley. 1994–95. Domestic Violence as a Human Rights Issue. *Albany Law Review* 58:1119–47.

U.S. Bureau of the Census. 1989. *Child Support and Alimony.* Bureau of the Census Consumer Income Series. Washington, DC: U.S. Government Printing Office.

Walsh, Joan. 1988. Take This Job or Shove It. *Mother Jones,* 30 September, 32–33, 52–54.

Weaver, R. Kent, and William T. Dickens, eds. 1995. *Looking before We Leap: Social Science and Welfare Reform.* Washington, DC: Brookings Institution.

Whitmire, Richard. 1993. Number of Never-Married Moms Stretches across Income Lines. *Gannett News Service,* 13 July.

Wilkerson, Isabel. 1995. An Intimate Look at Welfare: Women Who've Been There. *New York Times,* 17 February, A1.

Xinhua News Agency. 1992. Women Work Harder but Paid Less. 6 September.

STATUTES

Family Support Act. 1988. Pub. L. No. 100-485, 102 Stat. 2343 (codified as amended in scattered sections of 42 U.S.C.).

Family Welfare Reform Act. 1987. Hearings on H.R. 1720 before Subcommittee on Public Assistance and Unemployment Compensation of the House Committee on Ways and Means, 100th Cong., 1st sess.

Violence against Women Act. 1994 Omnibus Crime Bill. 42 U.S.C.A. §§3796gg–3796gg-5 (West 1994).

Welfare and Medicaid Reform Act (Welfare Reform Act). 1996. Personal Responsibility and Work Opportunity Reconciliation Act of 1996, Pub. L. No. 104-193, 110 Stat. 2105. (codified as amended in scattered sections of 42 U.S.C.).

Colo. Rev. Stat. §26-2-507(1)(a)-(b) (West Supp. 1995).

Fla. Stat. Ann. §409.933 (West Supp. 1995).

Va. Code Ann. §63.1-105.2 (Mitchie 1995).

Wisc. Stat. Ann. §49.50(7)(g), (h) (West Supp. 1994).

Contributors

June Carbone is Professor of Law, Santa Clara University Law School.

John Eekelaar is Professor of Law, Pembroke College, Oxford University.

Martha Albertson Fineman is Maurice T. Moore Professor of Law, Columbia University Law School.

Irwin Garfinkel is Mitchell I. Ginsberg Professor of Contemporary Urban Problems, Columbia University School of Social Work.

Marsha Garrison is Professor of Law, Brooklyn Law School.

Paul K. Legler is Assistant Commissioner, Office of Child Support Enforcement, U.S. Department of Health and Human Services.

Mavis Maclean is Fellow, Center for Socio-Legal Studies, Wolfson College, Oxford University.

Marygold S. Melli is Voss-Bascom Professor of Law Emerita, Law School, University of Wisconsin, Madison.

Daniel R. Meyer is Associate Professor, School of Social Work, University of Wisconsin, Madison.

J. Thomas Oldham is John H. Freeman Professor of Law, University of Houston Law Center.

Allen M. Parkman is Regents' Professor of Management, Graduate School of Management, University of New Mexico.

Judith A. Seltzer is Professor in the Department of Sociology, University of California, Los Angeles.

Andrea Warman is Lecturer in the Department of Social Work, Brunel University, Middlesex, England.

Index